A Thesis Resource Guide for Criminology and Criminal Justice

D0140993

Marilyn D. McShane
University of Houston–Downtown
Department of Criminal Justice

Frank P. Williams III
University of Houston–Downtown
Department of Criminal Justice

PEARSON

Prentice
Hall

Upper Saddle River, New Jersey 07458

© 2008

Library of Congress Cataloging-in-Publication Data

McShane, Marilyn D.
 A thesis resource guide for criminology and criminal juistice/Marilyn D.
Mcshane, Frank P. Williams III.
   p. cm.
 ISBN 0-13-236895-1
1. Criminology—Authorship. 2. Criminal jusitice, Administration
of—Authorship. 3. Dissertations, Academic. 4. Academic
writing. I. Williams, Franklin P. II. Title.
 HV6024.5.M37 2008
 808'.066364—dc22

                                             2006035343

Editor-in-Chief: Vernon R. Anthony
Senior Acquisitions Editor: Tim Peyton
Editorial Assitant: Jillian Allison
Marketing Manager: Adam Kloza
Production Editor: Patty Donovan,
 Pine Tree Composition
Production Liaison:
 Barbara Marttine Cappuccio
Managing Editor: Mary Carnis
Manufacturing Manager: Ilene Sanford

Manufacturing Buyer: Cathleen
 Petersen
Senior Design Coordinator:
 Christopher Weigand
Cover Design: Kevin Kall
Cover Image: © Jamie Kripke/Getty
 Images/Photodisc
Formatting and Interior Design:
 Laserwords Pvt. Ltd
Printer/Binder: R.R. Donnelley & Sons

Pearson Education, Ltd., *London*
Pearson Education Australia Pty. Limited, *Sydney*
Pearson Education Singapore, Pte. Ltd.
Pearson Education North Asia Ltd., *Hong Kong*
Pearson Education Canada, Ltd., *Toronto*
Pearson Education de Mexico, S.A. de C.V.
Pearson Education—Japan, *Tokyo*
Pearson Education Malaysia, Pte. Ltd.
Pearson Education, Upper Saddle River, *New Jersey*

10 9

ISBN 0-13-236895-1

To graduate students everywhere who really want
to make a difference.

Contents

INTRODUCTION/PREFACE xi
ACKNOWLEDGMENTS xiii

SECTION ONE   PREPARING FOR THE THESIS 1

1   WHY DO A THESIS? 3

The Thesis Process 3
    The Social Aspects of a Thesis 6
    Constructing a Time Line 6
    Taking the First Step 9
Choosing a Topic 10
    Neutral Perspective 11
    Just the Right Size 11
    The Right Methodology 12
    A Good Fit for the Committee Members 12
    The Study Needs to Be Done 13
Putting Together a Committee 13
    Types and Functions of Committee Members 14
    Best Case Scenario 15
Purchase Supplies in Advance 15
Using a Style Guide 16
Confronting the Demons of Self-Paced Writing 18
    Exercises for Goal-Oriented Writing 18
    Feedback and Edits 19

2   GETTING STARTED 20

Types of Theses 20
    Legal Thesis 20
    Theoretical Thesis 22
    Program Evaluation Thesis 23
    Policy Analysis 25

Historical 26
Content Analysis 27
Cost-Benefit Analysis 28
General Methodological Types 29
Case Study 30
Survey Research 31
Scales and Assessment Instruments 33
Experimental and Quasi-Experimental Design 34
Summary 36
References 36

3 DEVELOPMENT OF THE RESEARCH QUESTION 37

Forming a Question 37
Locating and Assembling Information .39
Secondary Data 40
Locating Good Data 44
References 51

4 THE INSTITUTIONAL REVIEW BOARD AND THE HUMAN SUBJECTS
REVIEW COMMITTEE 52

The Nature of the IRB 52
No Human Subjects 53
Human Subjects 53
Full Review 54
IRB Exempt Categories 54
Submitting a Proposal for Full Review .58
Informed Consent 58
Additional Application Materials 61
Theses Resulting from Ongoing Departmental Research 64
Summary 65
References 65

5 SUGGESTIONS FOR CITING AND WRITING 66

Academic Writing and the First Person 66
Avoid Plagiarism 67
Avoid the Overuse of Quotes 67
Vary Phrasing and Avoid Repetition 70
Avoid Unnecessary Verbiage 71
Write Clearly 72
Use Original Sources 73
Ensure Your Sources Are Reliable 74
Final Proofreading 74
References 75

SECTION TWO   THE PROSPECTUS OR PROPOSAL 77

6   Introduction and Problem Statement 79

Historical Background and Current Issues 80
   Historical Background 80
   Current Issues 80
Facts and Figures versus Case Examples 81
   Facts and Figures 81
   Case Examples 81
Constructing an Outline for Your Introduction 82
The Purpose of the Study Is. 84
Limitations 84
Transitioning from the First Chapter .85
Summary 88
References 89

7   Literature Review 90

The Purpose of a Literature Review .90
Organizing the Literature Review 91
Generalized Findings versus Specific Results 95
   Generalized Findings 95
   Specific Results 96
Summarizing the Results and Checking Citations 100
Concluding Your Literature Review .102
   The Contents of a Conclusion 102
   How Do You Conclude? 103
Summary 103
References 103

8   Methodology 105

Explaining Your Methodology 105
   The Advantage of Explaining Your Methodology
   in the Prospectus 106
   The Essential Contents of a Methodology Chapter 106
The Two Major Methodological Types 107
   Quantitative Methodologies 107
   Qualitative Methodologies 108
Writing Up the Essential Elements 108
   Overview of the General Research Design 108
   The Research Setting and Population from Which the Sample
   Is Drawn 109
   Source (or Sources) of the Data and Sampling Procedures 110
   Suggestions for Coding 111
   Statement of Hypotheses or Research Questions 114

Methodology for Collecting Data 116
Variables Used in the Analysis and Their Description 121
General Statistical Models to Be Applied 123
Methodological Limitations 125
Acknowledging Your General Limitations 126
Specific Limitations in Your Data 128
Defending Your Methodology 129
Summary 130
References 130

9   THE PROSPECTUS AND THE PROSPECTUS DEFENSE 131

Setting a Date 132
The Prospectus Document 133
Content of a Thesislike Approach 135
The Content of an Independent Document Prospectus 136
General Elements Found in All Prospectus Formats 136
The Presentation 137
Considerations in Preparation for the Prospectus Defense . . .139
What to Do and What Not to Do 140
Summary: The Prospectus Milestone 142

**SECTION THREE   ANALYZING INFORMATION AND DRAWING
CONCLUSIONS** **143**

10   ANALYZING AND PRESENTING YOUR DATA AND FINDINGS 145

Bivariate Statistical Analysis 146
Less Complex 147
More Complex 148
Multivariate Analyses 149
Controlling for Variables in Tables 149
Controlling Variables Statistically 151
Regression 152
Partial Regression 152
Multiple Regression 154
Logistic Regression 155
Hints for Special Parts of the Analysis Chapter 157
Creating Tables and Figures 157
Using Variable Names in Text or Tables 158
Writing Up Your Findings 158
Using Quotes from Interviews 159
Summary 160
References 161

11 CONCLUSIONS, IMPLICATIONS, AND LIMITATIONS 162

The End versus the Beginning 162
The Summary Section 163
The Discussion Section 165
The Conclusions Section 165
Implications for Policy 166
Implications for Research 168
Limitations of the Interpretations and Implications 169
The Big "So What?" 170
References 170

SECTION FOUR   THE FINAL DEFENSE AND BEYOND **173**

12 THE FINAL DOCUMENT AND THESIS DEFENSE 175

The Document 175
Proofreading Checklist 175
The Abstract 177
Table of Contents 177
Front Material 177
The Presentation 181
Choosing a Presentation Style and Format 183
The Results of the Defense 184
References 185

13 REVISING YOUR THESIS INTO ARTICLES AND PRESENTATIONS 186

Paper Presentation 186
Possible Scholarly Venues 187
Paper Competitions and Awards 188
Organizations Typically Sponsoring Student
Paper Competitions 188
Publications 189
Publishing a Journal Article: What to Expect 190
Outlets and Time Frames 191
Preparing a Manuscript for Submission 192
Reducing the Size of the Thesis 192
Revising Thesis Terminology 193
Cover Letter 193
Determining a Suitable Journal Outlet 193
Some Journal Suggestions 194
A Few Last Rules 195
Examples of Student Publications from Thesis 196

Final Remarks 197
References 197
LITERATURE REFERENCES AND RESOURCES .198

Introduction/ Preface

Most students, and even some faculty, tend to think of a thesis as an exercise in doing research—a way to fulfill the requirements of a Master's degree. A few still cling to the notion of "producing a work of importance to the field" or challenging themselves to write more and at a higher level than ever before. Regardless of one's motivation, a thesis is actually a demonstration of the ability to engage in critical thinking. Empirical research fits under the critical thinking umbrella because science is quintessentially a process of critical examination. Any other structure for critical thinking is appropriate as well. Historical investigation, legal research, theory construction, and policy analysis are all forms of critical thinking.

Why is critical thinking important enough to be the hallmark and purpose of the thesis? It is because a graduate degree is not about the mere accumulation of more information but instead the ability to process, or even produce, information and determine whether and how it should be used. For this reason, the culminating project of a graduate degree is a demonstration of those abilities. With this in mind, we encourage thesis students to apply critical thinking to their projects rather than just proceed through a series of formulaic steps and pronounce a hypothesis accepted or rejected.

This book is designed to orient students to the thesis process so that they are more confident and organized while accomplishing their research goals. You will find an overview of the most common and general steps, processes, and products. However, to allay the concerns of faculty who serve on committees, this guide is meant to dovetail with the traditional student-thesis chair and committee relationship, rather than supplant or preempt it. The purpose of this work is to provide advice on the thesis process, while providing an overview of the structure necessary to complete the work. Some of the most common questions are answered, particularly those that may arise prior to meeting with and seeking the advice of a committee. Students are encouraged throughout this text to talk with their committee at each of the major decision points. The material provided here presents a framework for addressing some of the common concerns students have, so that time spent with committee members can be more focused and productive. Just realizing that almost everyone is experiencing the same stresses and dilemmas that you are can make the thesis task more comforting and less threatening. And insights into the resolution of these problems can keep you moving without time-consuming delays.

We welcome your feedback on this text and any suggestions you may have for any future revisions. We caution that not all suggestions work for everyone, and each thesis process is different, as is each student. The compromises we have made to simplify examples and the generalizations we have engaged in are by no means intended to limit the imagination or boundaries of scientific inquiry. Personally we have always enjoyed working with students on theses and wish the best to all of you as you begin what promises to be a very rewarding journey.

Marilyn D. McShane
Frank (Trey) P. Williams III

Acknowledgments

We would like to thank the many graduate students we have worked with throughout our careers for their enthusiasm and trust. We have learned much along with you, and we are very proud of you all. Our special thanks to Frank Mortimer for his faith in this project. Also thank you to the reviewer Melissa A. Loque from St. Joseph's University. And finally, we would like to acknowledge all those who research against the wind, those who pick the politically unpopular, controversial, and critical "windmill" topics, who forsake funding, tenure, and administrative favor to take on the meaningful questions and investigate what really needs to be investigated.

Section One
PREPARING FOR THE THESIS

This section provides an introduction to the thesis and an overview of the types of decisions you will make before you begin writing. There is much to think about and plan in order to ensure a more streamlined, efficient, and less frustrating experience. Chapter One guides you through some background on the thesis process and toward a generic understanding of the characteristics of a good thesis topic. The best way to go about constructing a committee as well as some tips and exercises for writing on a schedule are also included.

Throughout this book, the work of graduate students from all over the country will be used in order to give you insight into the techniques and approaches that have been part of the thesis tradition for many years. The chapters in this first section will help you begin thinking about how your thesis project might take shape. We hope to give you ideas about the issues you should now be discussing with your fellow students, the graduate faculty in your department, and your graduate coordinator.

In Chapter Two we help you begin the thesis process, and consider your initial choices. This includes the type of thesis and the methodology that will best answer your research questions. Subsequent chapters include information to help you develop a research topic and question, find sources of data, meet human subjects' review requirements, and write more effectively, all of the tasks necessary in the thesis process. The format attempts to address the range of choices you have at each point and the best ways to avoid potential problems.

The decision to participate in the thesis process is not just a valued academic tradition, it is also a scholarly benchmark that sets you apart from other students who hold graduate degrees but did not complete a thesis. Many agree that the process works best when friends, family, and colleagues from work support the commitment you make to the challenges represented by the thesis. Feedback and encouragement from fellow students is also a key support factor in this process, and, hopefully, you will have all these resources as you embark on this meaningful journey. We expect that you will find this guide to be useful, and invite your comments and suggestions on ways to make it better.

1

Why Do a Thesis?

Most graduate programs offering or requiring a thesis view it as a culminating experience which allows the student to apply the skills of scientific analysis and inquiry that will be needed later in management and leadership positions and in more advanced graduate work. While many students see the thesis as an exercise that helps them prepare for possible doctoral work, it is also useful in developing skills necessary for effective policy analysis in public agencies and private organizations.

Today's criminal justice professionals are not only involved in conducting opinion polls, policy and program evaluations, grant writing, and developing needs and risk assessments, but are also critics and consumers of this type of work when it is done by others. The thesis experience sensitizes employees to the time, energy, and potential difficulties in various methods of conducting research their agencies might consider undertaking. In this way, one becomes a valuable resource for consultation on various research issues in criminal justice.

Because of the many uses of research skills in our highly competitive workplaces, students' success in completing a thesis instills confidence in their ability to initiate and complete a wide variety of reports, investigations, or evaluations later in their career. It also helps students become more efficient at screening meaningful information from the vast array of materials that come across their desks.

THE THESIS PROCESS

The thesis should be viewed as a process rather than as a product. Some faculty view the document as the final product while others view the defense itself as the actual evidence of completion. Either way, you will have both products completed at the end, and you should prepare for both of them, aware of the differences in the requirements of each. Thus this book addresses both and guides you through some of the traditional difficulties in producing each. The use of examples based on the work of former, successful graduate students illustrates how each task can be undertaken and completed.

The thesis appears much less intimidating if one views it as a series of tasks. Though each department and program will vary on how they would like the thesis done and in what forms, some generalizations can be made about the steps. The model we use here divides the process into chronological and cumulative efforts. None of the individual steps are much different from the types of assignments and research projects you have completed during the course of your degree work. The difference for most students is the more independent nature of the thesis effort, the appearance of less structure, and fewer deadlines. For these reasons, breaking the thesis down into steps and setting your own deadlines for each task is a more familiar route to take and has worked successfully for many students.

The model may be viewed in some varying form of a game board where you must proceed along from Step 1 to the prospectus defense, as in Figure 1-1.

After the prospectus stage, different types of theses will proceed differently. Depending on the type you have, your style of gathering, analyzing, and writing up information, particularly the number of chapters you have and how they are organized, will differ. However, it is safe to say that the basic remaining steps will go something like this:

- Finish gathering information, observations, or data documenting any problems.
- Analyze your materials and organize your findings in a logical format.
- Write up conclusions, implications, and suggestions for future research.
- Draft final copy of thesis and begin editing.
- Defend thesis.

This order is recommended for a number of reasons. First, the sequential character of thesis development allows you to avoid making an early mistake that contaminates subsequent work and even your results. By verifying your ideas against the literature and previous research, you have a supported basis for your proposal grounded in past empirical findings and sources that your committee can verify are legitimate. By scrutinizing the topic, the methodology, and the rationale for the methodology in the beginning, you have not wasted time and effort on material that will have to be revised and reformulated. Second, it maximizes feedback and interaction with your committee members, so that you can benefit from their input, and even allows you to continue working and moving along while they are reading and editing the previous sections. Finally, while there are some students who can work in a less structured and naturally organized fashion, this route has been time tested over years of graduate program history.

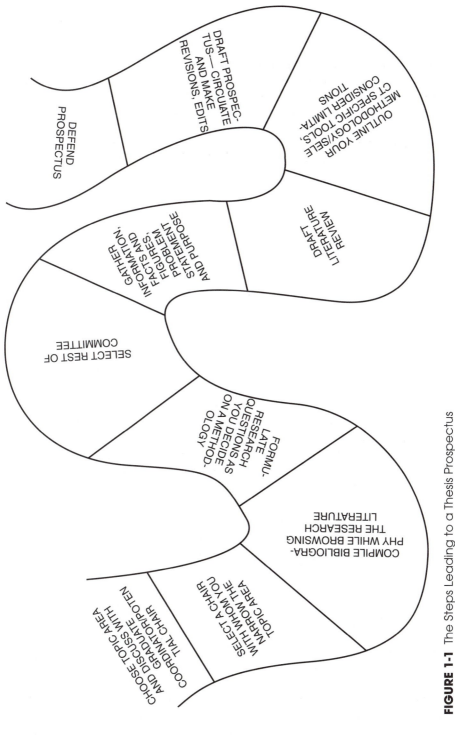

FIGURE 1-1 The Steps Leading to a Thesis Prospectus

Content within the figure:

CHOOSE TOPIC AREA AND DISCUSS WITH GRADUATOR/POTEN COORDIAL CHAIR

SELECT A CHAIR WITH WHOM YOU NARROW THE TOPIC AREA

COMPILE BIBLIOGRA-PHY WHILE BROWSING THE RESEARCH LITERATURE

FORMU-LATE RESEARCH QUESTIONS AS YOU DECIDE ON A METHOD-OLOGY.

SELECT REST OF COMMITTEE

GATHER, INFORMATION AND FACTS, FIGURES, PROBLEM STATEMENT AND PURPOSE

DRAFT LITERATURE REVIEW

OUTLINE YOUR METHODOLOGY/SELE CT SPECIFIC TOOLS, CONSIDER LIMITA-TIONS

DRAFT PROSPEC-TUS— CIRCUATE AND MAKE REVISIONS, EDITS

DEFEND PROSPECTUS

For those who are more visually oriented, the thesis process can be tracked according to the diagram in Figure 1-2.

Steady progress on the completion of the steps in the thesis process should be viewed as an accomplishment in and of itself and should continue to motivate the student toward the ultimate completion of the work. It is important to remember throughout the thesis that academic growth—particularly in graduate work—is, by nature, a social process.

The Social Aspects of a Thesis

The first five steps of the process involve a considerable amount of interaction with your professors, your fellow students, and professional colleagues in the field in which you intend to research. It is helpful to discuss your ideas and your intentions with a sufficient number of people to get as much feedback, suggestions, cautions, and insights as possible. This is the time to hear the stories about what to look for and avoid, what potential problems might arise, what the advantages and disadvantages of certain types of approaches and methods might be, and how others react to your choice of topic. You may want to organize a meeting time with other beginning thesis students to "brainstorm" about research ideas. These exchanges are invaluable in learning from others and with others. Having the support of professors, students, and colleagues will make the process seem less intimidating and stressful. Naturally, some students may have a strong personal preference for learning on their own, using the Internet and library resources for exploring their subject options, and that is what they should do. The important thing is not to isolate yourself if you are unsure of what you are doing and how to go about doing it. Obtaining meaningful feedback early in the process of topic exploration can reduce the amount of time and energy you spend getting started, so find a method that works for you and evaluate your ideas. Go ahead, order a couple of pizzas, and invite your professors and classmates to join in the discussion of potential research topics!

Constructing a Time Line

Very early in the thesis process a student should construct a time line that is best suited for their particular circumstances. In any group, students will vary on the pace at which they can complete the thesis and the factors that are pressuring them to do so. A time line should be realistic but firm. You should develop a time line to which you can commit. A history of pushing back the deadlines and delaying completion of one task after another can make the process more frustrating and unsatisfying. Don't be overly concerned, though, if one or two deadlines are missed—other people are involved, and some circumstances are beyond your control.

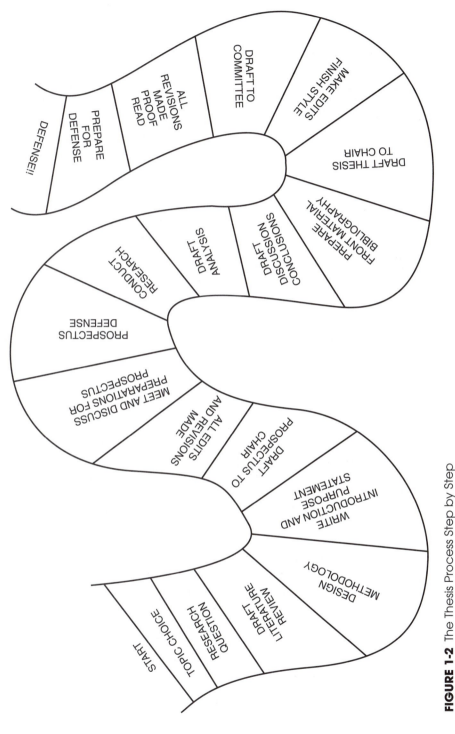

FIGURE 1-2 The Thesis Process Step by Step

7

For example, one student developed a time line that would allow him to complete his thesis in one academic year. It looked like this:

Fall Semester Begins	August 22
Bibliography Developed	September 12
Draft Problem Statement and Purpose	October 1
Draft Literature Review	October 14
Draft Methodology	October 28
Draft Prospectus	November 7
Defend Prospectus	December 7

(Get real—You are going to have to work on this all through the holiday break . . .)

Winter Semester Begins	January 5
Complete Analysis of Information	February 17
Draft New Chapters/Analysis	February 26
Draft Conclusions and Recommendations	March 13
Final Copy Thesis	March 26
Defend	April 23
Turn in Final Copy to University Repository	April 26

Though there are many little steps in between, as well as meetings, phone calls, or e-mails going on throughout this process, the most important dates and activities are shown. Keep in mind that even though you may move on and begin writing a literature review or the methodology, you are still expanding, refining, and editing all of the parts as you work toward the total prospectus product.

Any time line you develop needs to be sensitive to the normal working pace of your committee. Some members may take longer than others, and some may have varying commitments that interrupt the flow of their participation. This is something to which your chair can help you adjust. There are always other tasks and parts of the document you can be working on while you wait for feedback. And, even though the steps listed move from drafting the prospectus to defending the prospectus, the reality is that in between those two a carefully orchestrated sequence of circulating your materials through your committee must take place. It will be best to find a schedule for submitting materials to your committee members that works well for your particular group, but here, too, there are generalities that will likely work for you. A schedule should be proposed to minimize wear and tear on your committee, to avoid receiving conflicting edits, and to keep the smooth process flowing. Thus, when your chair talks about turning in your work before you defend your prospectus, he or she is really imagining something like the schedule used for Lorraine (see Box 1-1), which indicates that there was almost a month from when the draft of the prospectus was completed until it was defended.

BOX 1-1 EXAMPLE TIME LINE FOR EDITING

Draft prospectus to Chair	November 7
Chair's comments back to student	November 14
Revisions and edits made and submitted to other two committee members	November 17
Comments back from committee members	November 24
Edits and revisions made	November 28
Meet and discuss preparations for prospectus defense; work on prospectus presentation	November 30
Make final copies of prospectus and hand out prior to or at defense	December 7

The same schedule for submitting drafts and receiving edits and corrections from the committee could be used for the final thesis document.

As the schedule in Box 1-2 demonstrates, just because you complete your draft does not mean that you can turn around and defend it at the next possible date. The edit process is a valuable part of the learning experience. The committee can strengthen your writing, point out inconsistencies or potential problems, and redirect your attention to important sources you may have overlooked.

It is best to consult your graduate student handbook or thesis guidelines for official requirements governing the deadlines in the process in your department. University regulations may dictate how close to graduation a thesis must be completed. While some schools may let you defend quite late in the semester and certify the degree based on a successful defense, others may require all final bound copies to be produced prior to commencement.

Taking the First Step

As one Masters' graduate, Wes, explained, "Every great adventure begins with a single first step and the will to do it." He commented that "though it seems like eating an elephant, it is just one bite at a time. At the beginning it appears to be an enormous project. But starting early, allowing enough time, and constant work (even in small regular tasks) makes it doable." And, another student, Amiee, adds, looking back, it is a meaningful experience.

> Completing the thesis helped me to own my Masters Degree because I know the dedication and perseverance it took to complete it and the enormous amount of academic application it also required. I look at the paper degree hanging on the wall and it doesn't do justice to the educational experience I had. It wasn't as scary as I thought it would be, and is something that to this day, I am proud to have accomplished.

BOX 1-2 SAMPLE CALENDAR FOR COMPLETING THE THESIS

SUNDAY	MONDAY	TUESDAY	WEDNESDAY	THURSDAY	FRIDAY	SATURDAY
1 APRIL	2 Draft of all completed chapters to Chair	3	4	5	6	7
8	9 Comments back from Chair	10	11	12	13 All edits made and sent to rest of committee	14
15	16	17	18	19	20	21
22	23 Results from committee	24	25	26	27 All edits made, meet w/Chair to prepare defense	28
29	30	31				
		MAY	1 DEFENSE	2	3	4

One of the repeated themes that you will hear from successful graduate students is the importance of picking an appropriate topic and then following through with consistent effort at each step. Therefore, we continue to focus this book on the steps for completing a thesis and some suggestions and techniques for staying organized throughout the process.

CHOOSING A TOPIC

What makes a good topic? There are at least five qualities to a good thesis topic: a neutral perspective, a proper size undertaking, the right methodology, and a good fit for the committee. To these qualities add one final requirement, a study that needs to be done—that is, the study would make a meaningful contribution to our knowledge and understanding of our criminal justice system. Let's explore these features in more detail, and see what they mean for you in your selection process. One of the keys for staying on track and completing the thesis in a timely manner is that you go through the initial steps thoughtfully, aware of their importance so that you do not have to go back and start over later.

Neutral Perspective

By a neutral topic, we mean that it is not something that you feel emotionally or politically invested in. A student who has been a victim of sexual abuse or domestic violence should probably avoid those research topics. The thesis process alone is stressful enough without introducing strong emotional reactions and judgments. Most faculty would be very reluctant to approve topics that have the potential tension such work would involve. For example, a student who had served in a federal law enforcement agency was involved in a very high-profile sting operation that resulted in a major national scandal. He wanted to write about the incident and tell his side, in a part organizational analysis (case study), part historical exposé. This was not recommended by his committee. His emotional investments in the ensuing employee disciplinary actions as well as the media and public criticism meant that he might not be able to develop the academic perspective needed for a thesis. Could he write his version of the events as a memoire for a mainstream press? That is always possible, but as a thesis topic, the content will be challenged, critiqued, and moved toward a balanced discussion by the committee which would likely be a frustrating and stressful experience for the student. It is better to pick a topic with a more neutral perspective.

Just the Right Size

There are some topics that are too big and others that would be too narrow or small. For example, attempting to explain crime or even one type of crime or the differences between males and females in criminality would be too involved a topic to treat adequately in the size of a thesis as would a study that seeks to determine the relationship between drugs and delinquency. Instead of starting with "Which theory best explains . . ." it would be more practical to choose a single theory and see whether it is capable of explaining the phenomena selected for your study. Further, the phenomenon selected for study should not be crime in general, but a specific type or by a specific group of offenders such as delinquents or the elderly. In many cases, the sample size, if one is collecting his or her own data, is also one that is manageable for a thesis—one that would not take too much time or money to collect.

For these reasons, thesis topics will often acknowledge the appropriate size and scope by defining the project right from the start as a "preliminary assessment" or a "pilot study." This implies that the project has been "scaled down" and that the findings may not have generalizability beyond certain boundaries. It may also be sufficient to develop an instrument and conduct some reliability and validity tests on it without further surveying a large random population. Your committee will help you assess the proper size of a project. If you are working with faculty members on a large, long-term research project, they will often assist you in fractioning off a piece of that as a manageable thesis size investigation. Using a secondary data set allows one to trade off the loss of original collection with larger size samples that may be national in scope.

Narrowing a subject is a necessary but difficult task which is a process of reducing the topic to a certain type of crime or aspect of crime under certain circumstances among a more specific population or to a certain number of variables that may be suggested by a theoretical perspective. Often you will see this in theory testing, such as when researchers isolate and work with Hirschi's bond of attachment rather than the entire social control theory itself.

The Right Methodology

The correct methodology would hopefully fit both the student's abilities and the requirements of the data or the type of question asked. First, a look at the literature will tell you what methodologies have been used for similar types of research in the past and what the problems encountered there have been. Aside from your specific topic, there may be methodologies that are considered more productive for other aspects of your study such as your population (children or victims), your variables (criminal histories or dollar amounts of crime costs), and the amount of time that you have (a longitudinal design versus a single point in time). Read up on the methodologies that you are considering to ensure that they (or one of them) will fit your needs before presenting the approach to your committee. Methodologies are discussed in more detail in the following chapters.

A Good Fit for the Committee Members

Your chair and your other committee members, whether from inside your department or outside, should be comfortable working in the area you have under consideration. They need not be experts in the topic nor even have researched it before, as long as they have an interest in the topic and are capable of providing the necessary feedback whether it is on your methodology and data or on your theoretical assumptions or conceptualization of the problem. It is not uncommon to put together a committee where the different members each bring different strengths and experiences to the project. It is best to have honest and frank discussions with your members to ensure that they also feel that their participation is a good fit for the undertaking. This would mean that they are comfortable not only with the topic and the line of inquiry you are pursuing, but also they will work effectively with the other members on the committee as well.

It would be important to also discuss your anticipated time line with potential committee members. Often faculty have scheduled future commitments, such as administrative service appointments, sabbaticals, or international teaching assignments that may make it difficult for them to participate on committees that run longer than they initially programmed for or committed to. Again, realistic and frank discussions about the thesis time line are necessary to ensure a smooth and uncomplicated process. Though no one can ever ensure that emergencies will not arise, having to stop and appoint a new member in someone's absence is always stressful.

The Study Needs to Be Done

Researching the topic in advance is the best way to ensure that you not only have the right methodology, but also are aware of the gaps that remain in our knowledge base, how we could further our understanding of the topic, and what missing pieces of research have been identified by others who have worked in this area. Often at the conclusion of published studies, the author suggests, as you will at the end of your thesis, ideas for future research. This is often a good place to look for potential topics as that study has laid the groundwork for a logical extension to be developed. For example, after completing a study on the effect of segregation on prison inmates, Peck (2004) noted that further research might explore the question: "Does segregative architecture affect the presentation of mental illness? . . . Do inmates in the newer architecture require mental health transfers more or less often than their segregated peers in different architectures?" By looking through existing research in areas of interest, you may find some potential research questions. Those suggestions become part of your justification for that topic and would be cited to support your claim that the study needs to be done.

The way to determine if you have selected a good topic is to use the criteria discussed in your preliminary idea formulations. Discuss with others and your potential committee members how your project appears to fare with these criteria, and consider any other additional criteria that they may suggest. Remember that differences are also individual and that what might be an appropriate size project for one person may not be as desirable for another. Your time constraints, research interests, and experiences should weigh in on this decision as well.

PUTTING TOGETHER A COMMITTEE

Once you have a topic idea, you should discuss it with faculty members who may serve as your chair. After you have identified a chair, the two of you can refine your idea, narrow the focus to a research question, and determine the most appropriate methodology for investigating the problem. Then, when you have formulated a method of inquiry you will be ready to add your other committee members. In most programs this is a formal process that is solidified in the form of a written agreement which all parties sign. This document is usually part of the record of a thesis process and must be approved at levels above the committee chair. Normally, changes are only considered under extenuating circumstances so it is best to give this matter considerable thought. As discussed earlier, your additional members should complement your chair and provide the balance and support that is essential to the successful thesis. To assist you in making these choices, an in-depth discussion of the role and functions of the committee members is provided.

Types and Functions of Committee Members

Chair

The chair is the person that you interact with most frequently and the person who will guide your decision making as you plan and carry out your study. By directing your materials through the chair, before disseminating to the rest of your committee you will organize the review process so that you do not receive contradictory or overlapping types of directions and edits. When each phase of your material is ready, your chair will have you send your work to your other members either one at a time or simultaneously. Your chair will also help encourage their reviews and will often communicate directly with them if problems arise. The chair is a facilitator and a mentor; choose your chair carefully.

Committee Members

Your committee members are responsible for ensuring that your work proceeds according to accepted scientific practices. As you move through the thesis process, they will raise issues that you can work with your chair to resolve. Often committee members will have special expertise and skills for the project, and you will coordinate directly with them on those features. Then, as always, it is best to bring those issues and options back to your chair to ensure that the oversight is consistent. Some committee members are more comfortable assisting you with cleaning your data or performing sophisticated statistical analyses. Your chair may be able to give you some helpful advise about selecting the other members of your committee. Listen carefully.

Outside Member

Some departments will require you to have an outside member on your committee, while others may simply encourage or tolerate that. There are many benefits to having an outside member but also some potential problems as well. An outside member may have certain skills or an expertise that is important to your project as when a professor from a math or statistics department is brought on to assist in more complex data analysis or when someone from computer science helps with geographic mapping. As an interdisciplinary science, criminal justice has many close ties to other academic fields that have related interests in the topics of crime, justice, agency administration, behavior, and law.

EXAMPLE

Dr. R was the former head of research for the probation department where Susan worked at the time she began her thesis. Susan had heard about Dr. R's previous research evaluating an innovative drug program. Susan decided to do a replication or follow-up evaluation of that program to see if any improvements suggested by the earlier evaluation had made an impact. Dr. R was an excellent choice for an outside committee member not only because of her previous research on the topic but also as a person who had worked for the same agency as Susan and as an academic with a degree in statistics.

Best Case Scenario

The best case scenario for any thesis is undoubtedly a good fit between the chair and the student. This means that they both want to work on that topic, with that method, in the agreed-upon time frame. Optimistically, the two might have personality styles, work styles, and writing styles that are compatible. A successful team will also agree on many of the areas described below for you to consider. In assessing your potential for thesis progress and the effectiveness of your interactions with your committee, you may want to find out how your committee members want to work relative to the following topics:

Contact:	Some chairs and committee members want more, some less. It is to your advantage to have regular periodic contact so you need to find out what level is best for working with your chair, weekly, bi-weekly, monthly?
Meeting Format:	Some professors prefer to work in person, via phone, or e-mail—find out which your prospective committee members would utilize.
Editing Format:	Some may want products in hard copy form or computer files, and some may want to make edits on hard copy or in some type of word editing program for text.
Degree of Oversight:	Some committee chairs will want to see work incrementally, some not until entire sections are completely drafted. As you adjust to the work schedules of your committee, you may want to adjust your style so that the process flows—for example, if two or three weeks elapse before your new work is reviewed, you may want to hold off and submit larger chunks of work.

It is a good idea to explore these process issues ahead of time so that you are not surprised later by problems that might arise which could have easily been foreseen due to differences in working styles.

PURCHASE SUPPLIES IN ADVANCE

Properly equipping yourself for writing and researching is essential for minimizing mistakes and rewrites. Accordion file folders and other organizational aids will help you keep a variety of printed materials where they can be easily referenced. Various colored Post-it notes and highlighters can also be adopted into schemes that code types of sources and where they are to be used. You may want to have a file system that divides work by chapters or by topics.

Whatever organizational system you adopt, try to be consistent in its application throughout your research.

As you work, keep multiple backup copies of your electronic files, and back up your work on a regular basis. Keep each chapter in a separate file to minimize your risk of losing material. As much as possible, limit the exposure of your work files to potentially contaminating sources. You may also want to consider keeping a current spare copy of your electronic files in a separate location such as at work, on the web or a mainframe, or at a relative's house in case of some emergency. It is better to be safe than to find yourself re-creating your entire text. Be sure to have paper, other printing resources, and access to photocopying arranged prior to starting your project. Many professors prefer to read hard copies of your drafts so be sure to determine committee preferences for reviewing your work in advance. Adopting an accepted style manual before you begin is also important.

USING A STYLE GUIDE

The most efficient way to implement a format style into your document is to do it in the very beginning. It is not an effective use of your time to have to go back and reformat and adapt a style after your work has been written. Before you begin writing, purchase whatever style manual your committee or department requires and begin incorporating the elements as soon as possible. Make sure you have the most recent version, as earlier editions may be superceded, and you will end up having to revise your document later when you may not have the time.

The two most common areas for directions in style are in **page formatting** and for **bibliographic references.** There are many nuances to track throughout the text, including variations in bolding, italics, capitalization, and use of certain punctuation as well as citations within chapters. By adopting a style early on, you will develop a pattern for entering the correct reference information, and it is less likely that you will leave out necessary elements of the citation (page numbers, publisher, publication city, etc.) which may be difficult to go back and locate later. Early attention to spacing and margins also means that your document more accurately reflects how it will look as completed, which is a helpful guide along the way. Avoiding surprises is important as revisions and adaptations take valuable time and energy. Examining your headings and subheadings as you go ensures that your organization and flow remain logical. With an accurate identification of your heading levels, committee members can help you discern where to elaborate, condense, or reorder information.

Some of the most common style guides or publication manuals are listed below.

APA: American Psychological Association (2001). *Publication manual of the American Psychological Association.* 5th ed. Washington, DC: American Psychological Association. (Because APA heading styles are oriented toward articles, a thesis heading style is provided in Box 1-3.)

BOX 1-3 SUGGESTED HEADING STYLE FOR APA-BASED THESES

The APA Manual's description of manuscript headings and subheadings (which are for *journal articles* only) are a bit confusing. If your department has no other specific instructions, we propose the following guidelines for your thesis.

Level of Heading	Justification	Special Fonts	Font size
Title of chapter (T1)	Centered	All caps, bold	16
Main heading (H1)	Centered	Initial caps, bold	14
Second heading (H2)	Left	Initial caps, bold	13
Third heading (H3)	Left	Initial caps, italics	12
Fourth heading (H4)	Left with one tab	First word cap, italics	12
Fifth heading (H5)	Left with one tab, same line	First word cap, italics	12
Normal text	Left with beginning para tab	None	12

Example:
(6 empty lines from top)

CHAPTER TWO   T1

(1 empty line)

REVIEW OF THE LITERATURE   T1

(3 empty lines)

Methodology for the Review   H1

(2 empty lines)

Meta-Analysis as a Form of Review   H2

(1 empty line)

Description of Meta-Analysis   H3

(1 empty line)

Nonstatistical forms of meta-analysis

(1 empty lines)   H4

Tabular presentation: An alternative method, which is not   H5
precisely within the contemporary definition of meta-analysis is . . .
(0 empty lines)

CHICAGO or TURABIAN: University of Chicago Press. (2003). *The Chicago manual of style*, 15th ed. Chicago: University of Chicago Press.
MLA: Gibaldi, J. (2003). *MLA handbook for writers of research papers*. 6th Ed. New York: Modern Language Association of America.

Also, there are many Web sites with style information. For example, look at this one from the University of Colorado.

http://ucblibraries.colorado.edu/about/citing.htm

Talk to your chair early about what style you should use and how much emphasis they place on style issues. Having the necessary supplies, organizational aids, and a consistent style in place will make your writing much smoother and less frustrating. Safe handling practices for electronic files and data will also keep your project on track. Advanced planning and preparation ensures that the decisions you are now ready to make will be easier to put into action.

CONFRONTING THE DEMONS OF SELF-PACED WRITING

Oftentimes getting an idea and a committee together are not nearly as difficult for a student as the prospect of self-paced writing, or completing a project without the usual constraints of class deadlines. Some students find that they are just not able to produce the stream of output necessary for a work the size of a thesis. This includes the picky person who struggles for just the right words and fusses over the phrasing to the point that they are producing one perfect paragraph a week, the person who feels they have to have the entire section conceptualized in their heads before they put down any words, or those who stare at the empty page for a while before they are distracted by a walk, a friend, or a much anticipated TV rerun. For those having difficulty writing at a more effective pace, some exercises might be in order.

Exercises for Goal-Oriented Writing

The reluctant writer and the timer technique. Set a clock or kitchen timer to sixty minutes and sit down and write. At the end of sixty minutes, count your words, and if you have a sufficient amount, say a whole page, give yourself a reward and restart the timer. Be conscious of the need to keep up at least the same pace as you originally set and perhaps even increase it to the point where you have maximized your write over rewrite ratio. Go back and edit the pages you have written, judging whether writing using a modified or different system would increase your efficiency. Sometimes just having the background constraints of a timer bell or the competition of a friend or family member also attempting to complete a project might help spur the reluctant writer along.

The can't find time writer and the "countdown" approach.   Another technique would be to make a tear-off pad of the number of pages you need to complete by a certain date, and hang it in a prominent place. At the beginning of the week, establish a schedule of times each day to write and work toward the goal of tearing off those pages as you complete them and move closer to the goal. Sometimes a constant reminder of the goal and the progress motivates the person to completing the task. Remember, some of the world's most prolific writers are not persons who are extremely talented per se, but those who are disciplined and set and follow strict standards for how many words or pages they must produce each and every day.

Feedback and Edits

Another writing problem is the student who writes but does not want to turn anything in to his or her committee members until it is "perfect." This results in slow downs just like the problems described earlier. Discussions with your chair and other committee members may help you come to some agreement about what type of feedback and input schedule will work best. If you wait too long to show your material to your committee, expect more problems to arise. Perhaps the worst time to turn in delayed materials is the end of a semester. Professors may not feel familiar or comfortable enough with a work to approve its progress and may resent the pressure of being expected to approve something quickly. Feedback from your professors will frequently be very encouraging if you are turning in work in a timely fashion. Moreover, their comments will help clarify how soon sections will be considered "finished" or ready. The best thing to do is to explain to your professors that you do have concerns about the early "draft" condition of your work, but ask them if they would like to see it even if it is "preliminary." Many will ask to see it, just to make sure you are on the right track. Experienced committee members will be aware that your work will be in draft form for some time. As a word of caution, be cognizant that work in draft form is not examined as closely as work approaching the final copy. For that reason, you should expect that "approvals" of draft work will not preclude changes later.

Throughout the process, you will need to have an agreement with your members about whether they will be doing "technical" editing or just editing for substantive content. It may even be helpful to have a trusted colleague or associate review your pages before you submit them (just make sure you are confident in their reviewing and proofreading abilities). Even if that person is not familiar with your area and methods, their review of grammar, punctuation, and spelling might make it easier for you to turn material in to your committee, and your committee will appreciate not having to address that level of editing.

It is now time to begin the process of selecting a topic.

2

GETTING STARTED

Throughout the course of your graduate work, you may have been thinking about ideas for your thesis. The decision should be a practical one based on your interests and abilities, the strengths and interests of your faculty mentors, and the availability of information and resources with which to work.

While you may have already decided on a type of thesis, the examples presented may help you test whether your current choice is really the best format for your topic. This chapter also aids in your assessment of whether you are prepared to meet the expectations of a particular design and in providing some ideas you may not have considered. You may even want to adopt another methodology or even another topic. Not all possible thesis formats are discussed here, just some of the ones most commonly used. They are presented as an overview which you can further discuss with your graduate coordinator or potential thesis chair.

TYPES OF THESES

Legal Thesis

A legal thesis would involve research on proposed legislation, existing laws, and constitutional concepts using case law decisions and the work of legal scholars. Analysis of precedents and comparisons of rulings in various jurisdictions have been part of this approach. New legal trends such as the use of certain defenses or the interpretation of a new law also make good topics for theses. Often students in criminal justice will prepare an analysis of legal liabilities which may be involved in management decision making. Another approach would be to prepare an updated analysis of the legal aspects of new or anticipated policies and procedures for use by local agencies.

A single case study may be used as the focus of the research—as is found in Leo Carroll's (1998) study of the impact of the sweeping correctional reforms derived from *Palmigiano* v. *Garrahy* in the state of Rhode Island or Mary Parker's (1986) analysis of the effects of *Holt* v. *Sarver* on the Arkansas Prison System. Another approach would be to trace a legal issue over time (such as parental liability for delinquency or airport baggage searches) to explain the current role of the concept, or to predict its future role. Such analyses help practitioners anticipate the policies that may be more likely to comply with trends in judicial thinking on a given subject.

EXAMPLES

Some of the research questions that have been explored in a legal thesis are explained below.

1. Kristen analyzed *Brewer* v. *Arizona,* the first post *Furman* capital case in that state. This was a landmark decision not only in terms of the uncontested execution of the defendant but also as one of the first on the issue of fetal homicide. Kristen was able to interview each of the principal legal players in the case in depth—the judge, the prosecutor, and the defense attorney—which made her chronicle of their thinking and decision making a critical part of the work. Her research questions were (a) what factors influenced the outcome of *Brewer* v. *Arizona,* and (b) looking back, how do the principles view the decisions made in that case?

2. Valerie looked at the legal liability issues surrounding the practice of off-duty police working in private ventures in a major southwestern city. This was a particularly timely issue because the newspapers had been covering a series of scandals related to the abuse of authority and the use of deadly force during off-duty employment. Her search of the case law led her to focus on the issues of course and scope of employment, immunity, and concerns regarding workers' compensation. Her research questions were (a) what are the legal issues and controversies most commonly raised concerning off-duty police extra-employment, and (b) what are their implications for policy?

Some books that may be useful in your exploration of ideas for a legal theses are cited below.

CARROLL, L. (1999). *Lawful order: A case study of correctional crisis and reform.* New York: Garland.

DERNBACH, J. C., SINGLETON, R. V., WHARTON, C. S., and RUHTENBERT, J. M. (1994). *A practical guide to legal writing and legal method.* 2d ed. Littleton, CO: Fred B. Rothman & Co.

EDWARDS, L. H. (2003). *Legal writing and analysis.* New York: Aspen.

GARNER, B. A. (2002). *The elements of legal style.* 2d ed. New York: Oxford University Press.

KUNZ, C. L., SCHMEDEMANN, D. A. , DOWNS, M. P., and BATESON, A. L. (Eds). (2000). *The process of legal research.* 5th ed. New York: Aspen.

NEUMANN, R. K. (2001). *Legal reasoning and legal writing: Structure, strategy, and style.* 4th ed. New York: Aspen.

OATES, L. C., ENQUIST, A., and KUNSCH, K. (2002). *The legal writing handbook: Analysis, research and writing.* 3d ed. New York: Aspen.

PARKER, M. L. (1986). *Judicial intervention in correctional institutions: The Arkansas odyssey.* HUNTSVILLE, TX: Unpublished doctoral dissertation, Sam Houston State University.

PECK, L. (2004). *Hoeing a long hard row: Longterm administrative segregation of a cohort of Texas prison inmates.* Huntsville, TX: unpublished doctoral dissertation, Sam Houston State University.

SHAPO, H. S., WALTER, M. R., and FAJANS, E (2003). *Writing and analysis in the law.* 4th ed. New York: Foundation Press.

SLOAN, A. E. (2003). *Basic legal research: Tools and strategies.* 2d ed. New York: Aspen.

WREN, C. and WREN, J. (1986). *The legal research manual: A game plan for legal research and analysis* (2d ed.). MADISON, WI: ADAMS & AMBROSE Pub.

YELLIN, A. & SAMBORN, H. (2003). *The legal research and writing handbook: A basic approach for paralegals* (3d ed.). New York: Aspen.

Theoretical Thesis

A theoretical thesis might use data related to a criminal justice issue to test a traditional or contemporary theory of crime, providing an empirical analysis on one or more of the constructs or variables involved in a theoretical relationship. Alternatively, a theoretical critique, while similar to a theoretical test, focuses on the arguments that can be made for an alternative approach to an existing theory. It may be similar to theory testing, if data are used for analyses, but it is more likely to involve a more qualitative assessment and display of logic, or a theoretical thesis might attempt to construct a theory or modify, integrate, or add to an existing one. The theory testing approach is a fairly common version of the thesis and, other than making sure the constructs to be tested are reasonable, is among the easier forms of thesis that graduate students might attempt. On the other hand, the theory construction form is among the most difficult of theses because of the original nature of rigorous thinking required, and theory critique is almost as difficult for the same reasons. We say this not to discourage students from attempting these latter two approaches, but to make sure students who are considering these are aware of the effort involved and nature of the task.

EXAMPLES

1. Frank wanted to test lifestyle theory looking at vehicle theft in the college town where he was a police officer. In taking reports, Frank noticed that many students who originally reported "no idea" what happened to their vehicle, later revised their report to more accurately reflect that it was used without permission by an acquaintance, or that it had originally been loaned but was not returned, or it was damaged. This prompted the fearful student to report it as stolen, or to revise their version of events to cover up binge drinking or activities that made the victim vulnerable to the theft of the car. Frank was able to obtain all of the vehicle theft reports for a three-month period from his department and set about analyzing them for variables related to lifestyle theory, namely, age, occupation, time and place, day of the week, neighborhood, as well as victim and offender activities if known. His research question was "To what degree was vehicle theft in this college town explained by lifestyle theory?"

2. Sheila worked in the inmate legal services office of a large state prison system. She wanted to test conflict theory in the context of detainers or holds placed on illegal immigrants in the system. Conflict theory would be supported, she maintained, if less powerful groups like immigrants were further punished by federal immigration laws while serving state prison sentences. Her research question asked whether inmates who had immigration detainers served longer state sentences under more harsh conditions (no contact visits, no outside duties or recreation, no promotions beyond

the minimum level, etc.) than their counterparts with similar state sentences for similar offenses and similar criminal and incarceration histories.

3. Judith had read a number of works on the regulation of the homeless from the perspective of the "academic anarchist." She wanted to critique some of their assumptions and findings based on her own experiences as a pretrial officer in a large urban jurisdiction. She used four or five or their basic tenets to organize her thesis and structure her responses, concluding with her own theoretical model. Her research questions were (a) do formal and informal responses to the homeless in Houston differ from the framework posited by the academic anarchists in the critical criminology literature, and (b) if so, how?

4. Jermaine was convinced, after taking an advanced course in criminological theory, that many theories were correct but only partially so. He reasoned that if a few of those theories could be combined, then a stronger explanation would result. After thoughtful reading and discussion with some of his faculty, Jermaine took three theories he thought would be compatible and attempted an integration. The theories were social learning, drift, and exchange theories. He carefully investigated the assumptions of the theories, critiqued their separate positions, and noted where they tended to fall short. He then derived a list of propositions from the theories and demonstrated how some of the propositions from each one would assist the shortcomings of the others and allow for the development of an integrated, logical model from the results. His research question was, "Can social learning, drift, and exchange theories be integrated into a more powerful model for explaining criminal behavior?"

Program Evaluation Thesis

A program evaluation is one of the more practical formats for a thesis. Many Master's degree students work in agencies that provide services and programs requiring periodic review and outcome reports. Most state and federal grants have mandatory reviews incorporated into their funding, and many specify that outside agents be used for that purpose. This was how Wes came about his thesis topic. "I worked in the research office of county probation which had received state funding for an experimental program. The funding required a program evaluation. I was able to place myself in the position of coordinator of the research design and implementation." Faculty may also be involved in program reviews that would provide a graduate student an opportunity to conduct his or her thesis research in conjunction with the research effort.

Within the context of program evaluation, there are various categories of investigations that might be done. Most common is the **outcome evaluation** where the focus of the study is summative and the overall results at the end of the treatment are measured. Some may also refer to this as an impact study. The dependent variable is often recidivism, rearrest, or the cessation of some type of target behavior such as domestic violence or drug use. To conduct a meaningful evaluation, programs must keep accurate data that would allow researchers to make scientific assessments (with adequate controls) about the relationship between a treatment and an outcome.

Sometimes it is not possible for the student to wait for an appropriate number of program outcomes to be accumulated because of time constraints on completing the thesis. At other times agency officials may seek out an intermediate assessment of their program's progress. In both cases the student may want to consider an evaluation of the treatment integrity or the program's implementation. Such an analysis allows potential problems to be detected and rectified early enough to put the program back on the right track. Research done under these conditions is called a **process evaluation** or an **implementation evaluation.**

The focus of the analysis in these studies is formative, and researchers are not concerned about the future outcome of the subjects or participants. Instead they look at operations, staffing, budgeting, schedules, and other procedures that may be influencing the eventual outcomes, thus threatening the validity of predictions about the relationship between the treatment and the subjects' status or behavior.

Program evaluations will often use multiple information gathering strategies in the course of the investigation, including surveys, interviews, focus groups, archived or file data, current records, and observations (overt or covert, participant or nonparticipant). In some instances a researcher will conduct observations in a manner that keeps him or her out of the activities to avoid potential influence over the behavior of the subjects—which we refer to as "unobtrusive measures." These approaches are generally preferable as the biases introduced in the process of research are considered a potential threat to validity. However, researchers should also avoid the use of misinformation, spying, secret, or misleading roles in the process of gathering information—as directed by most ethical guidelines.

Some examples of program evaluation designs and resources that may be useful to you in further investigating this type of thesis are listed below.

EXAMPLES

1. Laura worked as a probation officer and was interested in the county's drug court program. She was able to obtain data that had already been gathered on the outcomes of a cohort of participants who had already come through the drug court program and then compare them with a similar group of drug offenders who, during the same time period, went through regular probation and not the drug court program (her control group). Her research question asked if the drug court participants had greater success on probation (i.e., if they were less likely to be revoked than nondrug court probationers or if they had fewer subsequent drug arrests or revocations for drug use).

2. Steve worked as a chaplain for a large county probation system. One of his duties was to develop a mentoring program for delinquent boys. Though it would take a long time before the effectiveness of the program might be determined, he was able to conduct an "implementation evaluation" or a study of how successful the program had been to date in effecting its objectives and activities. He was going to survey newly recruited and trained mentors, as well as administrators and some of the youth participants. He was also set to review program documentation, including recruitment and training procedures, the minutes of meetings, all related regulations, and budgets. His research question was, "Has the implementation of the youth mentoring program to date met its goals and objectives?"

RESOURCES

BERK, R. A. and ROSSI, P. H. (1998). *Thinking about program evaluation.* 2d ed. Thousand Oaks, CA: Sage.

CHEN, H. T. (2004). *Practical program evaluation: Assessing, improving, planning, implementation and effectiveness.* Thousand Oaks, CA: Sage.

FITZPATRICK, J. L., SANDERS, J. R., and WORTHEN, B. R. (2003) *Program evaluation: Alternative approaches and practical guidelines.* 3d Ed. Boston: Allyn and Bacon.

LITOSSELITI, L. (2003). *Using focus groups in research.* London: Continuum.

MORGAN, D. L. (1996). *Focus groups as qualitative research.* (Volume 16, Sage Qualitative Research Methods Series). Thousand Oaks, CA: Sage.

POSAVAC, E. J. and CAREY, R. G. (2002). *Program evaluation: Methods and case studies.* 6th Ed. Upper Saddle River, NJ: Prentice Hall.

ROSSI, P. H., LIPSEY, M., and FREEMAN, H. E. (2003). *Evaluation: A systematic approach.* 7th Ed. Thousand Oaks, CA: Sage.

ROYSE, D., THYER, B., PADGETT, D. K., and LOGAN, T. K. (2000). *Program evaluation: An introduction.* 3d Ed. Belmont, CA: Wadsworth.

WATT, J. H. (1999). Internet systems for evaluation research. In G. GAY & T. L. BENNINGTON (Eds.), *Information technologies in evaluation: Social, moral, epistemological, and practical implications* (pp. 23–44). San Francisco: Jossey-Bass.

WEISS, C. H. (1997). *Evaluation.* 2d Ed. Upper Saddle River, NJ: Prentice Hall.

WHOLEY, J. S., HATRY, H. P., and NEWCOMER, K. E. (Eds.) (2003). *Handbook of practical program evaluation.* 2d Ed. Thousand Oaks, CA: Sage.

Policy Analysis

In a policy thesis, one might study the effect of changes in administrative procedures, agency functions, or legislative initiatives. The focus is on measuring intended or unintended consequences of official changes in law and policy. While policy analyses will often use some of the other methods indicated here, such as survey research, cost-benefit analysis, and legal research, they are unique in their attempt to provide empirical evidence for the support of a particular social or administrative course of action. These studies are particularly geared toward the information needs of organizations and government leaders. It is important, then, to make sure that a policy analysis is written in clear, general language.

EXAMPLES

1. Lynn proposed to study the effect of legislative efforts to reduce drunk driving by examining a secondary data set with the results of surveying two thousand Texas residents. She theorized that harsher penalties, the prohibition of open containers in vehicles, and the raising of the drinking age would all lower self-report incidences of DWI or knowledge of the DWI experiences of others. Her general research question was, "Have recent legislative efforts at reducing DWI actually lowered citizen exposure to DWI?

2. Clete was interested in the degree to which judges and police officers supported the enforcement of tobacco laws, particularly those governing the sale of tobacco products to minors. He surveyed judges and officers in several jurisdictions to measure their attitudes toward the tobacco laws and the importance of enforcing those laws. He hypothesized that most law enforcement officials would view violations of

tobacco sales law as minor infractions and that those officers and judges who smoked would be even less apt to see the value in sanctioning these less serious offenses. His research questions were (a) how do judges and police officers view the enforcement of tobacco sales to minors laws, and (b) do these views affect their willingness to cite these cases (officers), and sanction these cases (judges)?"

References for this section that may help you examine this type of thesis are listed below.

RESOURCES

BARDACH, E. (2000). *A practical guide for policy analysis: The eightfold path to more effective problem solving.* New York, NY: Chatham House.

BARTLETT, R. V. (1989). *Policy through impact assessment: Institutionalized anlaysis as a policy stratgey.* Westport, CT: Greenwood.

LEMPERT, R. J. (2003). *Shaping the next one hundred years: New methods for quantitative, long-term policy analysis.* Santa Monica: Rand.

STOCK, J. H. (1989). Nonparametric policy analysis. *Journal of the American Statistical Association, 84,* 567–575.

VAN MAANEN, J. (Ed.) (1998). *Qualitative studies of organizations.* Thousand Oaks, CA: Sage.

YANOW, D. (1999). *Conducting interpretive policy analysis (Qualitative Research Methods).* Thousand Oaks, CA: Sage.

Historical

A historical thesis will take an event or series of events and provide a detailed, rich context from which we can understand not only how and why they occurred but also how similar events may have come about in the same way or been prevented by alternative courses of action. Someone doing a historical study is comfortable conducting extensive archival research, including tracking down newspapers, official records, books, journals, and government records. The author of a historical work will describe the complex interaction of social, political, and economic forces that shaped the attitudes, policies, and customs of the time when certain events took place.

EXAMPLES

1. Jim's great grandfather was the highest ranking police officer (a deputy chief) ever killed in the line of duty in the city of Houston. In 1910 he was shot by a former officer in a downtown restaurant. Jim proposed to develop the context of the events of that time, hoping not only to better understand the department and the city in the early 1900s, but also the outcome of the trial, in which the gunman was acquitted. He obtained many historical accounts of the events from newspapers, as well as from books about the city at the turn of the century. His research questions were (a) how do we explain the events surrounding the very public murder of a deputy chief, and (b) does that understanding differ from sensational crimes and trials today?

2. Nikkos studied the history of polygamists in this country from the origins of the Mormon religion through the most recent prosecutions of members of fundamentalist sects formed after the church's official denunciation of the practice of plural

wives. By tracing the social forces that influenced government responses to polygamy and the fundamentalists tactics to evade criminal charges, he hoped to clarify the options for future policy and predict the success of each. His research questions were (a) what forces shape social responses to polygamy, and (b) have fundamentalists' reactions to government intervention changed over time?

Some references that might help you to understand the process and support the use of this methodology are included below.

RESOURCES

CONLEY, J. (1993). Historical perspective and criminal justice. *Journal of Criminal Justice Education*, 4(2), 349–376.
GRAY, W. (1991). *Historian's handbook: A key to the study and writing of history.* 2d ed. Long Grove, IL: Waveland.
HARVEY, C. (1996). *Data bases in historical research: Theory, methods and applications.* New York: St Martin's Press.
HOWELL, M. and Prevenier, W. (2001). *From reliable sources: An introduction to historical methods.* Ithaca, NY: Cornell University Press.
MARIUS, R. (1999). *A short guide to writing about history.* 3d Ed. New York: Longman.
McDOWELL, W. H. (2002). *Historical research: A guide.* New York: Longman
REAGAN, P. D. (2002). *History and the internet: A guide.* Boston: McGraw Hill.
STOREY, W. K. (2004). *Writing history: A guide for students.* New York: Oxford University Press.
WILLIAMS, R. C. (2003). *The historian's toolbox: A student's guide to the theory and craft of history.* Armonk, NY: M. E. Sharpe.

Content Analysis

Content analysis is a research approach using coding schemes to categorize information from similar sources in a systematic way. Newspapers, magazines, books, television programs, and art are but a few of the media used in content analysis. The technique attempts to analyze the appearance of some phenomenon in an existing information source to assess its importance or perhaps its potential impact on our society, groups, or individuals. The social problems literature frequently uses content analysis as a way to indicate that certain phenomena have gained or lost status in the competition for social capital. Agencies compete for funds based on perceptions of the criticality of their topic or interest, all of which can be measured by content analysis.

Most frequently, a content analysis is done on media accounts. The presence or absence of events, attitudes, and topics in the paper, television, song, and film are a measure of the attention they garner in society and thus an indication that they may be ripe for analysis, action, change, or reconsideration. For example, one might count the references to drunken driving, gangs, or drug activity prior to an election or before some important piece of legislation is proposed. While most subjects of content analysis are fairly objective, such as the number of pictures of minorities as offenders in criminal justice textbooks, others such as incidences of violence in a series of Saturday morning cartoons may be dispute-prone or suffer from inter-rater differences in the detection of certain types of violence or its coding as either major or minor violence. In other types of content analyses, police or probation reports, performance reviews, or other narrative materials may also used.

EXAMPLES

1. Susan worked in the probation department and was interested in evaluating a somewhat controversial practice adopted by one of the DWI courts. Probationers were sentenced to complete a daily notebook of newspaper articles related to DWI in the hopes that the assignment would have some cognitive therapeutic impact. Though a previous evaluation had shown little difference between these program participants and regular probationers in terms of recidivism and successful completion of probation, Susan suspected program integrity was an issue, and that the program could not possibly be successful if the criteria were not being followed. She proposed a content analysis of completed notebooks to see whether participants were really completing the task each day according to the specified criteria. The court turned over a year's worth of completed notebooks to Susan, whose research question was, "to what degree is the assignment for completing a daily notebook entry being followed by probationers in this program?"

2. Shakira was a correctional worker in a state penitentiary. She became interested in cartoons after noticing them in older issues of practitioner magazines. Shakira wondered if the cartoons, particularly the ones commenting on crime and delinquency, were accurate reflections of the views of their time. She used the library's collection of three major popular magazines, set up a coding scheme, and analyzed every cartoon from 1920 to 1960. In addition, she used the correctional literature to determine the general trends of correctional change during that same period. Her research question asked whether cartoons in major magazines reflected the trends in correctional practice over the past century or other identifiable social trends.

Some resources that may help you in your exploration of this type of research are listed.

RESOURCES

HOLSTI, O. R. (1969). *Content analysis for the social sciences and humanities.* Reading, MA: Addison.

KRIPPENDORFF, K. (2004). *Content analysis: An introduction to its methodology.* Thousand Oaks, CA: Sage.

POPPING, R. (2000). *Computer-assisted text analysis.* Thousand Oaks, CA: Sage.

NEUENDORF, K. A. (2002). *The content analysis guidebook.* Thousand Oaks, CA: Sage.

WEBER, R. P. (1990). *Basic content analysis.* 2d Ed. Thousand Oaks, CA: Sage.

Cost-Benefit Analysis

The need for cost-benefit information is a product of the competitive nature of the public administration funding process. While it is difficult to quantify many outcomes or benefits of the work done in criminal justice, such as safety, crime prevention, and punishment, the costs may be easier to identify and calculate. Researchers can choose from varying levels of costs from the more direct, such as salaries and equipment, to the more indirect, such as training, health problems, and absenteeism. Though researchers do not always agree on the best parameters and criteria for conducting a cost-benefit analysis, as long as one is clear about the things included in his or her calculations and the rationale for using them, then great latitude is usually allowed.

EXAMPLES

1. Angela was a police officer who was assigned to a mounted patrol unit for a number of years. Though the equestrian unit was traditionally showcased at high profile events, there was periodic talk about eliminating it as it may be less effective than in earlier days. With access to all of the department's financial records and budgets regarding the mounted patrol unit, she proposed a cost-benefit analysis that would be useful to her supervisors in making decisions about the use of mounted patrol in the future. Her research question was simply, "what are the costs and benefits of the mounted patrol unit?"

2. Chia-Hsing was interested in the use of closed circuit television as a way to reduce property crime. His police department in Taiwan had adopted the technology but had yet to evaluate it. Using crime data from before and after the installation of CCTV, Chia-Hsing wanted to assess whether there was a reduction in crime and the calculated cost of that reduction. He also included a number of brief interviews with law enforcement officials for their expectations about what the cost-benefit ratio should be. His research questions were (a) what are the direct and indirect costs of CCTV monitoring in the city and (b) what have been the expected and actual direct and indirect benefits?

Helpful resources and references pertaining to this type of research follow.

RESOURCES

ADLER, M. and POSNER, E. A. (1999). Rethinking cost-benefit analysis. *Yale Law Journal, 109*, 2,165–247.

ADLER, M. and POSNER, E. A. (Eds). (2001). *Cost-benefit analysis: Economic, philosophical, and legal perspectives.* Chicago: University of Chicago Press Journals.

BOARDMAN, A. E., GREENBERG, D. H., VINING, A. R., and WEIMER, D. L. (2000). *Cost-benefit analysis: Concepts and practice.* 2d ed. Upper Saddle River, NJ: Prentice Hall.

DOMPERE, K. K. (2004). *Cost-benefit analysis and the theory of fuzzy decisions: Fuzzy value theory.* New York:Springer.

EARL, C. J. (2003). *Cost-benefit analysis: Just the basics!* New York: Resource Management Systems, Inc.

GRAMLICH, E. M. (1997). *A guide to benefit-cost analysis.* 2d ed.. Long Grove, IL: Waveland.

LAYARD, R. and GLAISTER, S. (Eds.) (1994). *Cost-benefit analysis.* 2d ed. Cambridge: Cambridge University Press.

LAWRENCE, S. and MEARS, D. P. (2006). *Benefit-cost analysis of supermax prisons: Critical steps and considerations.* Washington, DC: U.S. Department of Justice.

NAS, T. F. (1996) *Cost-benefit analysis: Theory and application.* Thousand Oaks, CA: Sage.

GENERAL METHODOLOGICAL TYPES

While some of the thesis types demonstrated earlier are based on specific methodologies, there are some more general methodologies that can be used across many thesis types. Depending on the thesis approach or research question you choose, you will have a variety of methodologies at your disposal. The nature of the research question is the primary ingredient in directing you to the most appropriate methodological strategy. As the examples indicated, students chose a type of study and then applied appropriate methods or techniques for answering their research question within that context. Some of the most common methods or formats for conducting a research study are case studies, survey research, experimental design, and participant observation. Each is briefly discussed below with reference to sources that may help you determine if any of these approaches would fit with the topic of study you are considering. A more detailed discussion of these methodologies can be found in later chapters.

A criterion that may influence your choice of a method is the amount and type of information available on a given subject. The newer the topic, the more restricted you may be in the type of study you can do effectively. One example is a topic such as the Minutemen who have taken up positions along the southwest to "guard the border." These activities seemed to develop in spring of 2005, so by fall of that year, it would still be too new to be studied using several of the common approaches. It would also be too soon for theoretical discussions or the use of existing data sets to analyze for patterns or trends. Thus, newspaper accounts may be all that would initially be available, and you might be able to perform a content analysis of those articles to begin a theoretical framework or to predict what types of legislation, case law, or policy may be adopted in reaction. Another option would be to broaden the topic to include a wider range of citizen responses to illegal immigration concerns and have the Minutemen play a smaller role in the work. There may be a data set from public opinion polls on views on illegal immigration issues, or one could explore the topic historically using other forms of vigilantism or militia type responses to perceived threats. An alternative approach, particularly useful with newer issues, is to use participant observation to record and understand the motives and intent of participants in the movement. Another possibility is to find a single typical or notable case—such as the leader of the movement—on which to focus and develop the issues. Because of these limitations, it might be wise to consider another topic, and let this one wait.

Case Study

The case study or life history method is a staple of the early positivist tradition and has been used in the Chicago School, as well as in many later classic studies with which you are probably familiar (Clifford Shaw's *The Jackroller,* Edwin Sutherland's *Professional Thief,* as well as the Richard Dugdale's *Jukes* and Henry Goddard's *Kallikaks*). While many of these noted case studies focus on an individual, a delinquent, serial killer, or organized criminal, the scope of possible case study topics is much broader. In many disciplines, an incident or event can also constitute the basis of a case study, such as the activities of a particular political organization or the analysis of a notable occurrence. The author may construct events leading to an incident or assess the way officials handled the effects of a disaster, such as K. Erickson's *Everything in Its Path.* Erickson's award-winning essay examined the aftermath of a deadly mining area mudslide and relief efforts that ignored neighborhood and community networks. Other examples include Mark Hamm's analysis of the Oklahoma City bombing of the federal building using extensive media accounts and court papers.

Today, some researchers doing case studies continue to use ethnographic techniques to more vividly illustrate the lives of their subjects. Examples you may want to review include Jennifter Toth's *Mole People* and Jeff Ferrell's *Crimes of Style.*

Other sources for the use of case studies are listed below.

STAKE, R. E. (1995). *The art of case study research.* Thousand Oaks, CA: Sage.
YIN, R. K. (2003). *Case study research: Design and methods.* 3d ed. Thousand Oaks, CA: Sage.
YIN, R. K. (2003). *Applications of case study research.* 2d ed. Thousand Oaks, CA: Sage.

Survey Research

Surveys use a variety of methods to develop profiles of how people view issues and to generate trends in opinions. When samples are of appropriate size and construction, one may be able to predict from them or to generalize to other populations based on their results. Politicians, policy makers, and academics are all interested in public opinion, and managers often use surveys to gather information about best practices and the most effective procedures. Certain types of theses, particularly policy analysis, program evaluations, cost-benefit analyses, and theoretical inquiries, might rely on survey information in order to answer research questions.

Survey research usually requires a knowledge of sampling theory and some sophistication in interviewing techniques or survey construction so that bias is minimized if not eliminated. Students may want to use an existing survey or instrument in order to test the replicability of an earlier study or to note changes in attitudes and opinions to the same questions over time. Some research methods classes may assign the development of a questionnaire that could later be used as the basis for a thesis. If you are developing your own instrument, there are many resources available to help you avoid errors and maximize the utility of your questionnaire. However, it is better to use existing research instruments and questions so you can avoid the difficulties inherent in developing reliable and valid measures.

Questionnaires

A needs assessment is one type of study that would utilize a questionnaire. An opinion poll or attitude survey is another. Some theses have surveyed agencies throughout the country to discern changes in policies generated by awareness of liability, new crimes, or new laws. Attitudes or opinion surveys are sought by management on issues such as work conditions, experiences on duty, and ways to improve performance. Generally the less sensitive the topic (i.e., career plans versus sexual harassment) the more likely survey participants are to return questionnaires and to have answered them honestly. For criminal justice students, there are many existing survey instruments dealing with everything from fear of crime to police professionalism—all of which can be borrowed for thesis research. In addition, questionnaires have been the basis for self-report studies in criminology, though asking people about criminal behaviors is becoming progressively more difficult to get approved by Institutional Review Boards.

EXAMPLES

1. Ricardo was interested in surveying members of his community college on their attitudes toward the use of community policing strategies by campus police officers. His premise was that the success of any community policing initiative the campus might be considering would ultimately hinge on the beliefs, attitudes, and expectations of the campus community. He developed a survey that would be administered to students, faculty, staff, and administrators at a large urban campus where he worked. His research question was, "do community college constituents support the values and principles of community policing?"

2. Shoshona read articles on the effect of media on people's behavior and wondered what that effect might be on their fear of crime. After reading the literature on measuring both media and fear of crime, she found several questions and scales to use on a questionnaire. The university had a survey research program with an ongoing quarterly survey, and she was able to have her questions included. Her research questions were (a) does media affect fear of crime, and (b) if so, does that effect vary by type of media (newspapers, television, and radio)?

Interviews

The ability to conduct a scientifically valid and reliable interview is a valuable research skill. There are many considerations if you decide to gather data from interviews. This technique is really much more complicated than it looks, so be sure to read some of the basic sources on doing research (not counseling) interviews before you decide on this approach. The specifics of the interview process depend on the type of thesis you intend to do and the particular research question to be answered.

Interviews may be highly structured or less structured and more open-ended or free-flowing. In some cases you would not need to ask everyone the same questions in the same way, or report the answers in similar fashion because the information you would seek from each would vary depending on their relationship to the subject or their different ranks and job positions. On the other hand, if you are answering a theoretical question or doing a treatment evaluation, it would be important to have consistency between each interviewer, the questions, and the way information is coded or recorded.

Once you have developed an interview instrument, it would be important to pretest the questions in the order you intend to ask them for clarity of understanding and any unanticipated answers or responses. Following the pretest, items that need to be reworded can be revised.

EXAMPLES

1. Mark Hamm's work on *American Skinheads* required that he interview a number of self-professed skinheads who had committed a variety of violent offenses. The interviewing process took time, and, even before beginning the interviews, he had to know a great deal about the skinhead culture in order to ask the right questions and understand their answers. Hamm used the interview results to develop a theory of contemporary hate crime.

2. Jaime's concern was public attitudes toward the police. She knew from her studies that different groups tended to view the police differently. Together with her advisor, she constructed a series of questions to be asked during a random sample of the public in a phone interview. Her research questions asked (a) whether experience with the police affected opinions about the police, and (b) if so, which experiences had the greatest effect.

Scales and Assessment Instruments

Most likely your chair would advocate the use of a preexisting scale to measure a concept related to crime or criminality. By using existing scales that have validity and reliability scores attached, you are able to concentrate on the administration of the instrument in a way that reduces threats to validity and reliability and obtaining an adequate sample of usable responses. One source for instruments is the *Yearbook of Mental Measurements*. Other sources for specific instruments include research articles in scholarly journals, dissertations, and textbooks.

EXAMPLES

1. Jose worked as a campus police officer at an alternative school. He was interested in the increasing number of physical attacks students seemed to be making on teachers and wondered if these could be better predicted and perhaps prevented. He searched the *Yearbook* for instruments and found the Antisocial Behavior Scale and the Social Competence Scale. He liked that one measured a trait traditionally associated with violence in the literature while the other measured what subculture theorists had argued to be a lack of skills leading to frustration and perhaps violence. He made arrangements to have both administered to a group of students as they entered the alternative program along with other testing materials. Jose was never given the students' identities and only the program's counselor matched the scores to behavior records six months later. His research question was, "how well does the Antisocial Behavior Scale and the Social Competence Scale predict attacks on teachers and staff in a small sample of alternative school youths?"

Or, for example, another student decided to focus on the preliminary development of an instrument as suggested by the literature.

2. Armand was interested in predicting school violence, particularly shootings such as at Columbine and Red Lake. He had a copy of the FBI's list of characteristics of youth based on a small sample of offenders who committed school shootings from

which he decided to develop an instrument. This means that he would convert the rather vague and ambiguous traits listed by the FBI into more discreet and measurable, if not already available, data from school records. While it would not be feasible to attempt to administer this instrument at public schools, he was able to receive permission to administer it to a small sample (field testing) of youth at a detention center.

Some references that might help you through the process are included below.

ALRECK, P. L. and SETTLE, R. B. (1994). *The survey research handbook*. 2nd ed. New York: McGraw Hill.

BABBIE, E. (1990). *Survey research methods*. Belmont, CA: Wadsworth.

CHURCH, A. H. (1993). Estimating the effects of incentives on mail survey response rates: A meta-analysis. *Public Opinion Quarterly, 57*, 62–79.

CONVERSE, J. M. and Presser, S. (1986). *Survey questions: Handcrafting the standardized questionnaire*. Thousand Oaks, CA: Sage.

DEVELLIS, R. F. (2003). *Scale development: Theory and applications*. 2d ed. Thousand Oaks, CA: Sage.

DILLMAN, D. (2000). *Mail and internet surveys: The tailored design method*. 2d ed. New York: John Wiley.

DILLMAN, D., TORTORA, R., and BOWKER, D. (1998). *Principles for constructing web surveys*. Pullman, WA (SESRC Technical Report 98–50).

DILLMAN, D., SANGSTER, R., TARNAI, J. & ROCKWOOD, T. (1996). Understanding differences in people's answers to telephone and mail surveys: New directions for evaluation. *Advances in Survey Research, 70*, 45–62.

FINK, A. and KOSECOFF, J. (1998). *How to conduct surveys: A step-by-step guide*. 2d ed. Thousand Oaks, CA: Sage.

FOWLER, F. J. (1995).*Improving survey questions: Design and evaluation*. Thousand Oaks, CA: Sage.

FOWLER, F. J. (2002). *Survey research methods*, 3d ed. Thousand Oaks, CA: Sage.

FREY, J. (1989). *Survey research by telephone*. Newbury Park, CA: Sage.

GROVES, R. M. (1989). *Survey errors and survey costs*. New York: Wiley.

MANGIONE, T. W. (1995). *Mail surveys: Improving the quality*. Thousand Oaks, CA: Sage.

NARDI, P. (2002). *Doing survey research: A guide to quantitative research methods*. Boston: Allyn and Bacon.

NESBARY, D. (2000). *Survey research and the world wide web*. Boston: Allyn & Bacon.

REA, L. M. and PARKER, R. A. (1997). *Designing and conducting survey research*. 2d Ed. San Francisco: Jossey-Bass.

SALANT, P. and DILLMAN, D. (1994). *How to conduct your own survey*. New York:Wiley.

SAPSFORD, R. (1999). *Survey research*. Thousand Oaks, CA: Sage.

TSE, A. (1998). Comparing the response rate, response speed, and response quality of two methods of sending questionnaires: E-mail vs. mail. *Journal of the Market Research Society, 40*, 353–361.

Experimental and Quasi-Experimental Design

Experimental designs are a good methodology for testing causal propositions, that is, answering a cause and effect question. Usually, these designs require that the independent variable is manipulated within the research setting. Program evaluations are among the more common uses for experimental designs in criminal justice. In their basic form, these designs have a "treatment" group and a control group, with random assignment to each group from the same pool of subjects. Random assignment, however, is usually the stumbling block for using experimental designs in criminal justice, particularly in field settings so quasi-experimental designs are frequently used instead. Even without random assignment, quasi-experimental designs can be quite rigorous but also complex, and students need to be aware of the various threats to validity before using one.

EXAMPLES

1. Randy worked in a parole unit that handled drug offending parolees. The state had decided to implement a "foster home" arrangement to keep parolees from returning to the same preprison environment. Because there were more parolees than available foster homes, Randy was able to convince his unit supervisor to randomly assign parolees to the new "treatment," with the remainder going to regular parole. He also collected information concerning their general demographics and offense records. His research question was, "does assignment to foster homes result in a lower failure rate (return to prison)?"

2. Sophia, who was a teaching assistant, wanted to know if there was a difference between taking online and classroom courses. She received permission to measure outcomes in two introductory classes she was teaching. One was taught as a normal face-to-face class, and the other was taught as an online course. Both classes were afternoon courses and, because she was teaching both, received the same information content. Her research question asked whether the average grade distribution in the online course was different from the classroom course.

Some good sources of information on experimental and quasi-experimental design follow.

GARCIA-DIAZ, A. and PHILLIPS, D. (1995). *Principles of experimental design and analysis.* New York: Springer-Verlag.
MONTGOMERY, D. (2004). *Design and analysis of experiments.* 6th ed. New York: Wiley.
SHADISH, W., COOK, T, and CAMPBELL, D. (2001). *Experimental and quasi-experimental designs for generalized causal inference.* Boston: Houghton-Mifflin.

Participant Observation

As mentioned earlier, a theoretical thesis or a program evaluation may rely on data gathered from participant observation. This is a research technique long rooted in the tradition of the Chicago School, and many students opt simply to observe phenomena in their natural settings and attempt to objectively interpret what they see and what it means. It is often favored in settings where the population is small and the data gathered must be in-depth. In many cases, a theoretical approach can inform the questions that researchers ask and the particular behaviors or cues that they look for in the environment. It is generally used to capture more of the context of issues where there is an emphasis on understanding processes that are taking place. There are many great examples of participant observation studies to draw on. The main threat to validity in this type of method is the bias introduced by the observer—which one must consider carefully and formulate ways to address.

EXAMPLE

Paulette had visited the drug court in her area several times and was impressed by how informal and chaotic the environment seemed. She was also struck by the high rate of individuals opting not to participate or being revoked. After reviewing the literature, she felt that existing evaluations had either just accepted uncritical data from the programs or drawn most of their information and feedback from judges or court representatives, and, consequently, the results were overwhelmingly supportive and positive about the character of the courtroom. She decided to adopt a symbolic interactionist's perspective, and, by observing the sessions from the audience, she would attempt to categorize the interactions between the various "actors." She wanted to determine if the setting was similar to that described in the literature and if both verbal and nonverbally communicated messages could be linked to scenarios of success and failure. Her research question was, "will participant observation and a symbolic interactionist perspective lead one to assess the drug court experience differently than existing drug court literature?"

You may want to visit one of the following works for further clarification and examples of this type of research.

DEWALT, K. M. and DEWALT, B. R. (2002). *Participant observation: A guide for fieldworkers.* Walnut Creek, CA: Alta Mira Press.
SPRADLEY, J. (1980). *Participant observation.* New York: Holt.

SUMMARY

The types of theses and methodologies introduced in this chapter were intended to be food for thought. A graduate student who begins to consider a thesis is usually not quite sure what to do or how to do it. We have discovered the best approach is to provide numerous examples of theses that have already been done and the methods by which they have been accomplished. In the process of looking through these examples, something is likely to stand out as a possible idea or approach. We reiterate, however, that the methodology does not come first—the subject of the thesis, and its attached research question, determines the methodology to be used. If the former were true, a thesis would be a case of a methodology in search of a problem to study. We hope the thesis student has a genuine intellectual curiosity about something, rather than a mundane concern with getting the task done.

REFERENCES

DUGDALE, R. (1877). *The Jukes: A study in crime, pauperism, disease and heredity.* New York: Putnam.
FERRELL, J. (1993). *Crimes of style: Urban graffiti and the politics of criminality.* New York: Garland.
GODDARD, H. (1913). *The Kallikak family: A study in the heredity of feeblemindedness.* New York: Macmillan.
SHAW, C. (1930). *The jackroller.* Chicago: University of Chicago Press.
SUTHERLAND, E. H. (1937). *The professional thief: By a professional thief.* Chicago: University of Chicago Press.
TOTH, J. (1993). *Mole people: Life in the tunnels beneath New York City.* Chicago: Chicago Review Press.

3

DEVELOPMENT OF THE RESEARCH QUESTION

This chapter explores the development of a research question for a variety of theses types according to the criteria described in the previous chapter. You should spend some time exploring as many options for original data collection as well as the use of secondary data sets as possible. It is important to understand the advantages and disadvantages of each and to be able to assess the viability, particularly in terms of quantity and quality, of any data set you might consider using. You must also be aware of the conditions and limitations on the use of many existing government data sets.

To many, the formation of a research question that is an appropriate size and depth is one of the most critical aspects of their work. The research question delineates the parameters of the study and the degree of depth that will be needed. A carefully chosen question will keep the writer focused and on track throughout the research process.

FORMING A QUESTION

As discussed earlier, the research question that becomes the basis of your thesis should be the appropriate size for a thesis, and your chair will help you adjust your topic to ensure that it is. One way to work your way to a question is to decide the general topic area and then narrow it down to topics or issues within that area first (see Figure 3-1).

Once you have the first two steps completed, it may be necessary to determine what data sources and research methods might be appropriate

TOPIC AREA
Domestic Violence

SUBTOPIC or ISSUE
Police Response to Domestic Violence

QUESTION
Does response time have any effect on the charge filed in a domestic disturbance call?

FIGURE 3-1 Forming a Research Question

before you decide on a specific question. As Goldilocks discovered in her analysis of the three questions, one was too big, one was too small, and only one was just right (see the examples in Box 3-1). One way to avoid having a question be too narrow is to avoid those that could be answered with a simple yes or no.

Thus, hints for a good research question might include the following:

1. The wording of the question does not reflect an ideological position or frame of reference, it is value neutral.

   Don't do: *Because sex offenders cannot be cured, how do we prevent them from gaining access to innocent children ?*

   There are several problems with this question, including the use of unnecessary, value-loaded descriptors like "innocent." Another is the assumption that sex offenders are "incurable"—this is more opinion than factual and should be omitted. As the term "sex offender" encompasses violators of a broad and diverse grouping of many different crimes, it is probably not an accurate choice for any study. If the author wants to concentrate on pedophiles' access to children, then he or she would have to ensure that the sample or data had enough cases with that particular offense, which is often difficult to obtain. In fact, a lack of cases sufficient for analysis is one of the primary reasons many topics have so little existing research (this can be thought of as a "red flag" as well—very few research studies suggest that the topic is a problem area and perhaps not the best choice for a

BOX 3-1 EXAMPLES OF CORRECT THESIS QUESTIONS

TOO BIG:	How has corruption influenced police organizations?
TOO SMALL:	Do the citizens of Fort Stickton view their police as corrupt?
JUST RIGHT:	*What factors affect citizen perceptions of police corruption?*
TOO BIG:	What types of treatments work best to rehabilitate offenders?
TOO SMALL:	How successful is the RIO program at X-box prison?
JUST RIGHT:	*Of the three drug treatment programs used in the Jute County Probation Department, which has the most promising results?*

thesis). There would also have to be some thought to operationalizing a vague concept like "access to children." A more defensible question might be:

DO: *What are the characteristics of recidivism among paroled sex offenders?*

By using "recidivism" one avoids the whole vague notion of "curing" or "access to" and simply focuses on the concrete legal parameters of reoffending. Also, by using a parole sample, the researcher has official data on reoffending as well as offender and offense history which are easily interpreted and analyzed.

2. The question is not worded in such a way that it assumes an outcome or finding.

Don't Do: *How bad is racial inequality in court sentencing?*

As the example shows, the author has already made a determination that there is racial inequality, and now is attempting to assess just how "bad," another value-laden term, it is. While we can all agree that racial inequality is an undesirable outcome in any process, a scientific assessment would simply be looking for a significant level of evidence of inequality that is best explained, after eliminating other potential sources of difference, by race. Given the researcher's findings, it would be up to the readers to interpret the social value and cost of that evidence. Therefore a more appropriate question would be phrased:

DO: *Does race affect the length of sentence in felony convictions for homicide?*

3. Avoid questions that promise to provide results beyond the scope of the research.

Don't DO: *This study will answer the question, "Why do arsonists set fires?"*

The wording of this question is simply too definitive in terms of the outcome of the research. Realistically, we may "contribute to our understanding of the concept of arson"; we may explore, examine, and investigate some of the motivations, but we are not going to come up with the final and absolute answer. Thus, a proper perspective on the study might look more like this:

DO: *What motives are expressed by a sample of arsonists interviewed in a mandatory treatment setting?*

Just in case, we should probably note that the questions as phrased here are research questions, not hypotheses. You shouldn't mistake the two, and they are not phrased the same (see Chapter Eight for examples of hypotheses).

LOCATING AND ASSEMBLING INFORMATION

The first choice you need to make in locating data is whether to gather your own or to use an existing or secondary data set. If you have plenty of time, some available resources (funds, access to supplies, and copying), and a potential population for sampling, then you may want to collect your own data. The advantages of doing so are that you have more control over the definitions and conceptualization of the constructs and you can more accurately identify any potential threats to validity in the collection process. If it is not practical or realistic to do so, you may want to consider using secondary data.

Secondary Data

It is not uncommon for a Master's thesis to be based on the use of existing data from some previous research project or a government agency. Searches of government Web sites and the academic literature will help you identify some of these eligible data sets. In addition, any standard research textbook will address the issues related to the use of secondary data. Some of the advantages of secondary data are listed below:

1. Data sets are particularly useful with phenomena that is difficult for a researcher to directly observe, such as crime and deviance.
2. Because large data sets are expensive to collect, using existing ones is relatively efficient in time and money.
3. Many data sets offer easy access and can even be downloaded from online public databases.
4. Many printed versions of data are very easy to code, with standard categories already provided.
5. Previous research can be built on or expanded, and researchers can help broaden bases of previous research with the same data.
6. Previous findings can be verified for policy decisions, instruments validated, or results challenged with modifications of the analytical approaches.
7. Because secondary data sets are often large, national samples:
   a. They may be drawn from multiple sites at the same time, thus allowing for greater generalization.
   b. They are useful for analyzing small subpopulations and rare events.
   c. They may also be longitudinal ones, allowing multiple time periods of analysis for the same sites.
   d. Finally, they may represent more culturally diverse areas than the researcher would normally have access to.

Students should also be aware of potential disadvantages.

1. Data may not be representative of other subjects, locations, or times.
2. There may be validity issues with thesis constructs (what you want to measure) that are not a good match for variables in the data set (what has already been measured), which encourages poor conceptualization and operationalization.
3. Data may not be adequately kept, cleaned, or coded.
4. Variables may already be aggregated at a level that creates problems for further analysis.
5. There may have been changes in the way the data were collected or coded over time in the original study.
6. And, in what most researchers view as the biggest problem, you probably don't know all of the details of the data collection, and, therefore, you may make interpretation mistakes while using it.

Ironically, even though secondary data analysis is problematic, it is probably one of the most common used for graduate theses and is often recommended because of the time, expense, and access problems faced by students trying to conduct research (which, of course, are some of the same issues faced by faculty). Prior to browsing the Web to look for secondary data, we suggest you take a look at an excellent discussion on secondary data at the

University of Wisconsin-Madison's Data and Program Library Service (*http://dpls.dacc.wisc.edu/types/secondary.htm*). To help you with your search, there is a list below that provides some of the major data sets in which you might be interested and where information regarding their use can be found.

Assessing a Data Set

You may want to examine a number of potential data sets before deciding what to use for your thesis. The following discussion covers some of the factors you may want to consider.

How Do You Find a Potential Data Set?

There are many sources for criminal justice data, some easier to locate than others. In addition, some have data in formats that are not very amenable to analysis and require that you recode the data before it can be used. Others come in proprietary formats and, while analyzable, may not permit the type of analysis needed to answer your thesis question. The best ones are those created by researchers and available in a downloadable file already in the format required by the statistical program you intend to use for your analysis. After this discussion, you will find a list of criminal justice sources and some notations about their usability.

How Do You Get Access to a Data Set?

The answer to this question varies by the source. Many of the better data sets are available from a few government Web sites, thus making it easier to browse what is available. The primary source is the National Criminal Justice Data Archive, a repository of data sets on crime and justice issues sponsored by the federal government. See the comments below for more information on this source. Other sources are more difficult to gain access to. Local agencies are likely to require access permission from their research office or committee (if they have one) or the head of the agency. In these cases it is best to use a contact within the agency who can smooth the path for you. In any event, you have to make a good case for why they would want to release data to you. This usually requires at least a letter and, frequently, the filling out of forms and a copy of your research proposal. It is usually best to go through your thesis supervisor to do this. When data are not available from a public online source, such as NACJD, you also need to be prepared for disappointment. Many agencies are very zealous in protecting their information. Therefore, we suggest you have some backup strategies just in case your request for data is rejected.

How Were the Data Collected?

Because the greatest difficulty in using secondary data is in determining what the data really represent, you need to be sensitive to both the way the data are collected and the way the data have been coded (transferred from the original information to a database of some sort). The first is a methodology issue. Remember that agencies, while they have an interest in the accuracy of their data, are collecting data for their own purposes. Because it is unlikely that you and the agency have the same thing in mind, their data will, at best, be an approximation of what you need. Furthermore, they are not concerned with the same kind of issues researchers are, particularly the important concepts of reliability and validity. The data may also be incomplete, a "sample" of information that is clearly nonrandom, or in some cases erroneous (for your purposes). You need to ask the people who collect the agency data how they do it and what they are recording to understand what the data represent and what the potential problems might be. The issue of coding is equally important. Many agency clerks record information as required by "higher-ups" but do not have a need for that information themselves. The tendency is to record that information without a real interest in its accuracy. Labels are also attached to such data that sometimes make the deciphering of individual codes very difficult. On the whole, we come back to an earlier point: use researcher-collected data whenever you can.

Will There Be a Cost?

Most of the online databases are free of charge. Sometimes there is a fee for downloading a particular dataset or the one you choose may be quite large and available only on CD. In these cases you may have to pay a small charge for processing, shipping, and perhaps for the cost of the CD itself. Some data repositories require membership, such as the Inter-university Consortium for Political and Social Research (ICPSR). Your university may be a member of the consortium so check to see if that is the case. ICPSR also has some areas of "free" data, such as the National Archive of Criminal Justice Data (NACJD), which are paid for by the federal government. There are also fee-based data repositories in the private sector, and their cost can be quite steep. Unless there is no other source for the data, or the data have been compiled from multiple sources and doing the same yourself with the original, free data would be too time-consuming, it is best to avoid these sources. If you want to see what these sites have, simply "Google" the generic type of data in which you are interested, and click on some of the results. Our recommendation is to go with the free, government-sponsored Web sites.

Overall Considerations

Here are some things we suggest you ask about any data set you are considering.

1. How big is the data set? How many *complete* cases are there?
2. How recently were the data collected? Have any significant historical events or changes altered the way these data would be perceived or valued? Are the concepts and variables measured still relevant and useful now?

3. Does sufficient information exist about the collection procedures so you can make a judgment about the quality of the data?
4. Are the variables sufficiently defined? Do you know what each one represents, and are there any special circumstances you must know about the coding procedures?
5. How much effort would be involved in preparing the data set for the type of analyses you intend to do? What condition are the data in?

If the data are electronic:

6. Are the data available to the general public? Is their use restricted?
7. What electronic format are the data in? Is a proprietary or special program required to access the data? If the latter, can the data be output in a standard format for use in standard programs?
8. What statistical package, if any, is necessary for their use? Do you have access to that statistical package and are you familiar with it?

Once you have evaluated the data set in terms of these questions, you will be able to decide if it is worth pursuing. Ultimately, a good data set would meet the following three criteria:

1. **Full documentation is available.** This means that those who originally collected the data have supplied detailed descriptions of the procedures followed in the initial research study. You would clearly understand all aspects of the data collection process. You would be able to recognize any threats to validity raised in that process and would be able to answer questions about the way variables were developed, operationalized, and measured.

2. **The number of cases is of sufficient size** to allow for meaningful application of the statistics that you intend to use. This means that once you attempt to do statistical analyses, you will not have cell sizes so small that the results would be useless (too much error). Your chair will help you determine what might be an adequate size, based on the type of question you intend to explore and the answers you need. If you are examining a subpopulation within a data set, try to determine the size of that group. For example, one student was able to obtain a large data set from a state parole system. There were five thousand parolees in that data set, but only twenty-eight female gang members, much too small a group for analysis and making comparisons to the general parole population.

It is also important that the data set is of sufficient size relative to the population from which it was drawn from. There are sampling charts you can use to determine, based on your allowable error rate, the sample size you need. Keep in mind the subsample problem mentioned earlier—an allowable error rate for the entire sample is not the same for any subpopulations contained in that sample.

3. There are **multiple measures of the important constructs.** A single variable is frequently not a good measure of the concepts you want to analyze. You also need to realize that the variables in the data are the *only* sources of those important concepts—you are stuck with whatever the

original researcher or data collector measured. For instance, if you want to ask questions about how stress affects police performance, you may find a survey data set in which the question was asked, "Do you feel stressed as a result of your job?" That single variable, perception of stress, would be a poor indicator of stress. You would prefer a data set with various indicators of stress, including physiological and psychological information. Similarly, the measurement of police performance should not be a single item. Another issue here is that with multiple measures you can create a scale or index of the important construct. You can then test the reliability of that scale with statistics available in almost any popular statistical package. A single item does not permit any estimate of reliability.

The Issue of Quality Data

There are several ways to address questions about the quality of a proposed data set. One is that government data sets, such as those that were generated by grants funded by the National Institute of Justice, the National Institute of Health, and those archived by the National Archive of Criminal Justice Data have already undergone intense scrutiny by experienced researchers before funding was awarded. This means that the research proposal and design underwent peer review and was monitored at several points, including final reporting, to ensure that rigorous defensible methodologies were employed. Such mechanisms constitute adequate assurance of a quality data set.

Another way to judge the quality of the data set is that the original authors have already published their results from the data set in a peer-reviewed journal. The appearance of an article in a reputable journal using a process of blind peer review would indicate that the data are acceptable and can be used in a meaningful way.

Locating Good Data

The government often makes data available from research that has been sponsored with taxpayer funds. Usually there are not many restrictions on access and use of the data sets for the purposes of academic research, but there are cases in which the use of certain data sets may be more difficult and even more problematic because of complexity or confidentiality issues. The sources listed below include the most common criminal justice sources available at this time. There are also specialty agencies and Web sites not listed here that you may want to explore for possible data on specific types of crimes such as alcohol and drug abuse, white-collar crime, domestic violence, and sex offending. For example, Chip Burns and Mike Lynch (2005) describe how to do environmental crime research using the Environmental Protection Agency's (EPA) Web sites and databases in their resource book.

Criminal justice data can be found in numerous governmental agencies and opinion polls. The list that follows will give you a general idea of where you might look.

- Uniform Crime Reports
- National Incident-Based Reporting System
- Sourcebook of Criminal Justice Statistics
- National Prisoner Statistics
- Juvenile Court Statistics
- Vital Statistics of the United States
- Uniform Parole Reports
- Public Opinion Polls
- NIJ/Bureau of Census Studies
- Criminal Justice Expenditure and Employment Data
- National Jail Census
- National Survey of Inmates and Local Jails
- National Census of Juvenile Detention and Correctional Facilities
- National Crime Panel Victimization Data
- Offender Based Tracking Systems (OBTS)

On the other hand, one can use the Internet to locate data quickly. Some, if not all, of the listed sources have made data sets available at Web sites, and, in many cases, the data are already in a machine-readable format. This latter aspect means that you would have minimal effort preparing the data for statistical analysis. Even better than that, some sources actually have fully cleaned and documented data files in the format required by major statistical or spreadsheet programs—all you have to do is download them and begin the analysis.

The following data resources are comprised of downloadable data sets, web-searchable data sets, and statistical compilations or reports on various criminal justice subjects. We have grouped them in categories, based on the types of data usually available from the source. URL addresses were accurate as of 04-10-2006. In the event you receive an error notice from your browser, simply back up the address and erase the end part of the address to the next backslash (/). If all else fails, use a search engine (like Google) to see if the database name we list here is available somewhere else on the Web.

The Nation's Largest Criminal Justice Data Archives

The National Archive of Criminal Justice Data (NACJD) is the big one, a source for almost everything. There are at least two advantages for looking there first. Most federal government-sponsored research is required to place a copy of their data in the Archives. In addition, many other researchers have elected to make available copies of their data. This means that data from more than a thousand studies, covering almost every criminal justice and criminology subject, are available. Moreover, almost all the data sets have been cleaned of erroneous coding, and appropriate documentation is available. Short descriptions of the original research and the data are available to read as you peruse the listings. A search function will let you use keywords and topics to locate possible data sets of interest. Finally, all the data sets are in machine-readable form, with commands for both the SPSS and SAS statistical programs, and some actually are in the file format required by those programs, requiring that you only download the file and begin the analysis. Box 3-2 provides the procedure for downloading a NACJD data set.

National Archive of Criminal Justice Data

http://www.icpsr.umich.edu/NACJD/index.html

National Consortium of Violence Research—a source for the Uniform Crime Report (UCR), National Incident Based Reporting System (NIBRS), and National Crime Victimization Survey (NCVS)

http://www.ncovr.heinz.cmu.edu/Docs/datacenter.htm

General Criminal Justice and Criminology Data

The major datasets in this area include the UCR, NIBRS, NCVS, and various federal statistical compilations.

Bureau of Justice Statistics Clearinghouse

http://www.ncjrs.org/

Bureau of Justice Statistics (BJS)

http://www.ojp.usdoj.gov/bjs/

Corrections statistics

http://www.ojp.usdoj.gov/bjs/correct.htm

Death Penalty Information Center—Execution Database

http://www.deathpenaltyinfo.org/executions.php

Justice Research and Statistics Association

http://www.jrsa.org/

National Archives and Records Administration

http://www.archives.gov/index.html

National Center for State Courts—Court statistics project

http://www.ncsconline.org/D_Research/csp/CSP_Main_Page.html

National Consortium of Violence Research

http://www.ncovr.heinz.cmu.edu/Docs/datacenter.htm

Sourcebook of Criminal Justice Statistics

http://www.albany.edu/sourcebook/

Statistical Abstract of the United States

http://www.census.gov/statab/www/

BOX 3-3 DIRECTIONS FOR DOWNLOADING NACJD DATA SETS

1. **Search for data sets on the Web site.** Using the "Data Holdings" tab on the search window, search for data sets with the topics you are looking for, or search for a specific title, data set number, or investigator name.
2. **Examine the description of data sets.** Choose the data set you want or browse through several by clicking on "description" under the data set title before you choose one. Note that the description of every data set has tabs that allow you to "browse documentation" (look at the codebook and a more thorough description) or "download" the data set. There is also a tab for "related literature" that will list any published research based on the data set.
3. **Set up an account.** The first time you choose to browse documentation or download data, a screen will appear warning you of federal usage restrictions and asking you to either login (if you already have an account) or to create an account/login as a guest. If you think you might be downloading other data sets (a strong possibility if the one you selected turns out not to be what you think it is), create an account. Follow the instructions to login or create an account.
4. **Download the documentation and data set(s).** Be sure you select the codebook(s) associated with the data set(s). You usually have a choice of downloading either SAS or SPSS setup files with the data files. Choose the one for the statistical analysis program you will be using. Sometimes, there is a STATA setup file for that statistical program. Even better, if the choice is available, use files labeled "SAS transport," "SPSS portable," or "Stata system" because they require no further preparation on your part to be ready for analysis. Click on the ones you want (Step 1), select "all data sets" (Step 2), and then click on "Add to Data Cart" (Step 3). After that, click on "Download Data Cart" (Step 5), and save the file like any other download to your PC.
5. **Copy or print the listing of any related literature.** You will want to see what others have done with this data set.
6. **Prepare the data set for analysis.**
   A. Go to the folder in which you saved the data set zip file, and unzip it and the documentation.
   B. If the data set files were either "SAS transport," "SPSS portable," or "Stata system" files, nothing else is needed—you are finished. Just click on the file to open it into your statistical program.
   C. If the files are "setup" files, you need to do some preparation. Ask your thesis chair to help you. If you will be using the SPSS program, do the following:
      • Write down the file name that ends in ".txt"—this is the data file.
      • We recommend that you copy the data file to a single-depth folder on your PC, such as a folder named "data" on your hard drive (usually the "C" drive). This would appear as "C:\data" in

the command line.
- Click on the file ending with ".sps"—this is the command file.
- The SPSS syntax editor will open the file, and you are ready to edit.
- Scroll down to a line beginning with FILE HANDLE DATA / NAME= "file-specification," and edit it.
- Replace "file specification" with the folder location and name of your data file; be sure to leave the quotation marks. For example, if you have copied the data file to "C:\data" and your file is named "03355-0001-data.txt," the replaced text will read "C:\data\03355-0001-data.txt." Check to make sure you have used back slashes (\) and not forward slashes (/), that the quotation marks remain, and that there are no typos.
- Scroll to the last line. Add the command SAVE FILE OUT = "C:\data\myfile.sav." (Replace "myfile" with any name you want to use and make sure the line ends in a period that is outside the quotation marks.)
- Check the documentation to see if the missing values assigned to each variable (and any missing value recodes) are okay. If so, locate and remove the asterisk (*) in front of the MISSING VALUES command (and the MISSING VALUE RECODE command).
- Go to the menu bar at the top of the syntax editor, select RUN, and click on ALL.
- Once the file is created, save it (FILE, SAVE).
D. Finally, we have a piece of advice for you. Keep your original, saved file in a safe location, and work from a copy. Save your SPSS, SAS, or Stata file every time you make a change. If you have a number of changes to make, put a copy of the most recent file in the same location you saved the original. Sooner or later, you will be glad you have copies.

U.S. Government Printing Office

http://www.gpo.gov/

Child Abuse

National Clearinghouse on Child Abuse and Neglect Information

http://nccanch.acf.hhs.gov/general/stats/index.cfm

National Data Archive on Child Abuse and Neglect

http://www.ndacan.cornell.edu/

Drugs and Alcohol Abuse

National Clearinghouse for Alcohol and Drug Information (NCADI)

http://www.health.org/

National Institution on Alcohol Abuse and Alcoholism (NIAAA)

http://www.niaaa.nih.gov/

National Institution on Drug Abuse (NIDA)

http://www.nida.nih.gov/drugpages/stats.html

Substance Abuse and Mental Health Services Administration (SAMHSA)

http://www.samhsa.gov/

Juvenile Delinquency and Juvenile Justice

Major data sets located at some of these Web sites include the National Youth Survey, Monitoring the Future, National Youth Risk Behavior Survey, and National Longitudinal Survey of Youth. Most of these are also available in the NACJD.

Bureau of Labor Statistics—National Longitudinal Survey of Youth

http://www.bls.gov/nls/nlsy97.htm

Compendium of National Juvenile Justice Data Sets

http://ojjdp.ncjrs.org/ojstatbb/Compendium/index.html

Juvenile Justice Evaluation Center

http://www.jrsa.org/jjec/

National Council of Juvenile and Family Court Judges

http://www.ncjfcj.org/

Office of Juvenile Justice and Delinquency Prevention

http://ojjdp.ncjrs.org/

OJJDP Easy Access—online data display program for:
Juvenile Populations

http://ojjdp.ncjrs.org/ojstatbb/ezapop/default.asp

Juvenile FBI arrest statistics

http://ojjdp.ncjrs.org/ojstatbb/ezaucr/default.asp

NIBRS hate crimes

http://www.as.wvu.edu/~jnolan/nibrshatecrime.html

Psychological Scales for Juvenile Research

http://www.jrsa.org/jjec/resources/instruments.html

Police

While many local and state law enforcement organizations have made various types of data available, including GIS-based mapping information, there are two additional sites with major databases.

Bureau of Alcohol, Tobacco, Firearms and Explosives

http://www.atf.gov/stats.htm

Federal Bureau of Investigation

http://www.fbi.gov/

Victims

National Center for Victims of Crime—resources

http://www.ncvc.org/ncvc/main.aspx?dbID=DB_Statistics584

Legal Research

GSU College of Law—Meta-Index for U.S. Legal Research

http://gsulaw.gsu.edu/metaindex/

MegaLaw Legal Research, Case Law, Supreme Court

http://www.megalaw.com/

MSU Libraries Criminal Justice Resources Guide

http://www.lib.msu.edu/

National Archives and Records Administration Home Page

http://www.archives.gov/index.html

While there are many reasons, as enumerated earlier, for using secondary data, one of the best is a practical one—it can speed you through the human subjects review process with a minimum of issues arising. Though this is true for some secondary data sets, others may have specific requirements for each user that involves your institutional review board

(IRB). Some data sets, usually those containing sensitive information or unavoidable identifiers, are available only after a lengthy approval process which is separate from the actual IRB process. Therefore, we should now discuss the function of the IRB and how it may affect your research.

REFERENCES

BURNS, R. L., and LYNCH, M. (2005). *Environmental crime: A sourcebook.* New York: LFB Scholarly Publishing.

PECK Jr., L. (2004). *Hoeing a long and hard row: Long term administrative segregation of a cohort of Texas prison inmates.* Sam Houston State University, Huntsville, TX: Unpublished dissertation.

4

THE INSTITUTIONAL REVIEW BOARD AND THE HUMAN SUBJECTS REVIEW COMMITTEE

This chapter provides an overview of the process of human subjects review. Depending on the type of research design you use and the source of your data, you may need to follow your university's guidelines for this very important step. While many refer to this research oversight committee as the institutional review board (IRB), others may call it human subjects review. This chapter describes the basic elements of this process and provides some general examples for facilitating the research proposal review process.

THE NATURE OF THE IRB

Any research project involving the use of human subjects is accountable to a review system to ensure adequate protections for all involved. Evidence of this approval to conduct research is also a requirement for grant funding from most government sources. Concerns about the humane and ethical treatment of subjects used in research have been a public, government, and particularly educational issue since the early 1900s. The rapid expansion of science, technology and medicines, laboratory testing, and abusive experimentation especially during various wars has sensitized people to the need for oversight and accountability in research. More information about the history of these protections can be found in *The Belmont Report*, issued by the Department of Health, Education, and Welfare, titled "Ethical Principles and Guidelines for the Protection of Human Subjects of Research" (1979).

Depending on the type of research project you develop, you may need some type of interaction with the human subjects review committee at your school. This is also something to consider up front before you commit to a project if you have certain time constraints that may not be conducive to participating in the IRB process. All researchers who are in public institutions, or use public monies, are subject to these regulations, and most researchers will follow them regardless, out of respect for the spirit of the regulations and to qualify their efforts to those standards. No doubt, your chair, who will be familiar with the nature of the IRB review at your school, will be able to help you with this. Your university, no doubt, also has a Web site that will provide you detailed information about the review process you may need to follow.

NO HUMAN SUBJECTS

As noted earlier, certain types of research designs are less likely to encounter human subjects or the need for institutional review procedures. This would include historical research where the information collected would be from books and articles, newspapers, and government reports and records. However, if you intend to interview subjects from certain events, such as a prison riot, or civil rights protest, you will be using human subjects and need IRB approval. Other general research techniques, such as most content analyses, cost-benefit analyses, and legal research projects, typically do not involve human subjects as the basis of information.

Even students who choose an empirical design with quantitative data analyses do not always involve human subjects. The study may instead focus on materials, evidence, policies, or inanimate objects such as vehicles stolen, guns confiscated, or the types of court imposed conditions ordered for probation. While it may be difficult in some circumstances for a student to gain access to a sample of drunk drivers, it may be less problematic and equally as interesting to study the extent of damage to vehicles involved in DWI accidents, a possible proxy measure of the seriousness of the offense. For example, Mauricio conducted a program evaluation of a gun buy-back program. The focus of the research was the types and quantities of weapons over the span of the project in comparison to the census demographics of three different neighborhoods. Consequently, his research did not involve human subjects even though his analysis included a quasi-experimental design.

HUMAN SUBJECTS

Basically, there are two types of human subject reviews. One requires a full board review, and the other is made up of categories that are exempt from full review.

Full Review

If your project involves gathering information from or about people, including records, opinions, surveys, test scores, or other performance measures, you will most likely need to obtain a full review of your proposal. Particularly sensitive topics (sexual abuse, drug addiction, or domestic violence) or vulnerable populations (children, prisoners, victims, etc.) will no doubt draw a higher level of scrutiny and require more advanced preparation of methods and assurances from the researcher. Usually, for a thesis, it is a good idea to avoid research topics that ask respondents to disclose any criminal activity, potentially stigmatizing victimizations, or deviant behavior.

For example, even though Kristin was doing an historical/legal research thesis, her study was based on interviews with the principal parties in a particular death penalty case. She submitted a proposal for full review, including the questions she would be asking the attorneys and the judge as well as two newspaper reporters who covered the case. It was obvious that those selected to be questioned were either government employees whose professional responsibilities required them to be available for public questioning and whose rulings and opinions were already public knowledge or they were media representatives, also with a limited expectation of privacy concerning their published work. Thus the committee did not have a difficult decision to make in approving this research.

IRB Exempt Categories

Even if you believe that your research design is exempt from full review, you must still fill out an application, noting that you are requesting an exemption. These requests must still be forwarded to the chair of the committee so that the official determination can be made that the proposal is in fact, exempt. In that case, you will most likely receive a letter within a short period of time notifying you that your proposal has been designated as exempt. A brief description of the different categories for exemption is in Box 4-1. The information is part of the Code of Federal Regulations and is readily available in case you want to refer to the full document.

As the regulations indicate, if you are using secondary data, data from anonymous closed files, aggregated data, or records without identifiers, then you may be exempt from the full review, and a much shorter review will most likely clear your project to begin. Information that is subject to the *Open Records Act*, which includes official records of many criminal justice system agencies, fall into this category—which makes receiving an exemption much easier. The most common exemption for students doing criminal justice related research is under Category 4.

The term "existing data" usually refers to retrospective research where data have been archived, usually by the collecting agency or a research institution such as the National Institute of Justice. In addition, existing data must be stripped of identifiers so that individual participants cannot be recognized. This would include not only names but court case

BOX 4-1 EXEMPTION CATEGORIES

Category 1. Research conducted in established or commonly accepted educational setting, involving normal education practices such as:

A. research on regular and special education strategies; or

B. research on the effectiveness of, or the comparison among, instructional techniques, curricula, or classroom management methods.

Category 2. Research involving the use of educational tests (cognitive, diagnostic, aptitude, or achievement), survey procedures, interview procedures, or observation of public behavior unless:

A. information obtained is recorded in such a manner that human subjects can be identified, directly or through identifiers linked to the subjects; and

B. any disclosure of the human subjects' responses outside the research could reasonably place the subjects at risk of criminal or civil liability or be damaging to the subjects' financial standing, employability, or reputation.

Category 3. Research involving the use of educational tests (cognitive, diagnostic, aptitude, achievement), survey procedures, interview procedures, or observation of public behavior if:

A. the human subjects are elected or appointed public officials or candidates for public office; or

B. federal statute(s) require(s) without exception that the confidentiality of the personally identifiable information will be maintained throughout the research and thereafter.

Category 4. Research involving the collection or study of existing data, documents, records, pathological specimens, or diagnostic specimens, if these sources are publicly available or if the information is recorded by the investigator in such a manner that subjects cannot be identified, directly or through identifiers linked to the subjects.

Category 5. Research and demonstration projects that are conducted by or subject to the approval of department of agency heads, and which are designed to study, evaluate, or otherwise examine:

A. public benefit or service programs

B. procedures for obtaining benefits or services under those programs

C. possible changes in or alternatives to those programs or procedures; or

D. possible changes in methods or levels of payment for benefits or services under those programs.

Source: Code of Federal Regulations

numbers, medical record numbers, or social security numbers. Further, there should also be no way to link these names or numbers to financial or employment information.

In cases of Category 2 or 3 exemptions, questionnaires should be accompanied by a cover letter advising potential subjects that their participation is voluntary and that their privacy will not be violated.

To conduct a survey of college professors, Carlan (2005) sought an exemption under Category 2. His application explained the risks as follows:

> Based on personal perspective and the observations of colleagues, there are no identifiable risks associated with participation in the project. There are no sensitive issues on the instrument, and anonymity will be ensured by having the respondent return only a scantron answer form in a pre-printed addressed envelope. Once the data has been successfully transformed and tabulated, confidentiality of the responses will be accomplished by keeping the scantron sheets in a locked filing cabinet in the investigators office. The data sheets will be destroyed five years from the date of collection.

Because Carlan did not want to have individuals identify themselves by signing a consent to participate form, he added a request that such a step be waived, given the innocuous nature of his survey. He wrote

> It is requested that the requirement concerning written approval of all participating subjects be waived. In accordance with the written guidelines for Human Subject Review, the investigator perceives the proposed research to be consistent with the waiver requirements. Furthermore, those in academic environments understand well the nature of this research, and therefore, this protocol involves "no procedures for which written consent is normally required when performed outside the research context." In essence, the subjects would be doing merely what they do as a routine part of their everyday educational responsibilities.

When sending out a survey of this type, you would include a cover letter, reproduced on university/departmental letterhead, and provide your complete title, address, contact phone and fax numbers, e-mail address, and the university's Web site. Your cover letter should explain the purpose of your research, its intended benefits, the estimated time it would take to complete the questionnaire, and how it should be returned. You also need to assure participants that their responses are confidential, that participation is voluntary, and that questions are welcomed. Finally, you should include information verifying that university human subjects review committee approval has been granted and provide full contact information for the board (as per their instructions). An example of such a letter is in Box 4-2.

Attachments with your application should include materials that the subjects will receive in the course of the research so that the IRB committee has examined and evaluated the actual instruments. It would not be realistic to expect the committee to approve documentation they have not seen first-hand. This would be any test, survey, questionnaire, letters, descriptions of incentives offered for participation, and so on.

BOX 4-2 SAMPLE LETTER TO IRB REQUESTING APPROVAL
OF CATEGORY 2 EXEMPTION

Eastern Darwin University
Department of Criminal Justice
7000 University SuperHighway
Cartwheel, PA XXXXX-0001
Tel: 999.XXX.XXXX   Fax 678.XXX.XXX   www.edu.edu

October 7, 2007

Dear Criminal Justice Faculty,

I am writing to ask for your support in an effort to collect data that will provide a comprehensive look at measures of assessment currently being used in criminal justice programs in colleges and universities today. This research will solicit feedback from criminal justice faculty on the types of assessment being implemented and faculty experiences with the various measures, as well as their evaluations of its utility and problems with the development of meaningful learning outcomes. I firmly believe that the present research has the potential to be of great benefit to the academic discipline of criminal justice. Your participation is critical for ensuring that the study is comprehensive and representative.

The enclosed instruments (comprised of a questionnaire, answer sheet, and self-addressed return envelope) requires no more than fifteen to twenty minutes to complete. I am asking you as a *full-time criminal justice faculty member* to complete the instrument and return it in the attached envelope. The target date for the survey's return is November 29, 2007. Data collected from voluntary participants will be held in strict confidence, and any questions regarding the research are welcomed (contact information is listed at the bottom of the page).

This project has been reviewed by the Human Subjects Protection Review Committee, which ensures that research projects involving human subjects follow federal regulations. Any questions or concerns about rights as a research subject should be directed to the chair of the Institutional Review Board, Eastern Darwin University, 7000 University Superhighway, Cartwheel, PA (999) XXX-XXXX.

Thank you for consideration of this request. It is hoped that this study will be useful to your department as you resolve assessment issues in the future. The results will be posted on our department's Web site after March 1, 2008 (*www.edu.edu/cjd/research/assessprjc1.html*).

With Sincere Appreciation,

Rasputin U. Pickelosky, Ph.D.   (999) XXX-XXXX
Assistant Professor   Rupickel@edu.edu
Department of Criminal Justice
Eastern Darwin University

SUBMITTING A PROPOSAL FOR FULL REVIEW

When you need to submit for a full IRB review, you will most likely be asked to fill out a set of forms that constitute an application for human subjects review. Your committee will assist you, but you should be aware of the type of information that will be asked and the most common ways to properly respond. This application will likely ask you the following information:

1. Information on the Principle Investigator (PI)
   a. PI Address
   b. College
   c. Phone Number
2. Information on any Associate Researchers
   a. Address
   b. Affiliation/College
   c. Role in Project
3. Identification of Faculty Sponsor
   a. College
   b. Campus Phone Number
4. Type of Review
   a. New, or
   b. Renewal
5. Are you applying for an exemption? If so, what category?
6. Title of Project.
7. Project Dates.
8. Short summary of the project (100–150 words), including number of subjects, ages, gender, where the project will take place, statement of thesis, research questions, methodology. If a questionnaire is to be used, attach a copy.
9. Description of the source(s) of subjects, selection criteria, and the recruitment process. Specifically where did you obtain the list of potential subjects (agency, organization, etc.). Where and how will you contact them (100–150 words)?
10. Procedures: Step-by-step description of the procedures, including the frequency, duration, and location of each (100–150 words).
11. Risks: Description of any potential risks or discomforts involved (physical, emotional, or social), and the precautions you have taken to minimize those risks.
12. Benefits: Description of the anticipated benefits to subjects and the importance of the knowledge that may be reasonably expected to result from this research (100–150 words).
13. Informed Consent: Description of the consent process. You will also attach all consent documents, including cover letters.

Informed Consent

One of the most important components of research conducted with real people is the agreement between the researcher and their subjects ensuring their safety and well-being during the process and afterward. It is the researcher's acknowledgment that all attempts have been made to minimize any inherent risks in the process and to provide assurances that the rights of the participant have been protected.

Prior to the setting of contemporary standards, it was not uncommon for inmates to be used in the testing of chemical, medical, and technological products. It could be argued that given the nature of the incentives offered and the complexity of the procedures involved, the inmates' lack of education would make informed consent unlikely. Thus, the meaningfulness of informed consent is interpreted today not only in terms of what the participant is told, but also the context itself that makes it clear that their involvement is voluntary and uncoerced.

As Box 4-3 indicates, there are basically eight factors covered by informed consent. The overall intent is to ensure that researchers show respect for all participants and that no harm occurs to those involved. That is usually translated into the concepts of voluntariness (a lack of coercion), being adequately informed (most likely in writing), and having the ability to give full consent. Most review committees will want to see how you intend to achieve full informed consent—the written materials to be provided to participants and the explanations they will receive. You will need to explain how you will ensure that the subjects' participation is voluntary and how they may be able to withdraw or decline without any repercussions.

If you are interviewing subjects, then an informed consent script is usually read and signed by participants, or, if confidentiality is employed, their verbal agreement is noted. It is also important that the subjects receive a copy of the script, normally with the name and phone number of a responsible contact person should they later have questions or concerns. A sample of an informed consent script is provided in Box 4-4.

In mailed or written questionnaire designs, the informed consent is usually attached with a cover letter. It is easy to see that it is in everyone's best interests if volunteers are comfortable in their participation and understand the research process to which they are contributing.

BOX 4-3 THE BASIC EIGHT ELEMENTS OF INFORMED CONSENT

These items are required for the recruitment of subjects in verbal scripts/cover letters and in consent letters for activities not exceeding minimal risk.

1. Who you are
2. What you are doing
3. Why you are doing it
4. What subjects will be asked to do and how long it will take
5. That participation is voluntary
6. That there will be no penalty for nonparticipation or withdrawal from the study
7. How confidentiality/anonymity will be maintained
8. Who to call with questions or concerns about this study

BOX 4-4 SAMPLE INFORMED CONSENT LETTER

My name is Arnice Porter, and I am a graduate student at North State University. I am now collecting data to complete my thesis on the topic of neighborhood associations and control of graffiti. You have been selected to be interviewed because of your membership in the Parkside Neighborhood Association and because you signed a letter of interest in participating in this study that was distributed at the October 17, 2005, meeting of that association.

There are ten open-ended questions that I will ask you, and this interview should take no more than twenty-five minutes. I will ask you about your experiences in this neighborhood and with the association, some questions about your support for certain crime control measures, and then some questions about the relative value of certain types of services or policies related to crime and delinquency prevention. By participating in this study, you will help provide a greater understanding of how homeowner association members view their role in crime prevention and what types of responses to graffiti are perceived as most beneficial.

Confidentiality is a priority in this study, and I will make every effort to maintain the anonymity of each participant. This means that I will not use any names or identifying characteristics when recording the information your provide. The transcriber will not receive any information relative to the identity of each speaker, and numbers will be assigned to the various interviews. Further, the responses for each question will all be combined so that no one person's entire set of responses will be presented together. At the conclusion of this data gathering process, and once the interviews have been transcribed, the tapes will be destroyed. Until that time, they will be kept in a locked cabinet in the Criminal Justice Department Office.

Again, your participation is completely voluntary. You can choose to withdraw from this study at any point in time or refrain from answering any question that you are not comfortable addressing. There is also a ten-day period following this interview that you can contact me to withdraw your responses from the data set. If you withdraw, all information pertaining to you will be destroyed. If you wish to speak to my academic advisor or the Chair of the Human Subjects Committee their contact information is provided below. You are encouraged to keep this informed consent document. Because of our concern for confidentiality I will not have you sign any agreement, but when the tape begins, I will state the interview number that has been assigned to this collection and ask you to agree to participate under the terms we have just discussed.

Additional Application Materials

When you submit an application for human subjects review, you may want to include any support materials that explain your project's data gathering process. A copy of a letter of permission (see Box 4-5) is a good demonstration that the proper officials at an agency have sanctioned your research. Often it may be helpful to assist the agency supplying your data with the language for your letter of support. You may also be asked to submit a copy of your informed consent documents and a copy of any instruments you may be using to collect original data such as surveys or questionnaires.

In filling out a request for an exemption, you will still need to provide the assurances that the project you are undertaking meets the requirements for an exemption. A cover letter to the IRB committee would help to clarify this for the committee and thus would be an important part of your submission (see Box 4-6).

BOX 4-5 SAMPLE LETTER OF PERMISSION FROM AGENCY HEAD

Winifred S. Duncan
District Clerk
County Court of Simonis

July 13, 2006

Dr. Harmon S. Whippup
University of Margaritaville
Department of Criminal Justice
2299 Highway Ave
Dreamland, NW 00009

Dear Dr. Whippup,

This letter is to inform you that Andre Loosinit has the permission of the Simonis County Court, District Clerk's Office to use aggregate jury data drawn from 2002 and 2003 for a research project for his thesis. He will receive an export file of existing historical data that indicates only the zip code of the prospective juror and whether or not they appeared at the time of the summons. The data will not include any personal identifiers. No active cases will be used for this study. Existing data from closed files that are stored in aggregate files will be used and analyzed regarding the "failure to report for jury duty rate."

Sincerely,

Winifred S. Duncan
District Clerk

BOX 4-6 SAMPLE LETTER TO IRB REQUESTING APPROVAL OF CATEGORY 4 EXEMPTION

Dr. Morton V. Andrews
Chair, Institutional Review Board
University of A Mountain
788 Skylark Avenue
Romaine, BT 00002

To the Chair,

Enclosed please find my application for Human Subjects Approval for my thesis research. As the application indicates, I am seeking an exemption under Category 4 as the data will be from existing archived agency records and will not include any identifiers. My research examines the relationship between age and arrest for certain public order crimes in the downtown area, particularly drag racing, loitering, and vandalism over time. The data I am seeking from the Romaine Police Department will only include the date/time of offense/race, gender, and age of offender/and offense category. No names or addresses will be used. The data are identical to some of the information used in annual crime reporting and are generally available to the public.

I look forward to a favorable response on this application, and I can be reached at any of the contact numbers listed on the application should you have any questions. I thank you in advance for your time and attention on this matter.

Sincerely,

Elaine I. Auger
Graduate Student, Criminal Justice

Some examples may help you distinguish research designs that may need full IRB review, those that may be exempt, and those that would not involve human subjects. As each university and its IRB committee (the makeup of the committee membership normally changes in any given year) may interpret the criteria necessary to comply with the *Belmont Report* differently, these are just hypothetical examples to give you a general idea of the criteria that may qualify for certain types of review. It should be understood that you may find the standards and requirements are somewhat different at your school.

EXAMPLES

1. Silvia wants to do a study on identity theft. She proposes to test lifestyle theory, that is, whether someone's lifestyle (particularly being young and living in large urban areas) makes them more vulnerable to identity theft. With three different designs she could expect three different levels of human subjects involvement.

First Design

Sylvia proposes to collect her own data using a classroom survey of students from two college campuses, one rural and one inner city, asking them about identity theft victimization. For this design she would in most cases need to do a full human subjects review because she herself is approaching the students and asking them for the information that she would need to promise to keep confidential. She should be able to demonstrate to the reviewers that she could gather the information anonymously without using identifiers. Further, she should show how she would store the data in a way that would be secure until after the study when it would be destroyed. She would also have to submit the survey instrument with her proposal, as well as a statement specifying how she would ensure that she had each individual's informed consent to participate voluntarily. This usually means that whoever is administering the survey reads a prepared statement prior to passing out the instruments or provides everyone with a form letter for them to keep (see the example in Box 4-4).

Second Design

Sylvia proposes to use data routinely collected and filed by the local police department. This means that the police department's data technician downloads into a file only select case variables, that is, information that contains no identifiers. All variables (such as age, occupation, zip code) should be listed in the proposal so that reviewers can ascertain that none of them will disclose the identity of any of the victims. For this proposal, Sylvia may qualify for a Category 4 exemption. By definition, a Category 4 exemption is, "Research involving the collection or study of existing data, documents, records, pathological specimens, or diagnostic specimens, if these sources are publicly available or if the information is recorded by the investigator in such a manner that subjects cannot be identified, directly or through identifiers linked to the subjects."

The request that Silvia sends to the IRB committee will look like that in Box 4-6. Even though she may qualify for the exemption, she must still submit the formal application with all of the details of the study and ask that she be granted such an exemption. If the exemption is approved, she will receive written notice from the committee. She should maintain that notice with her research records and even include it as an attachment to her prospectus or final thesis document.

Third Design

Silvia may decide to use an existing data set from a survey the Federal Trade Commission conducted and published in 2003. The survey used nationwide random telephone interviews with more than four thousand persons over eighteen years of age, asking about identity theft. When the variables are presented in aggregate form, with no individual personal information or identifiable locations in the data, and the data are downloadable from the Internet by anyone in the general public, there should be no concern with human subjects review. Because interpretations of exactly which data sets must be reviewed still seem to vary from place to place, it would be best to consult with your chair and your university IRB if you have questions about data that may not require review. Though this particular design would seem like an expedient approach, this data set has a limited number of victims and usable variables—with even fewer directly related to the theory Silvia wants to test. In this case, the trade-offs between the advantages of using this design and data set were carefully weighed and discussed with her chair.

2. Andre would like to test the idea that as higher percentages of women are found in the workplace, levels of anomie that influence crime rates, as proposed by Merton, would decrease. He is also thinking of controlling for age as he believes the theory might be more powerful once young offenders are excluded.

First Design

Andre would interview female offenders in the local jail and administer Srole's Anomie Scale. Again, like in the first example, he would need full IRB review. However, in this case, because the subjects are offenders, there would be a higher level of scrutiny. No doubt an "inmate advocate" such as a jail chaplain or counselor would be consulted by the IRB committee to ensure that there were no potentially harmful ramifications to the research nor any punitive or coercive mechanisms involved in the strategy to draw a sample (the incentives proposed to gain participants). Andre would need to include a copy of the questions that would be strictly followed in his interview and a copy of the anomie scale instrument, as well as his informed consent paperwork. If inmate participants are to be given any incentive or gratutity for participating in the study such as snacks or vouchers, it must be stated clearly in writing. He also might facilitate this effort by including a letter from a jail administrator or staff member who supports the study and can verify the conditions under which it will be undertaken. He might also be sure to cite in detail similar studies that have been approved under similar conditions.

Second Design

In this scenario, Andre would use data from closed case files from the state parole office. The parole administrator would ensure that data downloaded onto a disk for the researcher would not have any identifiers and would only contain a limited number of case variables such as previous number of jobs, length of employment, prior salaries, education, criminal convictions, sentences, previous probations and paroles, and various demographic traits. The data would come from two different time periods, ten years ago and this past year. For this study, Andre would probably qualify for a Category 4 exemption, and his application would request such a designation. He would need to ensure that not only names, addresses, and social security numbers be omitted but also inmate numbers as well. Because the data are from preexisting files, and are stripped of any identifiers, he should be eligible for the exemption once it is clear that the data he will receive will meet these parameters.

Third Design

Andre may decide to use Uniform Crime Report Data and Census Data, both available off the Web to do his study. This design would not require any human subjects review. As in the previous example, there are trade-offs in such a compromise. In this case the use of these general data sets may cause him to lose the more direct theory component of anomie, and he would have to add assumptions (which would lead to concerns about validity) about levels of crime serving as an indicator of anomie. Still, he would have a larger, national data set with both female offenders and nonoffenders and aggregate information on employment, income, single-headed households, and so on. In addition, he could argue that national crime rates are more consistent with Durkheim and Merton's conception of the effects of anomie rather than the more individualized model investigated by Leo Srole.

THESES RESULTING FROM ONGOING DEPARTMENTAL RESEARCH

Finally, if a student is working with a professor on a research project that has already been approved by the IRB for data collection, than it is unlikely that the individual student would have to obtain a separate independent review for any further or varied analyses of that data. In most cases, he or she would simply attach a copy of that original approval as an appendix to the prospectus and/or the final thesis. Again, check with your chair and your university research office to be sure.

SUMMARY

While the research project you have in mind may seem harmless and inconsequential, and the IRB process may seem time-consuming and frustrating, the need to clear the participation of others is a fundamental expectation in modern science that protects you as well as your department and university from accusations regarding the use of an improper protocol and ensures that a neutral evaluator has deemed that subjects could not be foreseen to be harmed by involvement in the project.

The process of human subjects review is not without controversy in the social sciences. Many critics argue that normal research on offenders, victims, and delinquents is often impeded by the constraining interpretations of those who may be grounded in other disciplines. According to Gunsalus (2002), scholars often complain that stricter medical and clinical protections are often mistakenly imposed in areas where there is far less risk of physical harm.

There are more mundane issues as well. Some IRBs have improperly stretched their oversight to passing judgment on research methodology and other nonharm issues. In some cases, the determinations of committee members about what constitutes "proper" research design reaches the level of disciplinary bias—"this is what we do in our field and if you don't use that type of design your research should not be permitted." There have also been instances of committees mandating a specific type of statistical analysis and even requiring changes to the title of the research. Whether these problems occur in your IRB approval process will be a function of your particular IRB committee makeup and the university rules. Overreach, usually with the justification of decreasing legal liability, is particularly common outside of major research universities.

The debate on the proper degree of oversight will, no doubt, continue. Your task will be to navigate the process, allowing yourself enough time and patience to receive any needed approvals to conduct your research. Some Web sites that might be helpful to you in studying the review process are

www.hhs.gov/ohrp/humansubjects/guidance/belmont.htm

www.hhs.gov/ohrp/references/nurcode.htm

www.hhs.gov/ohrp/irb/irb_guidebook.htm

www.nsf.gov/bfa/dias/policy/docs/45cfr690.pdf

www.nsf.gov/bfa/dias/policy/hsfaqs.jsp

Also, if your university does not have a detailed IRB Web site, you might want to look at the Web sites for the University of Minnesota, the University of Texas, or the University of Southern Mississippi, and search on their detailed IRB Web pages.

REFERENCES

CARLAN, P. E. (2005). Personal communication.
GUNSALUS, C. K. (2002). Rethinking protections for human subjects. *Chronicle of Higher Education, 49*, 12. Accessed online at *http://chronicle.com/weekly/v49/i12/12b02401.htm*.

5

Suggestions for Citing and Writing

A few words are now in order to provide some helpful hints for improving academic writing skills. These suggestions are general, apply to all types of writing assignments, and are based on the errors editors encounter most often. Hopefully you have covered most of them in earlier course work though many students have not yet had to develop a system for editing and proofreading effective at the level of a thesis. A timely review of these cautions may help you organize your efforts according to the areas you feel need the most attention so that your writing progresses much faster and with fewer revisions by your committee.

ACADEMIC WRITING AND THE FIRST PERSON

As a rule, most academic writing is done in the third person. First person is more common in editorial pieces and in rebuttals though it is often used in ethnographies or observational research. Thus, while theses and dissertation supervisors often prefer the third person, or academic style of writing, your methodology may lend itself to some first person references. This is something that you should discuss with your committee early in your writing, particularly if you feel that first person writing would be more appropriate. There may even be parts of the thesis where the committee will support the use of first person accounts perhaps throughout the prospectus itself or in the methodology, depending on the design, or in the conclusions. A first person voice should only be used if it is indicated or preferable, not simply because it is easier. In fact, you may initially find it easier to write in first person just to draft your ideas but then convert it to third person in the editing process. Hopefully, once you become accustomed to the conversion, you will be able to adopt that writing style in your initial composing.

Depending on the type of prospectus your committee envisions, it may be suitable to use first person language in it as well as in the oral defense. The more your presentation is separate from your prospectus document, the more likely it may be that the first person style could be appropriately adapted. The same will apply for the final thesis presentation. Committees are usually more flexible about the style used in the defense while they may have very specific expectations for the style and tone of the thesis document.

AVOID PLAGIARISM

Keeping careful notes while you gather information for your literature review will help ensure that you are able to accurately reference all of your sources and that you reduce your risk of inadvertently plagiarizing any of the works you are using. Exactly what constitutes plagiarism is often misunderstood by students so ensure that you are fully informed about the proper use of quotes, citations, and paraphrasing before you begin gathering your literature and writing. One of the hints for minimizing your risk of copying material is to read it and try to recall the major points after you put the materials out of sight and write your recollections in your own words. Occasionally, students will have difficulty understanding parts of articles they read and, as a consequence, use quotes to avoid plagiarizing material they are unable to rephrase. This is one of the problems leading to an overuse of quotes.

There are a number of helpful Web sites that provide tips on avoiding plagiarism and using proper citation techniques. Most universities have one, and you should consult those at your school first or an on-site writing resource center. While specific Web addresses will change over time, key word searches on terms such as "how to paraphrase," "avoiding plagiarism," "tips for student research," "academic honesty," "writing resources," and "antiplagiarism" will usually yield sufficient information.

AVOID THE OVERUSE OF QUOTES

The over use of quotes is a weakness in writing style that will diminish as your writing improves. As much as possible, you should try to paraphrase findings from the studies you read in your own words and avoid the use of quotes. When you have finished a draft of your literature review, you should go back through and eliminate as many quotes as you can. Reserve the use of quotes for those special circumstances where the original language adds color, emotion, or powerfully unique expressions that would be lost in another phrasing or would diminish the impact in another form. You should not use quotes simply because you cannot think of another way to express the material or if you do not really understand the material well enough to rephrase it. Examples of the effective use of quotes are given below.

EXAMPLE 1

In a literature review on prison adjustment, one student relied on a quote which, as you will see, could just as easily been paraphrased and cited.

With Quote

While prison adjustment varies from offender to offender, some generalizations are appropriate. According to Santos (2003, p. 21):

> . . . most of the people who have served time in prison have come from the lower socioeconomic classes. They are undereducated and have little experience contributing to legitimate society. These offenders were least informed about and least prepared when the federal government began implementing changes in the law resulting from the *1984 Comprehensive Crime Control Act*. After 1987, the sentences offenders received were more rigid and less apt to be mitigated by extenuating circumstances.

In this case, the quote is simply stated information with no particular dynamic that would qualify it as "quotable." So, here, the author would have a smoother and equally informative comment without using a quote.

Without Quote

> While prison adjustment varies from offender to offender, the poor and less educated may be at a disadvantage when it comes to understanding changes in the law as it affects their incarceration status. For example, Santos (2003), explains that the *Comprehensive Crime Control Act of 1984* confused many prisoners when it resulted in their receiving harsher sentences with less consideration for mitigating circumstances.

In other cases, a quote may provide some qualitative drama or emphasis to a point as when Justice Oliver Wendell Homes wrote in a decision supporting the use of sterilization for the feeble-minded, "three generations of imbeciles is enough." Picturesque speech or colorful descriptions may enhance an image for a writer and provide some additional insights, as when the majority in *Kent v. United States* critiqued the juvenile court with the complaint that the youth "receives the worst of both worlds." This is the effective use of quotes. As another example, in a critique of the tobacco industry's marketing of cigarettes to children, Snell (2005, p. 63) wrote the following.

EXAMPLE 2

With Quote

Motions and legal arguments consume the time and financial resources of plaintiffs' attorneys. J. Michael Jordan was a highly successful attorney for R. J. Reynolds Tobacco Company in the 1980s. In an internal memo to his colleagues he stated,

> The aggressive posture we have taken regarding depositions and discovery in general continues to make these cases extremely burdensome and expensive for plaintiffs' lawyers. . . . To paraphrase General Patton, the way we won these cases was not by spending all of [RJR's] money but by making that other son of a bitch spend all of his.

The use of this quote is highly effective because it captures the essence of just how aggressive and ruthless this tobacco company lawyer really was and how deliberately they focused on delays and expenses to wear down the opposition. This section, you would perhaps agree, would be less effective if Snell had simply paraphrased as follows:

Without Quote

> Motions and legal arguments consume the time and financial resources of plaintiffs' attorneys. J. Michael Jordan was a highly successful attorney for R. J. Reynolds Tobacco Company in the 1980s. In an internal memo to his colleagues he stated that it was an effective practice to engage in delay tactics and other trial procedures that would add expenses to the plaintiffs' burden. Jordan assessed that they would eventually win these cases using this strategy originally advocated by General Patton, namely forcing your opposition to use up all their ammunition.

Though the later statements are accurate, they are less descriptive than the original information. The quote brings to life the warlike nature of these business practices and makes the very subtle point that it is difficult for the average person, or child to defend against such an army. Snell's quote also demonstrates another point (2005, p. 63) and that is the appropriate way to minimize the length of the quote, eliminating unnecessary or distracting verbiage with the use of ellipses. Without confusing or distracting the reader, you should be able to pare down a more lengthy quote into just the necessary elements. This is particularly useful when you are abstracting from speeches or government reports.

Jahmal was writing about the influence of the Christopher Commission on the Los Angles Police Department. In summarizing the mayor's charge to the commission, he was able to cut and paste the most meaningful parts of the document and still have a smooth reading flow by eliminating less pertinent information, such as the names and titles of all participants. He wrote:

> In his Charge to the Special Independent Commission, Mayor Bradley affirmed that "The time has come for a reasoned, objective, thorough and constructive examination of the structure and operation of our Police Department. . . . This is a citizens' commission of the highest order. . . . My hope is that it will recommend solutions that reflect a broad consensus and that . . . the commissions work will be primarily prospective, focusing on needed changes to the department's methods of selecting, training, promoting and disciplining its officers" (Bradley, 1991, pp. 132–133).

Jahmal was able to capture the essence of the four-page document with a few key phrases directly from the document that flowed smoothly.

It is important that quotes be used strategically, and not to fill space or to explain findings that you, as an author, cannot find a way to paraphrase due to a lack of understanding. If the methodology or the analysis used in a study is too complicated or sophisticated for you to put in your own words, then you should seek assistance from one of your professors before including it in your own literature review. If you do not understand it, it is unlikely that you will need that information for your study or that its importance would be effectively communicated.

The guidelines presented here for using quotes apply to your literature review and the use of source materials. When doing interviews as part of your research methodology, quotes that are part of your data are treated quite differently. The guidelines for using that material should not be confused with quotes from the literature. The reporting of quoted material from your data is covered in detail in Chapter 10.

VARY PHRASING AND AVOID REPETITION

Throughout the literature review make an effort to vary the phrasing you use to explain the different author's works. The use of citations throughout a literature review should not be a repetitious litany of "he said, she said." There are many stylistic ways to vary the reporting of research findings without confusing the reader or constantly referring to the author by name.

For example, what you want to avoid is:

> A second cognitive perspective has been offered by Walters and White (1989). Walters and White argue that criminal behavior is the product of faulty, irrational thinking and deny that environmental factors determine criminal behavior. Locating some eight "primitive cognitive characteristics" Walters and White (1989) examine the thinking patterns of lifestyle criminals and find that, from an early age, these individuals present chronic management problems. Finally, Walters and White argue that lifestyle criminals direct their behavior toward "losing in dramatic and destructive ways." (p. 8)

Though the writer here is trying conscientiously to attribute the ideas to the correct authors, the unnecessary repetition of their names is a stylistic problem. The paragraph might be edited to read:

> A second cognitive perspective has been offered by Walters and White (1989) who argue that criminal behavior is the product of faulty, irrational thinking and deny that environmental factors determine criminal behavior. In the process of locating some eight "primitive cognitive characteristics" they examined the thinking patterns of lifestyle criminals and found that, from an early age, these individuals present chronic management problems. The authors also maintain that lifestyle criminals direct their behavior toward "losing in dramatic and destructive ways." (p. 8)

As the example indicates, once you tell readers the names of the study's authors, you can then use a variety of references that will convey the idea that you are still referring to the same article (e.g., "The author argues that . . . ," "they also found . . . ," "he further adds that . . ."). The point is that the reader should always know whose work you are referring to, and they will continue to assume you are talking about the same work and the same author until you tell them differently. Usually within a single paragraph, if no new studies or authors are introduced it is assumed that you are talking about one study as the example below from a work by Yolanda Scott (2001, pp. 40–41) illustrates.

> Ortega and Myles' (1987) study of respondents residing in eight Chicago neighborhoods illustrates this point well. Keeping in mind that their fear measure

seems to better measure risk perceptions, using a general "fear" measure, they report that, of all race, sex, and age groups examined, African Americans were on the opposite ends of their purported "fear" continuum. That is, whites experienced medium average fear levels, relatively younger African American males were the least fearful while older African American females were the most fearful. Stated perhaps more accurately, these researchers report older African American females felt the most *unsafe*, while younger African American males, on average, felt the most *safe* at all subgroups. Whites' average *risk assessments* were found to be in between those African American citizens. Interestingly, the researchers report that when taking into account offense specificity, relatively younger African American males were actually found to be "fearful" of something—burglary. While this is merely a footnote in this study, this finding is important as it highlights the need for multiple-item measures, greater specificity and clearer conceptualization of the crime-reactions under study.

Rather than repeating "Ortega and Myles" throughout the paragraph the author's continuous stream of reference is implied in her discussion. Thus, the reader is never in doubt that she is talking about Ortega and Myles's study when she says "their fear measure" and "these researchers," thus the ideas flow naturally. Another point demonstrated by this example is how the author does not simply report on the findings but adds comments about the meaningfulness of certain points and how they lead to her conclusions about what further information is needed in this topic area.

AVOID UNNECESSARY VERBIAGE

Most students tend to use unnecessary words and phrases so attention to this aspect of your writing could eliminate the need for editing and thus wear and tear on your committee. The secret is to be concise. Almost any document can be shortened, so devote time to reading through your chapters and focusing only on superfluous terms. For example:

report back → report
in 30 years of existence → in 30 years
would be expected to impact upon performance causing → would cause
This is found to explain → this explains
Studies that have been done have found → studies have found
have resulted in the system being divided → have divided the system
variables that have been measured on a continuous basis → continuous variables

Some phrases can be eliminated entirely such as: "the amount of," "the case of," "the characteristics of," or "the occurrence of."

Another example of unnecessary information, particularly in a literature review, is the specific title of a work, the author's affiliation, or the title of the publication in which the research appeared. For example:

DON'T DO THIS: Dr. Janet E. Null, Professor of Neuropsychiatry at Fort Myers University Medical Center explains in her 2004 paper "The Onset of Superhero Identities in Adolescent Vitamin Abusers"published in the Florida Cable

Network Medical Guide that eight out of ten of those addicted to dietary supplements also had histories of delinquency.

DO THIS: In an admittedly small sample of adolescent vitamin abusers in Florida, Null (2004) found that most of those addicted to dietary supplements were also designated as delinquent.

Writers also fall into bad habits involving the repetition of certain phrases that are unnecessary such as "due to the fact that" or "as is the case with" or "in regards to." Some of these phrases are ingrained in our speech as well as in our writing, and it often takes the kind intervention of another to point them out to us. Be open to the chance that you might have some pet "wordy" phrases that you use and make an effort to eliminate them—yes, all of them.

WRITE CLEARLY

Writing clearly often means writing simply. One should avoid the use of multiple descriptors and compound sentences, particularly when attempting to explain complex ideas. Alternating longer sentences with shorter ones also may help readers catch up. Avoid wearing readers down by processing too many ideas at one time. Observe the differences between the two examples in each of the cases below. It is important to determine if any crucial information is lost by making statements simpler and the flow smoother. Does the use of the additional adverbs and adjectives, phrases and clauses, really improve the reader's understanding of your ideas? Or can the phrasing be streamlined for enhanced readability? These decisions are part of the art of writing clearly, and you will improve as you practice your writing.

DON'T DO THIS: Across the country, and in major cities specifically, public intolerance of misconduct within police ranks is low.

DO THIS: The public is unlikely to tolerate police misconduct.

In the example above, the use of "across the country" and "in major cities" is really unnecessary. The term "public" is general, and unless a designated area has already been mentioned, it is implied that this perception is widespread and not geographically specific, which is better for your scope of interest anyway.

DON'T DO THIS: Toward the development of unions, there were only weak and sporadic police movements for the next twenty years. According to Gammage & Sachs (1972) in Portsmouth, Virginia, the inactivity for twenty years was broken in 1937. That year, the American Federation of State, County and Municipal Employees chartered its first police local.

DO THIS: The movement toward police unions over the next twenty years was weak and sporadic. It wasn't until 1937 that the American Federation of State, County and Municipal Employees chartered its first police local in Portsmouth, Virginia (Gammage & Sachs, 1972).

The second example should sound much more direct and clear. When citing historical facts, it is much more appropriate to just relay the material and cite the source in subsequent parentheses. The use of "according to . . ." is more suited for something that is likely to be opinion, interpretation, or research findings. In addition, the first description seems to imply that the authors, rather than the union, are in Portsmouth, Virginia.

To write clearly means that you avoid **jargon, faddish words, slang, abbreviations,** and **acronyms** unless clarified and established in preliminary discussions. This means that if you are doing a thesis on DNA, rap music, motorcycle outlaws, or computer-generated simulations you should realistically incorporate the appropriate terms. Even here, though, you should take initial steps to ensure that the reader has been afforded definitions and explanations to fully appreciate the context. In such theses, the author will most likely devote some portion of the introduction or methodology to clearly defining these terms or variables. You may even want to put a list of abbreviations and acronyms in the front of the thesis in sequence with your list of tables and/or figures, should there be enough of them to warrant this approach. By having a friend or relative who is not conversant with the field read your drafts, you can receive feedback on clarity and familiarity of your terminology.

One final caution is to avoid the use of rhetorical questions. While handy for philosophers, a more efficient and effective mode for a thesis is to use affirmative statements. Inviting readers to think up their own answers always risks distraction at best, contradiction at worst. Simply state the point you are suggesting or arguing and avoid losing your audience's attention.

USE ORIGINAL SOURCES

Try to use original sources for your references as much as is possible. Avoid the use of textbooks or other secondary sources if the original versions are generally available. This also means avoiding the use of Web sites or online references if the same material has been published in print. Web-based materials tend to disappear quickly as URLs or Web sites change. By using printed sources, it is easier for readers, at any point in time, to track and obtain the materials in their original context. This is particularly true for government publications; most can be formatted into a full citation that will give the reader all of the reference information necessary to locate the material, regardless of the status of the Web site.

A major issue with web-based materials is the difficulty of citing what otherwise are desirable quotations when there are no page numbers. As an example of this difficulty, one frustrated chair was overheard telling a student to delete all materials for which there were no page numbers in the citation. Imagine the equal frustration of the student who was depending on those sources to convey part of the point she was trying to make. One of the corollaries to this issue is to make sure, if there is a choice between downloading an article in html or pdf formats, that you choose the pdf version—it has page numbers.

ENSURE YOUR SOURCES ARE RELIABLE

Using the most recent and most reliable sources will lend credibility to your work. It is trite, but true, that not all sources are created equal. Your committee members may have expectations about the types of sources you rely on, particularly given the nature of your topic, so be sure to consult with them once your bibliography is drafted. Be careful to attribute facts and figures to their originators, using primary sources whenever possible. If you are using a secondary source, clearly indicate that fact and use the proper referencing style designated by your style manual. Keep in mind that Internet sources are unlikely to have the level of review and scrutiny that peer-reviewed journals or reputable academic publishers offer. If you are in doubt about any piece of information, follow up with another source that you can substantiate; consider eliminating that item if no substantiation can be located.

Again, in attempting to maximize the use of primary sources, trace all relevant information to its original source, and use those original sources in your writing, as well as in your bibliography. This will also give you the opportunity to verify that the information is as the author meant it to be and was not misinterpreted by someone else. As in the old children's game of whispering a secret around the room, the end product may be an entirely different version of the initial wording. An excellent, and even frightening, example of the way statistics in particular can be distorted in subsequent usage can be found in Joel Best's (2001) classic piece "Telling the truth about damn lies and statistics."

FINAL PROOFREADING

As you prepare to turn in materials, proofread as much as possible. Often this means reading through several times in order to focus on certain aspects. Reading for punctuation, spelling, grammar, and phrasing may be separate than reading for continuity, flow, and substantive quality. Reading the paper aloud also helps to identify awkward or difficult-to-understand passages. Sometimes it is only when reading aloud that we identify nouns and verbs that are not in agreement or modifiers that are misplaced.

When you simply cannot read your thesis one more time, call upon your friends and colleagues to go over it a last time for you. Have a volunteer check the items in your bibliography while you call out the citations as they appear on your text page by page to ensure that you have captured all the references needed, including multiple works by an author or set of authors by year.

Finally, we offer a word of caution. Do not, under any circumstances, ask your chair to proofread your thesis for you. There are two major reasons for this. First, it is almost certain that the task will create frustration in, and potentially antagonize, the one person you want to be your champion. Second, proofreading is different than reading for substance and content. If your chair is focusing on minute detail, he or she will likely not be able to take a larger view of your work and help you strengthen your thesis with appropriate content, flow, and ideas. As a result, this economy measure (not using others . . .) will tend to backfire and reduce the quality of your end product.

REFERENCES

BEST, J. (2001, May 4). Telling the truth about damn lies and statistics. *Chronicle of Higher Education, 47,* 34, B7–9.

SCOTT, Y. (2001). *Fear of crime among inner-city African Americans.* New York: LFB Scholarly Publishing.

SNELL, C. (2005). *Peddling poison: The tobacco industry and kids.* Westport, CT: Praeger.

Section Two

THE PROSPECTUS
OR PROPOSAL

Undoubtedly, the best way to prepare for a thesis prospectus defense is to have attended at least one to get an idea about the process and what to expect, particularly at your institution. In retrospect, Rudy admitted that not attending a prospectus defense led him to get more nervous than he should have about this step. However, he was very grateful that he had taken a communications and presentations class that had perfected his PowerPoint skills. He advises everyone to obtain some type of formal PowerPoint training prior to their defense.

Each thesis advisor or committee will have specific expectations for the prospectus. Some may want the first several chapters of the document completed while others may want a shorter, briefer version of the elements of the first chapters. It is safe to say across the board, however, that all thesis prospecti will have at least the same basic information, enabling faculty to evaluate the feasibility of the proposed study:

1. An overview of the problem and its significance
2. A clear statement of the study's purpose and methods so that it is obvious to a reader that the methods used will be able to accomplish the intended purpose
3. Some background via the literature supporting both that you understand the problem and its related issues and the study you are proposing fits within the framework of not only what we already know but also what we further need to know

Therefore, in this section we discuss the elements of what are traditionally known as the first three chapters in a quantitatively oriented analysis or evaluation, as well as other types of study formats. Finally we discuss the prospectus defense itself and how you can smooth the process with a well-prepared presentation.

6

INTRODUCTION AND PROBLEM STATEMENT

The introductory chapter is an important outline of the rationale for the study, as well as a brief explanation of what will be done and why. You and your chair will decide how best to structure your introductory chapter, keeping in mind that it has the dual role of drawing the audience into the work and convincing them that you are dealing with a problem worth pursuing.

The following is a more comprehensive list of potential elements that may be in the first chapter. You should discuss these with your committee to determine which are appropriate for your work.

- Historical background
- Size and scope of the problem today
- Specific examples of how the problem effects us today
- What leading experts may say about the problem or issue
- Importance of addressing the issue or consequences of not doing so
- Summary of what we do and don't know from research on the issue
- What we need to know
- Why this study will contribute what we need to know
- General limitations of your study
- Brief outline of what you are going to do
- The organization of the thesis

Each of these elements are discussed in some detail below, with recommendations for topics and approaches where they are most appropriately used. Examples from various types of theses will help the student determine what elements would be best for the study he or she is undertaking.

HISTORICAL BACKGROUND AND CURRENT ISSUES

Some topics lend themselves better to an introduction that focuses on the current issues surrounding them, such as topics related to DNA evidence or cyber crimes, while others are better approached from the standpoint of their historical development. This is especially true where issues were shaped by successive political, social, and economic forces or in instances where practices have changed over time.

Historical Background

Developing the historical context of a subject gives a reader the ability to understand why we are now at a certain point with an issue or why something may have been valued or treated in different ways in the past. For example, the author of a thesis on the length of sentences served by illegal aliens in American prisons (by virtue of being held with an immigration detainer) might spend some time explaining the historical uses of the detainer. Similarly, someone doing a thesis on the law enforcement practice of seizing homes and cars of drug dealers might start out with historical uses of the law in asset forfeiture. Other examples include historical antecedents of community policing and delinquency prevention. The point is that background information sets the stage for a more thorough understanding of an issue as it now stands. It also can yield insights into alternative approaches to your topic or assist in a critique of the issue.

The opening of an historical thesis, for example, will set the stage for understanding the events to be described in the body of the work. Thus, in a thesis about the recent prosecution of polygamist sect members in Colorado City, Arizona, the author might begin by discussing the historical controversies over the practice of polygamy, the forcing of members out of Missouri and Ohio from 1833 to 1839, and the subsequent movement from the Nauvoo community in Illinois in 1844. The author might also describe the passage of the *Morrill (Anti-bigamy) Act of 1862* and the *Edmunds Act of 1882* and the ensuing convictions that were handed down between 1884 and 1895. This context allows the readers to see the parallels and traditions that offer a more holistic view of the legal, political, and historical issues involved.

Current Issues

If a thesis topic is a more current issue and the work will not be drawing on any significant historical background, a writer may want to open with a broader discussion of the significance of a topic in terms of current costs, numbers of people affected, or particularly notable cases that have had a high profile in the media. These are all ways to make the topic come to life for the reader where the importance of doing research on this subject becomes clear and makes the utility of the study obvious. For example, a thesis on the constitutionality of current detention procedures with suspected terrorists might begin with a discussion of the number of recent terrorists bombings, the number of people killed, the range of countries affected, and the ethnic backgrounds of the various terrorists arrested or detained to date.

A topic without at least some historical background, however, is relatively rare. Normally, a discussion of the historical background will begin your chapter, and then you will treat the current issues. The pairing of history and contemporary events makes for the best opening discussion.

FACTS AND FIGURES VERSUS CASE EXAMPLES

Facts and Figures

The purpose of any introductory chapter is to build a strong argument about the importance of a topic. One way to do that is to use facts and figures that are particularly illuminating or compelling. In criminal justice and criminology, these usually are derived from crime reports, government agency data, or statistics drawn from research studies. As an example, note the way Silvia (Iglesias, 2005) crafts an opening that will catch the reader's attention by making the less dramatic white-collar offense of identity theft reflect its true serious and widespread nature.

> Since Edwin Sutherland first defined "white collar crime" in 1939, the definition has been expanded to include a complex array of technologically-enhanced offenses and sophisticated financial schemes. In 1998, there were an estimated 400,000 arrests for fraud, over 110,000 arrests for forgery and counterfeiting, 17,000 arrests for embezzlement and close to 140,000 arrests for dealings with stolen property (FBI, 1999). One of the fastest growing white collar crimes is identity theft (Milne, 2003). In 1997, two-thirds of all inquiries to the Trans Union Corporation, one of the three major credit bureaus, were related to identity fraud. That same year, the Secret Service reported that losses relating to identity fraud totaled $745 million, a 75% increase over the figure for 1995. Within the same time period, arrests for identity fraud increased from 8,806 to 9,445 (Hemphill, 2001). In 2003, a survey by the Federal Trade Commission (FTC) found that three and a quarter million adult Americans had their identities misused. The FTC also found that one in every four United States households has been a victim of identity theft in the past five years.

The readers now have a sense that this crime has personally touched many people they know and could even happen to them. Thus, it makes an effective introduction to the topic.

Case Examples

Case examples are also an effective tool for introducing a topic. A brief outline of the Martha Stewart case or the Enron scandal could also constitute an appropriate beginning for a white collar crime thesis. Via a review of the case, a reader is reminded how big these issues can become and how they can consume thousands of media hours, becoming household discussion topics in the process.

Valerie incorporated several recent scandals and controversial incidents involving local police in off-duty employment in her introduction to a legal analysis of such practices. The use of these cases is an effective way to demonstrate to the reader that these incidents, day-to-day and month-to-month, may accumulate into a perception of serious patterns of misconduct that undermine public confidence in the police. She does a good job of illustrating this in the paragraph below (Krizan, 2004).

> Recently, five Houston police officers were accused of extorting money from local cantinas allegedly collecting $50 per night from over 40 bar owners. In return for the money, the five officers were allegedly expected to condone illegal activities such as the sale of drugs and prostitution and to warn the bar owners of impending raids by other law enforcement personnel (O'Hare & Olsen, 2003b). Another Houston officer fatally wounded a 15-year-old he was attempting to stop and question for cruising suspiciously through the movie theatre parking lot where the officer was employed off duty. (Crowe, 2003).

Case examples are also dramatic and create an awareness in the reader that inspires them to read more and learn more about the issue. Note the example used by Rudy in his thesis on juveniles and access to weapons (Hardy, 2005).

> In 1991, a 12-year-old student from northern New Jersey fired three rounds from a .380 semiautomatic handgun in a schoolyard during recess. The shots missed their target, but injured three other students. Upon questioning, the 12-year-old revealed that he had purchased the firearm on the street three days earlier for $300. During the investigation that followed, an agent from the Bureau of Alcohol, Tobacco, Firearms, and Explosives (ATF) asked the boy if, supplied with $300 and given 30 minutes, could he leave school and return with a handgun similar to the one that he had possessed earlier. The boy replied, "What do I do with the extra 15 minutes?"

CONSTRUCTING AN OUTLINE FOR YOUR INTRODUCTION

Your introduction should move cumulatively and logically toward the research question that you plan to ask. The chapter should move from the more general to the more specific, narrowing to your topic, and end with a clear statement of your purpose. When the reader finishes this first chapter, there should be a definitive picture of what you are and are not going to cover. A possible model for this would resemble radiating rings where you move the reader inward from the broader topic to the more narrow question in the bull's-eye or center (Figure 6-1).

For example, Lois analyzed data from the characteristics of a large sample of summoned residents who did not show up for jury duty (Dewey, 2005). As Figure 6-1 illustrates, her first chapter opened with a discussion of the importance of the Sixth Amendment, the original intent of the Framers of the Constitution, and the potential for undermining the basic concepts of

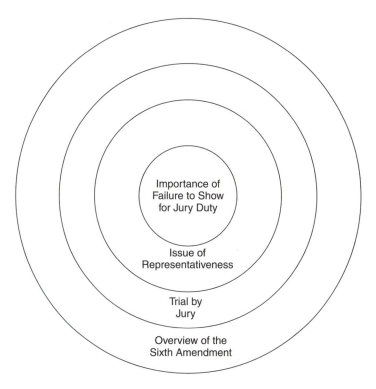

FIGURE 6-1 Narrowing an Issue until You Hit a Bull's-eye.

jury representativeness by not addressing the issue of those who failed to appear. It is very easy to see how a reader would be impressed by the level of significance of this study. She emphasized that if juror no-shows result in nonrepresentative juries for trials, then the very fabric of our justice system may be eroded. Thus her study attempted to identify and examine no-shows to see if they were generally representative of the population at large (which would imply less threat to jury representation), or if they tended to be from groups characterized by poverty, minority status, or other specific variables. She was also able to tie these concepts to recent investigations and public controversy over jury selection in capital cases, where concerns about jury representativeness constitute issues literally of life or death. Finally, she was able to argue that if we knew who the no-shows were, we might be better able to design incentives and support mechanisms to increase participation. Though a number of programs had been tried in the past, most were based on intuition or assumptions about who was not attending and why, and none appeared to be directly linked to any study identifying who was at greatest risk not to appear. This narrowing of the topics is also the proper flow for your headings and subheadings as you move through your chapter.

THE PURPOSE OF THE STUDY IS . . .

After identifying the problem and providing the reader with information about what is known, what has been done, what is still needed, and why it is all important, it is up to the writer to conclude with a concise statement of the purpose. One of the best ways to do this is to simply jump in and say "The purpose of this study is . . ." Dee clearly explained the focus of her study below.

> This theoretical analysis will assess support for existing explanations of female offending using secondary data and contemporary research on women and crime. A comprehensive review of the literature regarding female criminality will be followed by an isolation of selected perspectives (marginalization, victimization, and power-control) whose concepts will be examined further using an array of sources including current research, official, self-report and survey data. The specific perspectives covered here primarily focus on the commission of economic based offenses and common delinquency by females.

It is also important to remember that in the social sciences we are constantly exposed to a variety of perspectives and ideas on any given issue. We study these varying perspectives and propose different interpretations over time based on which evidence is available, or what data are analyzed from which sources. There are few universal truths or absolute findings. This caution and awareness of the relativity of results is important as you undertake a study and should be reflected in your purpose. Thus, we might say that we will "build on," "explore further," or "examine in more detail," but it is not realistic or practical to say that we are going to "prove" with any certainty or "establish" anything.

Some thesis chairs and committees ask for the statement of hypotheses or research questions in this section. If so, it would be a good idea to refer to any hypotheses as theoretical hypotheses, or propositions, at this point. You don't yet have a grasp of the actual variables you will be using and, therefore, cannot provide the specificity required for stating an operational hypothesis. Thus, it would be sufficient to say something like: "Males are likely to receive more severe sanctions in criminal justice processing than females." Later, in your methodology chapter, you can clarify a series of operational hypotheses based on the actual data you have available. These would be much more specific as, for example, "When bond is approved, males are required to post higher bail amounts than females."

LIMITATIONS

Every research study has limitations, yours included. You should include some statement of these limitations here. You will also be noting limitations again in other chapters, so keep these more general—perhaps we can call them *subject* limitations. This is the time to express that you will not be covering all of the possibilities of your topic, but instead will focus on a specific aspect.

One good reason for doing this is to narrow the parameters of what is expected of your study. For instance, in a study of female versus male criminality, it would be wise to say that you will accept standard definitions of both gender and criminality, as defined in research on the issue. This also means you are going to explore whether differences exist between male and female motivations to criminality, but will not develop a theory to explain any differences found. In regard to criminality itself, you are not going to deal with *all* criminality, merely the two offense types for which you will have data available. Further, your study will be limited to a specific area of the United States (Chicago, for instance), and you will not be discussing the potential cultural differences between Chicago and the rest of the United States, much less the implications of female criminality in other parts of the world.

Note that much of these sample comments are focused on what you will not be doing. This is frequently a good approach to limiting the scope (and expectations) of your thesis. If you don't tell readers (and your committee) what you are not planning to do, they might expect it anyway. In short, use this section to narrow the scope of your subject in a way that will help define your approach to the topic. Do not discuss, at this point, methodological limitations such as representativeness of your sample and other sampling concerns, response rates, definitions of your variables, and data limitations. Also refrain from discussing how the results of your study should be interpreted and whether extrapolation to other geographic or cultural areas, similar issues, or alternative data is proper. These two types of limitations, methodological and interpretational, are discussed in the methodology and conclusions chapters of your thesis.

TRANSITIONING FROM THE FIRST CHAPTER

The conclusion of the introductory chapter should *transition*, or lead smoothly, into the next chapter, the literature review. For instance, the example below accomplishes that in a brief paragraph.

> In the literature review which follows two main issues will be addressed. These issues are domestic violence myths and police responses to domestic violence. Initially, the history of domestic violence—in particular wife battering and stereotypical attitudes and beliefs about aggressive physical interactions in the home—will be presented. The chapter details some of the results of past research studies on the nature and prevalence of misperceptions about domestic violence and concludes with a brief summary of the types of responses required by law and typical of the police.

Another approach is to provide a short blueprint of the remainder of the work. This is especially helpful when a nontraditional chapter format is used. This is often the case in theoretical works where it is anticipated that multiple chapters on different theories might be offered, or in historical or legal theses where the breakdown of the analysis will help the reader understand the way the study is to be organized. The example below explains the format of a thesis with two "extra" chapters.

> This thesis explores the power of self-control theory to explain flagrant foul penalties assessed to basketball players across ages and across ethnic groups. If there is support for self-control theory, then coaches and players may be able to specifically address those issues in education and training programs and benefit individuals both on and off the court. Chapter 2 provides a review of the basic tenets of self-control theory as originated by Gottfredson and Hirschi (1990) and a summary of the findings of previous research on this perspective. Chapter 3 discusses sports violence, characteristics of players associated with violence, and traditional approaches to dealing with unsportsmanlike conduct. Chapter 4 explains the methodology involved in this study, the various teams involved, a survey instrument revised from Grasmick's Scale to probe the nature of fouls committed by the players, and the development of the data set. The data are analyzed in Chapter 5 using bivariate crosstabulation analyses. Chapter 6 is a summary of two special sessions held with the players and coaches to discuss the results and implications of the survey and then possible solutions and strategies for improving self-control measures by the players themselves. Chapter 7 contains a discussion of the outcomes of the study, the implications for possible programming and necessary considerations for evaluating any implemented measures, as well as the limitations of the study.

Having an idea how the entire thesis will flow is not something that everyone has at this point. If this is the case, don't worry. Over time, the organization will unfold. Often, one of the clearest ways to see this is by analyzing completed theses using hindsight.

For example, Dalila's (Mebane, 2002) thesis was a theoretical attempt to integrate the work of African American criminologists and sociologists into mainstream criminology from the same periods. She selected mainstream theories from the 1930s to the 1960s and compared them with writings during the same period by African American scholars Monroe Work, Franklin Frazier, Earl Moses, and W. E. B. DuBois. Eventually, she organized her work into five chapters that looked like this:

1. Introduction and Background
   a. Statement of the Problem
   b. Background and Purpose of the Study
   c. Importance of the Research
2. Mainstream Criminology 1930 to 1960s
   a. The Chicago School
   b. Social Structure and Crime
   c. Subculture Theories
   d. Social Structure and Anomie
   e. Differential Association
   f. Social Learning Theory
   g. Labeling Theory

3. African American Writings in Theory 1930 to 1960s
   a. Colleges and Universities
   b. Emancipation and Anomie
   c. Social Disorganization and the Negro Family
   d. Delinquent Areas
   e. Race and Economics
   f. Racial Attitudes
   g. African American Perspectives, 1950s and 1960s
4. Comparison of Theories
5. Conclusions and Recommendations for Research

Another theoretical thesis also compared perspectives, this time on the issue of female criminality. Over seven chapters, Dee (Warren, 2003) examined a number of biological, psychological, and sociological perspectives on female offending and then narrowed her theoretical examination to three: victimization, marginalization, and power-control theory, and the implications each had for explaining (and thus perhaps helping us in predicting, treating, and preventing) crime among women. Consequently, her final Table of Contents looked like this:

I. The Female Crime Problem
   a. The Scope of Female Crime
   b. Dynamics of Female Crime
   c. Study Focus and Implications
II. Literature Review
   a. Biological Perspectives
   b. Psychological Perspectives
   c. Sociological Perspectives
      1. Social Control Theory
      2. Opportunity Theory
      3. Strain Theory
      4. Theory Integration
   d. Discussions of Difference
      1. Aggression Theory
      2. Gender Theory and Research
         a. Liberation Theory
         b. Marginalization
         c. Victimization
         d. Power-Control Theory
III. Methodology
   a. Study Dynamics
      1. Power-Control Theory
      2. Victimization Perspective
      3. Marginalization Perspective
   b. Study Limitations
      1. The Use of Official Statistics
      2. The Problems with Survey Data

      c. Availability of Data

      d. Assessment of Data

  IV. Power-Control Theory

      a. Theory Description

      b. Examination of Data and Research Findings

      c. Ability to Explain Female Crime

   V. Victimization

      a. Description of Characteristics

      b. Examination of Data and Research Findings

        1. Studies with Control Groups

        2. Retrospective Studies

      c. Ability to Explain Female Crime

  VI. Marginalization

      a. Theory Description

      b. Examination of Data and Research Findings

      c. Ability to Explain Female Crime

 VII. Conclusions and Implications

Once again, do not be alarmed if you are still unsure of the layout of your thesis at this point in time. The examples are only provided to give you an idea of the types of organizational schemes that may ultimately result and to assure you that nontraditional formats may be the best fit for your work. In addition, theoretical theses, while difficult in other ways, are sometimes easier to sketch out in outline form. The issues are more conceptual and are not necessarily contingent on uncollected and unanalyzed data.

Generally, by the time you defend your prospectus, you should have a much clearer idea of the organization of the work and the order in which material will be covered. Still, as you progress you may end up combining shorter sections into one chapter and dividing longer sections into two separate chapters. How it evolves is something on which you will work with your committee. A logical flow to your thesis with balanced chapter coverage will make it more appealing to readers as it will be easier to understand.

SUMMARY

The key to a good introductory chapter is to make sure the readers know where you are going; in short, give them a good road map. You have to set the stage so that there is agreement that a problem exists and it is worthy of a thesis. Indeed, some faculty see the purpose behind a prospectus defense as determining whether the student has a "thesis-able" topic. The introductory chapter serves the purpose of convincing others that the topic is indeed something on which a thesis may be constructed.

Remember, the introductory chapter makes the case for your entire thesis. Be sure to adequately argue the significance of your problem, beginning with a broader, more abstract perspective and narrowing to your specific topic. This broad-to-narrow approach has an additional benefit: when you finish your study and are writing the conclusions, it can be done in reverse to "speculate" about the broader implications that result from your somewhat specific and more narrow findings. Readers will already be familiar with your arguments for doing so, thus the continuity is apparent.

Your introduction might incorporate a variety of statistical facts, figures, and case examples as necessary to illustrate your points. Don't take on the full burden of justifying your proposed study from scratch—use the literature on your general problem to help you make the case. Draw on the writings of experts who have already identified the needs related to this inquiry. And, finally, your specific problem statement and hypotheses/research question enable readers to pin down what you propose to do, and the limitations you add should remove any remaining doubts.

After the initial chapter (or section if it is a prospectus), you are ready to determine the way in which the problem should be approached. The next step is the literature review.

REFERENCES

DEWEY, L. (2005). *Juror "no-show": Examining the lack of citizen response to jury summons and its effects on jury representativeness.* Houston, TX: Unpublished thesis, University of Houston-Downtown.

HARDY, R. (2005). *An analysis of juvenile firearms confiscated in Houston, Texas.* Houston, TX: Unpublished thesis, University of Houston-Downtown.

IGLESIAS, S. (2005). *Identity theft: A test of lifestyle theory.* Houston, TX: Unpublished thesis, University of Houston-Downtown.

KRIZAN, V. (2004). *Legal issues of police off-duty employment.* Houston, TX: Unpublished thesis, University of Houston-Downtown.

MEBANE, D. (2002). *Integrating African American criminology.* Prairie View, TX: Unpublished thesis, Prairie View A & M University.

WARREN, D. (2003). *An examination of power-control theory, victimization and marginalization perspectives and female criminality.* Houston, TX: Unpublished thesis, University of Houston-Downtown.

7

LITERATURE REVIEW

At the master's degree level, a literature review is not simply a retelling of the studies that have been done on a particular subject to date. Instead, it is an analysis and assessment of the body of work in an area leading logically to the conclusion that not only does more need to be done, but also that the proposed study for the thesis is exactly what is needed. After the introduction and literature review chapters, a convincing argument should have been made that the study to be outlined in the subsequent methodology is of importance to the field. Further, the conclusions derived from the literature review should demonstrate precisely why this is so.

THE PURPOSE OF A LITERATURE REVIEW

The goal of any literature review is twofold. First, it assures the reader that the proposed study is grounded in a competent understanding of the issues, perhaps past, present, and future, related to the topic at hand. Or, by tracking studies done to date, one is able to see the relationship between the proposed study and policies and practices in the field, or further understanding and clarification of existing theories about crime and justice. This is the student's opportunity to demonstrate expertise in a subject area, to expand the readers' knowledge of the issues, and to bring them up to date on work done in the area which is both directly and indirectly related to the research question. The results of previous research should be explained and critiqued.

Second, the literature review provides information on which to base the methodology of the thesis itself. A well-done review suggests what works best in defining concepts related to the topic. Most issues have concepts that may be defined in various ways, and an overview of the literature usually allows one to see those alternative definitions and determine which work best for which purposes. Operationalizing those concepts exhibits a similar problem— which "variables" or groups of variables best represent the concepts? Finally, which methodologies appear to approach the issue best? A good literature review can clarify issues and provide suggestions for almost any thesis topic. In fact, one should not attempt operationization of concepts or propose a study methodology until a thorough awareness of the relevant literature exists.

A comprehensive literature review is a contribution to science in and of itself as it reflects the current state of the art in a given topic area. Readers who want to be familiarized with a topic can use a well-written literature review to gain a generalized understanding of what is known and what remains to be learned about that subject. As Jeff Walker (1998) explains, the purpose of the literature review should be stated clearly up front, and the writer should attend to that purpose throughout. He argues that through the presentation of the literature "sources may be compared to show how the current work overcomes the limitations of some research, expands and refines other research and complements still others" (p. iv). In other words, this is your opportunity to strengthen the argument for why your study should be done. It allows you to indicate, by comparison, the contribution your perspective on the topic will make in our field.

Among the benefits of a good research review are the following:

- A good review offers a general approach to your problem, for example, the techniques normally used for your problem and those that provide the best results,
- The review may suggest ways in which others have already "solved" your problem,
- You can compare your plans for studying the problem with what others have done and perhaps locate and correct problem areas,
- You may find sources of data with which you were not familiar.
- You may discover new ideas or generate new insights.

ORGANIZING THE LITERATURE REVIEW

Undoubtedly, one of the major, and most difficult, tasks in organizing the literature review is deciding how to proceed through the material to be covered. You need to determine whether it should be arranged by the types of issues or variables studied, the various findings or outcomes, chronologically (according to when the studies were done), or other groupings such as geographics, legal principles, or theories (see Box 7-1 for more suggestions). At a minimum, we suggest the following general organizational approach:

- Begin with a historical overview.
- Start with a broader perspective rather than narrow.
- Move from general or "classic" literature toward specific, narrow points and recent literature.
- Use headings/subheadings within your groupings if they are appropriate for your particular problem.

BOX 7-1 SUGGESTIONS FOR GROUPING STUDIES IN YOUR
LITERATURE REVIEW

Chronology—the most common approach. There are many ways to group studies and literature so that you can make sense of them, but one of the most common ways is to do it chronologically. This is because other authors and researchers writing on your topic have also done literature reviews and are aware of the literature that preceded their studies. Thus, they likely "added to" that previous literature. The reader is able to see the subject evolve, and understand the forces shaping the evolution.

Other approaches are used to make sense of important issues and shed light on differences and similarities among studies:

- Focus on different areas of the issue, such as those that influence police, courts, and corrections.
- "Newer" approaches versus "older" approaches to the issue.
- Ways in which the dependent variable is defined/operationalized.
- Ways in which the primary independent variable is defined/operationalized.
- Use of scales versus single measures of the independent or dependent variable.
- The use of certain "control" variables.
- Tests of single issues versus tests of multiple issues.
- Type of sample.
- Geographic location of samples or populations.
- Demographic differences between samples or populations.
- Use of certain types of methodologies (i.e., surveys, experiments, observation).
- Use of different types of analyses (i.e., percentaging, crosstabulation, bivariate, multivariate).
- Use of certain statistical tools.
- Differing foci on interpreting the results.
- Differing outcomes or results.
- Social context of the period during which the information was gathered.
- Political context of the period during which the information was gathered.

According to Walker (1998, p. iv) problems occur when the literature review is poorly organized or thought out. He tells us "Authors generally attempt to include as many references as possible (sometimes in semi-colon divided lists that run on longer than the sentence to which they are attached). What occurs with these kinds of reviews is that all but the most dedicated reader quickly tires of the discussion and moves on." He constructively lists two major errors to avoid in formatting the literature review (p. v):

- Composing a "long and rambling litany where it is difficult to determine where the author is citing previous works and where he or she is making new assertions."
- "Where the authors begin the article with positive, active writing and then change the tone completely in the literature review to a lock-step of phrases;

'So and so (1997) argued . . .' 'This and that proposed (1976). . . .' Nothing loses a reader quicker than a slice and bake approach to presenting previous works."

The construction of a literature review also is not restricted to a search for other studies *exactly* like the one proposed. Students frequently complain they cannot find any previous work on their proposed topic, or there is not enough research from which they can develop a comprehensive review. The fact is such comments come from a lack of understanding the nature of a literature review. For example, in a literature review prior to testing Travis Hirschi's social bond theory in the relationship between delinquents and schools (Eith, 2005), Christine separated the findings of previous studies by the variable(s) on which they focused or later found in their analyses to be significantly related. Her presentation flowed according to the outline of subheadings below:

A. Race
B. Gender
C. Age
D. Family Structure
E. Parent's Level of Education
F. Grade Point Average
G. Delinquent Peers
H. Substance Use

In each section, Christine was able to cover a number of important studies related to each variable while keeping the focus on some general conclusions about the strength of those variables. This allowed the reader to remember just which variables and relationships were important rather than trying to focus on a confusing number of authors, or an entire discussion of a single study. It also prepared the reader for why she chose to focus on certain variables in her research and not others, defending and supporting the choices she made in her own methodology and analysis. This is demonstrated in her section discussing grade point average (Eith, 2005, p. 20).

Academic performance is an important factor to consider given its predictive relation with future life outcomes. Research indicates there is a relationship between school bonding and academic performance as measured by grade point average (GPA). Academic performance is enhanced when students exhibit stronger bonds to school (Maddox and Prinz, 2003; Lopez, Ehly, & Garcia-Vasquez, 2002; Learner & Kruger, 1997; Wiatrowski, et al., 1982). Those students who exhibit higher grade point averages are found to report a stronger bond to school. While this relationship between academic achievement and the school bond is correlational, it can be argued that grade point average predicts a student's commitment to school. Academically successful students were found to be more likely to be committed to and involved in school whereas lower GPA students were found to reject the goals and values of education (Metz, 1979). Thus, it is expected that students with higher grade point averages will exhibit a stronger bond to school.

In the quoted section, Christine prepares you for why she will be looking at grade point averages in her research. Indeed, this raises an important point: do not be unnerved if studies have mixed findings or one contradicts another, just try to convey the gist of what was found and any important circumstances (specific sampling or validity threats) influencing the outcomes of atypical findings. Avoid having the reader struggle to remember which study found what by summarizing the most salient points at the conclusion of each section. Though someone may be tempted to simply relay the findings of each important study in chronological order, for Christine's research, that method would not have presented the clearest picture of what is known about her issue.

One graduate admits that the literature review was very difficult for him, particularly trying to determine how much was enough. In most cases, you will need to address research on all of the critical variables you have planned for your analysis. This is also the time to decide whether to include research on variables you will not be using or to explain why certain variables that others have focused on will not be included in your study. Your chair will help you assess just how much of the existing literature should be covered and just how broadly you should structure your discussion of what has been ascertained to date.

Keeping the literature review simple and clear is an important goal. Like the introduction chapter, the literature review chapter should develop inward from the broader outer ring of discussion to a more narrow, specific focus on your particular research question. The major difference in this chapter, however, is its focus on studies and research serving as the basis for an understanding of this subject. This allows readers to pick up general knowledge about this subject and build their understanding of what we have learned, and how we have learned it, as they move toward the more specific topic of the thesis. It also allows readers to assess the quality of previous studies and other factors, such as social forces that have changed since earlier research, that might be driving a need for new or better information.

For example, in a thesis on factors that predict recidivism among young parolees (Samuels, 2001), the author begins with a discussion of the history of the parole system and what it was originally intended to do (rehabilitate). She then moves toward an explanation of the decline of rehabilitation and the evidence that attitudes on the value of rehabilitation have changed. Transitioning to a discussion of the change from an emphasis on rehabilitation to assessing risk and preventing recidivism, she follows with a discussion of current methods of assessing risk and predicting recidivism and how effective those efforts have been (not very). The author concludes with the possibility that, by isolating special groups of parolees (young, old, female, sex offenders), we might be able to improve the accuracy of recidivism prediction. At this point, she would discuss any previous research indicating that special populations might have different risk indicators for related problems like continued drug use or unemployment, both of which

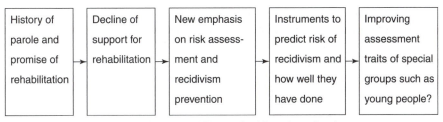

FIGURE 7-1 Logical Flow of a Literature Review

have been cited in the literature as factors related to parole success. This sets the stage for the study that she will do, testing whether younger offenders have other traits or characteristics that better predict failure on parole than the general population, standard instruments currently in use. Thus, we could diagram her flow in a logical progression that directly reflects how her headings and subheadings will look through the chapter (see Figure 7-1).

As a reminder, it is not necessary to say that there is "nothing out there" on this topic or that "nothing has been done" or "little has been done." If there truly were nothing on this topic, there would be concern as to whether it was an appropriate subject for research at all. There is a difference between there being fewer studies on the particular research question you have selected and there being no information on the subject. Students sometimes feel they have to argue that no similar studies have been done in order to justify their research, and this is not so. Careful wording should convey where the gaps in the literature are, what we do know, and how we can expand on what we know. For example, Terry is able to educate us about why there may not be many published studies to report on without appearing to complain that he could not find anything.

> The controversy concerning racial profiling in traffic stops often appears to have created a negative and hostile image of law enforcement officers. Often, departments have been reluctant to release their traffic stop data to the public for fear of misinterpretation and accusations. As a result, few examinations of racial profiling and traffic stops have been subjected to traditional and scholarly peer reviews. (Richardson, 2006)

GENERALIZED FINDINGS VERSUS SPECIFIC RESULTS

Generalized Findings

Generalizing your findings allows you to summarize the literature. This is especially helpful when there are a number of studies in the area under examination. There are basically two ways that research findings might be summarized. One way is best used when a number of similar studies have similar results. For example, Valerie Callanan (2005) chose this approach:

> With the exception of capital punishment attitudes, research on demographic correlates of punitiveness has usually produced weak and inconsistent

results (Cullen et al., 1985; Langworthy & Whitehead, 1986; McCorkle, 1993; Stinchcombe et al., 1980; Tyler & Weber, 1982).

Rather than going through each of the studies one by one, the author has, for efficiency, grouped them together to make her point. This helps us progress through a very large amount of literature in a way that is less confusing and keeps us from drifting from the major finding of those earlier studies—the bottom line is all we really need to know—that "demographic factors are weak or inconsistent predictors of punitiveness."

Another way to report research findings in a summary fashion is when studies of the same basic topic cite a number of easily distinguishable, different results. This helps to show how the studies actually build on each other and present a more sculpted product. For example, when discussing the research literature on women's attitudes toward punishment, Callanan (2005) wrote

> More recent research suggests that women are significantly more punitive than men. For example, they are more likely to think that adult sentencing is too lenient (Sprott, 1999), less likely to support parole for serious offenders, and half as likely than men to think prisoners' sentences should be reduced (Flanagan, 1996; Haghighi & Lopez, 1998). However, women appear to believe more strongly in the potential of rehabilitation than do men (Cullen et al., 1985; Haghighi & Lopez, 1998), especially if the intervention efforts start early, or if the offender is a juvenile (Sprott, 1999).

There are many instances when it will be necessary to elaborate on a specific study, particularly as you move inward—toward the core—in your layers of discussion. As you progress, you will be discussing and critiquing studies that are more closely related to the one you propose, so the need for more detail will be apparent.

Specific Results

Discussing the specific details of a study, or group of studies, is sometimes necessary. This is most common when discussing "classic" studies. Such studies can represent the original research on an issue, a major turning point in understanding, or even a methodological development that defines how research on the issue is to be approached. In each instance you would want to elaborate on the way the issue was conceptualized, the specific methodology and analysis that was used, and how this represented an innovation and why it was important at the time. Other detail-worthy studies are those that are particularly well done. These usually represent methodological and analytical approaches that are clearly better than run-of-the-mill research on the issue. Try using these general guidelines, no matter what type of study you are reviewing.

- Restrain the urge to quote from the material.
- Summarize the purpose, the data (sample, etc.), and the conclusions of the study.

- Critique the study—your comments are more important than *specifically* what the author of the study says. What could have been done to improve the study?
- Summarize what has been said and explain its significance for your research problem.

One good way to determine which studies should be detailed is to ask yourself the question "Is this an important study?" You can define "importance" in any way you would like, but it will clearly be a study that provides an example (even if it exemplifies the "wrong" way to research the issue). Box 7-2 provides some potential details worthy of discussion in an elaborated review of a single study.

One of the dangers of elaborating on specific studies is that it is easy to lose sight of how the details of one study mesh with others. A way to remedy this problem is to include a summary of the important details of those studies. One good approach is to develop a *research summary chart.* Such a chart may help you, your committee members, and potential readers sift through related research with a more visually oriented summary of the studies and their results. Even if you ultimately don't include the chart in your thesis, the construction of such an outline will help you in writing your literature review—especially when it comes time to make sense of the collective results. As students hardly have the time to sit down and write the entire literature review at once, the chart can be constructed over time allowing the researcher

BOX 7-2 EXAMPLES OF ITEMS FREQUENTLY DISCUSSED IN REVIEWS OF SPECIFIC STUDIES

Not all of these suggestions for discussion are present in every specific research review. In addition, while the terminology here is that of empirical research, analogies can be made to literature reviews in qualitative research, legal research, and logical critique theses.

- The way in which the "issue" is set up or defined.
- The time period of the study.
- Variables included in the research (independent and dependent variables, control variables).
- How the variables were operationalized from the problem concepts.
- If any, how scales were created and their reliability results.
- The methodology of the study (sampling method, sample size, research design, and problems encountered).
- The primary mode of analysis.
- Results of the analysis.
- Conclusions and interpretations based on the analytical results.
- Your assessment of the importance of the results (or of the study in general) and any critical limitations.
- How the study fits into the general picture presented by other studies on the issue, particularly if the results are different.

to work at his or her own pace without losing the continuity of comparing and contrasting the research being encountered. With a research chart at hand, you can continue to add studies until the relevant literature is exhausted, or until you feel comfortable in making assessments about the trends exhibited to date. In fact, after completing your research chart and in particular enabling an aggregate view of specific items, you may find it easier to sit down and write the literature review based on the chart.

An alternative, but similar, approach to a research summary is a *systematic literature review* designed to turn the information collected into "data" you can describe and analyze. The most sophisticated versions of this are called "meta-analyses," but, for your thesis at least, you don't have to go to that level of analytical skill. It is sufficient to use simple frequency distributions and cross-tabulations to make sense of the literature data. A listing of suggested steps for a systematic literature review is provided in Box 7-3.

As the first page of a sample research chart in Table 7-1 demonstrates, you can scan quickly through a large group of studies and draw

BOX 7-3 SUGGESTIONS FOR USING A SYSTEMATIC
LITERATURE REVIEW AS A GUIDE FOR A SUBSEQUENT
SECONDARY DATA ANALYSIS

Steps in the Process

1. Determine what your topic is.
2. Pose the general problem, and focus it to a narrower issue.
3. Gather as much of the research literature as you can get your hands on. Request anything not readily available from interlibrary loan.
4. Determine what you will use as "data" from the various studies (this will require you to read some of the studies and, in particular, reviews of the literature).
5. Construct a "codebook" of your variables. Use the following areas as a guideline and think about others you might want to include
   a. Publication information (year, type of journal, etc.)
   b. Subject information (what variation on your topic is covered, etc.)
   c. Methodological information (sample, method, statistics, etc.)
   d. Evaluative criteria (assessment of quality, etc.)
   e. Statistical results (significant result, size of correlation, etc.)
   f. Overall results
6. Code each of your studies according to your codebook. Revise if necessary based on the first few studies coded.
7. Analyze the "data" using:
   a. Frequency distributions
   b. Cross-tabulations
   c. Multivariate approaches, if possible
8. Draw conclusions from what your literature analysis says about your narrowed topic.
9. Refocus your topic to guide your own investigation.

TABLE 7-1: RECENT RESEARCH ON THE RELATIONSHIP BETWEEN DRUG ABUSE AND DELINQUENCY

Study	Sample	Relationship between Drugs & Delinquency	Other Variables Analyzed
K. V. T. Bui, P. Ellickson & R. M. Bell (2000)	3000 West Coast 10th & 12th graders	Early delinquent behavior more likely to predict later drug use	Emotional distress did not appear to predict either delinquency or drug use
Baron, S. W. (1999)	2,000 homeless male youths, Edmonton, Alberta, Canada	Parental drug abuse & physical abuse as well as drug-using peers related to drug abuse	Long-term homelessness, depression, & property crime also increase likelihood of drug use
Brook, J. & E. Balka (1999)	1,330 African American & Puerto Rican boys & girls, Harlem, NYC	More, early marijuana use increased risk of school drop out, delinquency, cigarettes, alcohol & fewer job skills	Also greater unsafe sex risk & HIV, and more deviant friends; perception of drugs as not harmful
Garnier, H. E. & J. A. Stein (2002)	198 youth (N. Calif.) followed 18 years	Teen drug use & delinquency related to peers with similar behaviors	SES indirectly related to delinquency; maternal drug use indirectly related to teen drug use
Engles, R .C. M. E. & T. Bogt (2001)	508, 12–18 year olds, 2nd generation Netherlands	Substance abuse & minor delinquency related to quality & quantity of peer relations	Better peer relations means less criminal activity; parental attachment & family climate have small effects on minor offending
Zhang, L., J. Welte & W. Wieczorek (1999)	Buffalo Longitudinal Survey of Young Men	Past delinquency predicts gang membership, prior drug use not predictive of gang membership	Gang membership influences subsequent delinquency & drug use for those without past involvements
Mackesy-Amiti, M. E. & M. Fendrich (1999)	13,000, 7–12th graders in Illinois in 1993	Inhalant users had more minor criminality & trouble behavior than other drug users or drinkers	Number of substances ever used & parents' lower education linked to troubled behavior

TABLE 7-1: *(Continued)*

Study	Sample	Relationship between Drugs & Delinquency	Other Variables Analyzed
Williams, J., C. Ayers, R. D. Abbott, J.D. Hawkins & R. Catalano (1999)	Longitudinal data from 808 Seattle students who were white and African American (15–16 years old in 1991)	Low academic & social skills predicted delinquency & drug use which was also predicted by peer & sibling influence	Results were similar for both white and African American youth

Source: McShane and Williams, 2003.

some summative conclusions about the studies that have been done to date and what they have found. You can group the studies by ordering in some way that makes their analysis easier, such as chronologically or by important variables or by samples or populations studied. This also helps you develop and defend later statements you might make about what is missing from existing knowledge and what your study will contribute toward this area.

Another example (Table 7-2) from part of a student's research chart shows how even though the focus of the student's topic is gender, it can be important in the literature review to discuss other related disparity issues. Here, the student can explain how gender may be correlated with other variables and how more specific analyses have or have not clarified those relationships.

SUMMARIZING THE RESULTS AND CHECKING CITATIONS

We strongly encourage some method of organizing your literature review, either by using charts, a spreadsheet, or some type of file system. This will help you recognize systematic differences between studies or even trace particular results to certain research methodologies. At the end of each point in your organization, however you develop it, a summary is in order. In summarizing look for what these specific studies (or general research type) have in common and where they might be different. Do the results depend on a particular methodology, a definition of the variables, or whether certain control variables were used in the analysis? Do differences appear associated with the type of sample, the geographic area of the study, or the time period during which the research was done? As you can see, there are many ways to make sense of the findings. Don't simply state that "of five studies on anomie, three were supportive and two were not" because that won't help you *use* the results of your literature review. Having results you can use is the primary reason for doing a review; they will tell you what needs to be done in your own study.

TABLE 7-2: RESEARCH ON GENDER AND SENTENCING DISPARITY

Study	Sample	Relationship and Gender	Race/Ethnicity, Other
Abwender, D.A. & Hough K. (2001)	Mock jury with 207 black, Hispanic, & white college students decide guilt based on gender/race/ attractiveness of accused	Women treated unattractive female defendant more harshly; men showed opposite tendency	Blacks used more leniency with blacks than whites. Hispanics were lenient toward whites & whites showed no race-based leniency
Curry, T. R., Lee, G. & Rodriguez, S. F. (2004)	Random sample 1,242 offenders convicted of assault, robbery, & homicide, from 7 largest counties in Texas	Judges viewed females as less blame-worthy, less dangerous, have greater family responsibilities, & better potential for reform than men	Relationship between victim & offender, racial combination & age differences had no effect on odds of incarceration, only amount of injury to victim
Daly, K. (1989A)	Analysis of 500 cases —11% female in Seattle & 2,000 (11% female) in New York	More lenient sentences for women are explained by family ties	Statistically, gender differences favoring women are more often found than race differences favoring whites
Daly, K. (1989B)	Interviews with 20 male & 3 female criminal court judges in NY & MA	Protection & maintenance of family unit is primary concern of most judges	Psychological well-being of children most important factor for judges
Farrell, A. S. (2001)	Analysis of senten-cing data from U.S. Sentencing Commission 1996–97 on 17,000+ drug trafficking cases, 87% male	Women more likely to receive downward departures & disproportionate decreases in sentence lengths	White defendants more likely than nonwhites to receive downward departures for providing "substantial assistance"
MacDonald, J. M. (2001)	85,600+ cases referred to the Hawaii family court between 1980 and 1991	Once past early stages of system, females receive more severe sentences & treatment than males	Disparity not limited to adults

Don't forget to track all of your sources carefully, recording the proper citation information needed for your references. Keep in mind that proper citation is not done merely for the sake of the reference style you will use but, more important, it will allow you to relocate the material quickly. This latter point is critical because it is common to find that you need more information during the process of writing and rewriting the thesis. Even in organizing your literature, it is common to find that the information you recorded for one of your studies didn't have a needed item. In addition, even if you don't deem something important at the time, one of your committee members may have questions about the way you have interpreted a study or want you to add more information.

CONCLUDING YOUR LITERATURE REVIEW

The Contents of a Conclusion

The conclusion of a literature review should be a succinct statement about what we know and perhaps what we do not. After taking the reader through a number of studies on racial profiling that moved from general research on profiling to more specific studies in the area of traffic stops and DWI stops, Terry summarizes what we know from the literature (Richardson, 2006).

> Minorities are the most likely targets for pretextual stops. They have a higher probability of being searched and arrested than whites. The previous literature suggests that minorities are stopped more at night and that African Americans get stopped the most. Furthermore, minorities, namely African Americans, are most likely to be arrested for violations in which whites receive citation tickets. In contrast, whites have a greater probability of being stopped and arrested for DWI. When compared with whites, minorities only account for a small proportion of arrests for DWI.

One technique for summarizing the overall literature review is to look across the various organizational categories you decided to use. Ask whether differences or similarities exist among and between categories or if different methodologies are used. In short, the same questions you might have asked to help you summarize the individual literature categories can be used to make sense of the overall results. Decide if certain methodologies best capture what you are interested in doing. Are some definitions of the variables more in line with your approach? Regardless of the questions you ask and answer, keep in mind that they set up what you should do in your own methodology. For example, if studies indicated that respondents in self-report surveys are unlikely to admit doing certain types of crimes or deviance, it would not be logical for you to propose to conduct such a study. Also remember that if you *don't* use the suggestions found in your literature review, an explanation is required.

How Do You Conclude?

Your final conclusions should transition the reader to the next chapter or section of your thesis. By summarizing what we know and emphasizing what we still need to know, you logically draw the reader to the obvious need for your study. Some traditional transitional devises can be used to introduce a discussion of the way your study is to be conducted.

In the final paragraph of his literature review, Weiss summarizes the existing studies on the problems defense attorneys encounter in their professional identities. He concludes by transitioning the reader to the next phase of the research, his methodology (2005, p. 32).

> It is as much for these reasons as it is to examine issues left unresolved by the existing research that a study asking public defenders why they do what they do would be a particularly useful contribution to the field. Before questions about what motivates public defenders can be addressed, however, a few words about methodology are in order.

SUMMARY

Remember that a good literature review doesn't just tell us about the state of the research on some issue, it constitutes an analysis, critique, and assessment of that knowledge. It should make sense of the research, determine what is good about the research, and suggest what improvements are still needed. Because all of this should tell you how similar research should be done, a good literature review is the cornerstone for setting up the methodology for your thesis.

If nothing else, you should have conducted an *analysis* of the literature so you know what affects the results of studies on this topic. By summarizing that analysis, you have the makings of a proposed methodology for your study.

REFERENCES

CALLANAN, V. J. (2005). *Feeding the fear of crime: Crime-related media and support for three strikes.* New York: LFB Scholarly Publishing.

EITH, C. A. (2005). *Delinquency, schools and the social bond.* New York: LFB Scholarly Publishing.

McSHANE, M., AND WILLIAMS, F., III (2003). Youth, drugs, and delinquency. In P. Benekos and A. Merlo, eds., *Controversies in juvenile justice and delinquency* (pp. 69–88). Cincinnati, Anderson Publishing.

RICHARDSON, T. (2006). *An analysis of drunken driving cases for potential evidence of police profiling.* Houston, TX: Unpublished Master's Thesis. University of Houston-Downtown.

SAMUELS, L. (2001). *An analysis of young parolees in comparison to their parole cohorts.* Prairie View, TX: Unpublished Master's Thesis. Prairie View A&M University.

SANTOS, M. (2003). *Profiles from prison: Adjusting to life behind bars.* Westport, CT: Praeger.

SCOTT, Y. (2001). *Fear of crime among inner-city African Americans.* New York: LFB Scholarly Publishing.

SNELL, C. (2005). *Peddling poison: The tobacco industry and kids.* Westport, CT: Praeger.

WALKER, J. (1998). The role of the literature review in publication. *Journal of Criminal Justice Education, 9*(2), iii–vi.

WEISS, M. S. (2005). *Public defenders: Pragmatic and political motivations to represent the indigent.* New York: LFB Scholarly Publishing.

METHODOLOGY

The methodology chapter of a thesis has two basic goals. The first is to describe clearly and in detail the method you have chosen to answer your research question. The second is to support your choice of method with enough justification to convince the reader that (1) it is the best approach to the study, and (2) by following these procedures you will undoubtedly be able to find the information you seek and process it in a meaningful way. The term "methodology" is, in one sense, another way to say that you are following a systematic, logical process to solve a problem. Any type of thesis will need the methodology explained, even a theoretical or legal analysis. The difference is that in some types of works, the explanation of methods, resources, and analysis may be shorter and not constitute an entire chapter.

While many students feel intimidated by discussion of methodology, it is easier to view it as a menu of items to be addressed—you simply have to determine which of the elements applies to your proposed work and explain them. There are many textbooks and examples to use to assist you in this process. One of the ways you have already begun this task is by pointing out during your literature review (1) what earlier studies related to your topic have already found, and (2) methodological weaknesses or unexamined areas of that research. A logical extension of your introduction, problem statement and literature review will lead the reader to the conclusion that your results will either be more meaningful or will continue to build on our knowledge by extending previous work in your topic area.

EXPLAINING YOUR METHODOLOGY

Usually, this section includes a short and clear explanation of the research methods you are going to employ, the type of data you will collect or use, and, for studies using statistical analysis, a description of the variables to be analyzed. This chapter is a blueprint for the research process in which you will engage.

The Advantage of Explaining Your Methodology
in the Prospectus

The essential content, if not the full chapter, is usually completed in the prospectus stage so that the committee might be able to assess whether the sources you have selected or your plan for data collection will, in fact, provide the information you seek. This will save you time and energy by eliminating any nonproductive avenues you might be considering. The committee will also be able to anticipate problems arising from the way the study constructs are operationalized. At the same time, concerns about how the information will be collected and analyzed can be resolved. The earlier this is done, the better, as your committee is determining whether the information you plan on gathering will be capable of adequately addressing your research question. The clearer and more detailed your explanation, the more readily your committee will be able to ascertain whether this project is a viable undertaking. They will also be able to determine whether the methods you adopt are the most logical, practical, and scientifically sound ways to go about researching this issue. Just because a study can be done, does not mean that it should be. In the best-case scenario, the specificity and detail you include will allow the committee to assist you in making small corrections and, sometimes, even collectively developing another, better approach.

The Essential Contents of a Methodology Chapter

To provide this detail, the methodology section of a traditional empirical thesis might include a discussion of any of a number of the following elements:

- Overview of the general research design
- The research setting and population from which the sample is drawn
- Source (or sources) of the data and sampling procedures
- Statement of hypotheses or research questions
- Variables used in the analysis and their description
- The form of analysis to be applied
- Specific statistical tests to be used
- Limitations of the research design

Each of these elements will be discussed according to their use in either a quantitatively oriented or qualitatively oriented framework. In addition, the types of points you may want to address include

- Is this a traditional type of methodology for this type of inquiry? Why or why not? You can simply refer back to your literature review if that information is covered there.
- Are there any ethical or legal complications involved? If so, how will they be addressed?

- Who are the pioneers or experts in this methodology? Are you consistently applying their approach to the methodology? Why or why not?

We now turn to a brief refresher on the major approaches you can use in designing your research.

THE TWO MAJOR METHODOLOGICAL TYPES

Quantitative Methodologies

As discussed in Chapter Two, quantitative methodologies can involve original data collection either through a survey, sampling of existing records (such as content analysis), or, most rarely in criminal justice, an experiment. The use of existing data, such as a data set from NACJD, is much more common than original data collection. If you have a problem or topic on which little has been done—usually rare—you would want to collect your own data. Or, perhaps, you have access to court or community corrections records as part of your job and have permission from the agency head to collect information from these records. Even if you are collecting your own data, insofar as possible you want to use an existing instrument so that you do not have to invent a new series of questions, scale, or approach to the collection. If the latter is necessary, you will be faced with determining the reliability and validity of your data collection instrument—a task that almost can be equivalent to doing another entire thesis.

Assuming that you have a thesis topic for which a research data set already exists in the NACJD archive, then a secondary data analysis would be proper. Keep in mind you do not want be analyzing the same issue as that done by the original researcher who created the data set you are using, unless you somehow have a new twist or analytical form that was not previously used. Your effort must be somehow different from the original researcher's, because you are using exactly the same data. Thus, one of your tasks will be to demonstrate exactly how your use of the data is different from the original. In addition, you will have to justify the use of this particular data set compared with others that might be available. One of the most likely justifications is that the variables in the data best match the ones you need to answer your research question.

On the whole, most students are better off doing a quantitative, empirical thesis—even though it requires the use of statistics. Almost all graduate programs teach a course in quantitative research methods and another in statistics, thus students already have been exposed to the important elements already. If a secondary data set is available, there is another, much more practical reason: time. You avoid the time spent in the design of data collection instruments and the actual collection of data. In addition, the format of such a thesis is much more organized and routine. Some departments or faculty even insist the only proper thesis is an empirical one.

Qualitative Methodologies

We are treating the concept of "qualitative methodologies" broadly in this book. Some research-oriented faculty will feel that a qualitative design is one that collects original data through the use of such methodologies as observation, ethnography, or a more contemporary approach frequently called "edgework." The key here is that you participate in one way or another in making observations that become your data. More broadly defined, qualitative research also includes legal analysis, historical analysis, and theory construction.

Whichever of these you might choose, all of them have in common a greater reliance on your own work and, usually, a lower degree of structure. Thus you have to explain in greater detail precisely what you did (or will do, in the case of the prospectus). The issues of reliability and validity remain but may be harder to see; you still have to explain how you attended to these potential problems. The lack of structure means you have to have a higher tolerance of ambiguity and a greater ability to self-organize, traits not all thesis students have.

On the other hand, qualitative designs can be more satisfying in their end product. The student will go through the entire research process and fully participate in developing everything (we can almost hear Frank Sinatra in the background singing the words of an old Paul Anka song "the record shows I took the blows and did it my way . . ."). Whether an observational design, a legal analysis, or a theoretical exposition, the increased intensity of involvement can be rewarding. However, the latter approaches are not for everyone precisely because much of the work is done on your own and is usually unstructured.

At this point though, unless you are still working on the methodology section of your prospectus, you already will have made the choice of an appropriate research design. What you need to know now is how to write it up.

WRITING UP THE ESSENTIAL ELEMENTS

Overview of the General Research Design

The first task of the chapter is to provide a brief overview of your methodology or research design. The purpose is to describe for the reader what lies ahead so he or she can better grasp what you are going to do. This is particularly critical for the members of your thesis committee. If they don't have a complete grasp of what you intend to do, we can assure you that the thesis will go off on tangents, useless analyses will be performed, and time will be wasted. If for no other reasons than these, *make sure your committee is aware of and approves every detail of your methodology*. This begins with the overview.

One of the things that many thesis students are concerned with is making repetitious statements. Don't worry, it is expected—and it is done to clarify your purpose. The problem statement chapter (see Chapter Six) normally has a statement of the problem and, frequently, your basic hypotheses. You will briefly state the problem again here and the hypotheses will also reappear, but now they will be tied directly to your variables.

Let's look at an example of a beginning paragraph of a thesis on parole recidivism among females:

> From the previous two chapters it is clear that parolee recidivism rates vary by both type of offense and characteristics of the parolee. In the case of gender, this effect is quite evident yet there is much less research on female parole recidivism than for males. Among the reasons is the difficulty of obtaining large enough sample sizes for analysis because, when compared to the total number of those incarcerated, the percentage of incarcerated women is fairly small, on the order of 10 percent or below. This study uses a random sample of 500 women parolees, which is sufficient to allow analysis of various factors that might affect female parolee recidivism. This chapter discusses the methodology used to select that sample, the variables available for analysis, the measure that will be used to define recidivism and the type of analyses to follow.

Thus, the introductory paragraph reaffirmed the purpose of the thesis, used the literature to justify the study, and told readers what will follow in the chapter.

The Research Setting and Population from Which the Sample Is Drawn

The next section should describe the setting in which the research was (or will be, in the case of the prospectus) conducted. This can be a valuable section because one of the limitations of any study is the representativeness of the data. Even though you might have a random sample, it was still drawn from a population that itself may be different from other populations and, therefore, difficult to generalize to other areas. Use this as your opportunity to describe the setting of the research within the general population or geographic area. Two problems usually emerge about a setting, both of which are a product of perception: the makeup and characteristics of the location and representativeness.

The first problem is that the actual makeup and characteristics of your research setting are not likely to be widely known among readers. As a result you want to describe the area, usually with data from the U.S. Census or other governmental reports. Say what the population size is, what the characteristics of the population are (gender, race, ethnicity, percent minority, and educational levels), where people live (the percentage urban, suburban, and rural), crime rates, the economic conditions (percent in poverty, median income and housing values, and dominant business types), and any other characteristics that might be important for your area (such as religion, political affiliation, general attitudes, and so on). You can use this information to compare with similar variables in your study and demonstrate that your sample is close to the population figures. Thus, you have a way of demonstrating that your sample is representative of the population (at least for the variables you can compare) and can be used to make statements about the population. Even if you find some unique population characteristics, it is best to make them public at this early stage and note that the results of your study will likely apply only to other areas with similar features (a statement you will reintroduce in the limitations section of the methodology chapter).

The second problem is that readers have perceptions about certain areas being relatively different from national or regional characteristics. In fact, someone is likely to raise this issue about your research setting regardless of where it came from (unless it is a national sample—and even there you can find international issues). By describing the setting with standard governmental data and comparing it to national figures, you can usually defuse the accusations of difference. As opposed to perceptions, most locations in the United States have very similar characteristics, particularly when compared with other locations of their size.

Source (or Sources) of the Data and Sampling Procedures

After you have described the research setting and population from which the data are derived, you should follow with information about the data you will be using. While we have labeled this section to include both source and sampling, you may be able to describe both at once or use a logical flow that moves from one to the other. If the data are being collected by you, then a description of the location of the data collection is in order. Here, you might talk about the agency, where the data are kept and who keeps them, what type records are used, and any other information that would help a reader to understand the source of the information.

If you are using secondary data, you should do the same thing to describe the source, but it often means having to locate additional information about the data set. Frequently this can be found in the literature by looking for research publications by those who originally collected the data. One advantage of NACJD data sets is that there is usually a good description of the data source and citations to published literature with more information. If your data come from one of the faculty in your department, prepare to sit down with the professor and ask questions until you have a good grasp of the data. In all likelihood, the professor can provide you with written information—take everything you can get because you don't want to make a mistake by thinking you have one thing and halfway through the thesis it turns out to be another. Many data sets are highly complex, and available information doesn't fully describe them.

As with the source of the data, you need to describe the sampling process. Specify what type of sampling was employed (random, stratified, or systematic probability samples; convenience, quota, proportionate or snowball nonprobability samples), and describe the exact process used to collect data. If you used a table of random numbers to construct a random sample, say how you used the table and where the table came from. If a random number generator on the Internet was used, provide the details of using that generator, the type of random sample it creates, and the Web site. No matter what type of sampling process you used (or plan on using in the case of the prospectus), be sure to describe every step taken to generate the sample. Don't exaggerate your process to make the sample look better or, if you are using a secondary data set, assume things you do not know for certain. While mundane, this is one of the most important parts of your methodology chapter.

A sample write-up of this section, based on the example we have been using on parole recidivism research, is below (McShane, Williams, & Dolny, 2002).

> The data were derived from the parole files of a western state. In order to allow for reasonable error margins in analyses, a sufficiently large random sample from the general statewide parole population was required. Because of time constraints, the necessity of having an outcome measure, and recent changes in parole policies (workload change, forthcoming policies on gangs, etc.), the preferred population for the study was parolees who had just completed their terms of parole or who had been terminated on parole within the period of November, 1997, to February, 1998. Pursuant to a request from parole headquarters, dead case files were "saved" by the parole units during the period of October through December, 1997. These files would normally have been destroyed 120 days after parole termination.
>
> There were four groups of parolees of special interest to the overall study: general population, females, sex-offenders, and gang members. Because the latter three groups represented relatively small proportions of the general population, a large sample was required to produce a sufficient number (at least 500) of analyzable cases in each. Even the general population was to be sub-analyzed in keeping with the purpose of determining whether there were subpopulations with differential predictability. Therefore, the case files were stratified into all four categories and three categories were disproportionately sampled until a minimum of 500 cases were reached. The final random sample drew cases from all 121 parole units in the state, constituting 4047 parolee files. The interest here is, of course, on the 546 female parolees in the sample.

From this example, you can see the source of the data, how the information was made available, and the sampling process. It might surprise you to know that, following the example text above, the source continues with more than another page on the data collection instrument, who the data coders were, what type of training they had, and how they coded the data. The original report, which was referenced in the article for further information, actually contained five pages describing the sampling process with another two pages describing the data collection instrument. The lesson here is to provide minute detail—this is the one place it is okay to bore your readers.

Suggestions for Coding

While we are discussing data, this seems a reasonable time to talk about coding. Coding is the process of transferring information from the original source to a machine-readable format (such as your computer and statistical program). If you are collecting your own data, whether responses to a survey, records to which you have been allowed access, or observations made while doing field research, there are a few hints for coding your data that will help.

1. *Create a codebook.* One of the first things you want to do is create a codebook that documents the data you have collected, or will collect. Such a codebook should be filled with documentation of each piece of information, precisely what the information means, how it was coded and what each value means, and what, if any, changes you had to make as you continued data collection. The key to a good codebook is having another person pick up your data set and, using the codebook, fully understand what each datum represents. Actually, it is common for a person who collected data to come back to it a short time later and forget exactly what each variable means—so, in reality, you are doing yourself a service to fully document everything. An example of a few codebook items appears in Box 8-1.

BOX 8-1 AN EXAMPLE OF A FEW CODEBOOK
INFORMATION ITEMS

Codebook for Parole Risk Assessment Study	
Item and Variable Name	Coding and Comments
1. Unit of initial release on parole (unit)	Record the parole unit administrative number assigned by parole headquarters (as per attached list).
2. Original Release Risk Score (risk)	Parolee's score on the current parole risk instrument. 0 = no risk 1 = low risk 2 = medium risk 3 = high risk
3. Parole result at 12 months (result)	1 = No return to custody—still on parole 2 = Returned to custody due to technical violation 3 = Return to custody due to new offense 4 = Parole violation and given new prison term 5 = Parole absconder 6 = Death before end of 12 months 7 = Discharge due to incarceration in other state 8 = Deportation 9 = Other (please specify)
4. Gender (gender)	1 = Male 2 = Female

2. *Collect the data at the highest possible level of measurement.* For instance, if you have date of birth information, you might want to collect age information. Even though you may plan to compare younger individuals with older ones, collect and code the data at the interval level (years of age). Afterward, it is easy to collapse the data into another variable which is coded into two groups, "younger" and "older." The lesson is that data originally recorded at the collapsed level can never be expanded to interval. This might prevent you from using certain types of analysis (e.g., a regression analysis or even a t-test) that require interval level variables. Keep in mind that follow-on analyses are dictated by logical questions that emerge from the first questions you ask (e.g., "If young parolees fail on parole more frequently than older parolees, does this apply to all 'young' ages or is there some age group that might perform better or worse?").

3. *Code all categories of an item.* Most items (or variables) have clear categories, and you already know what they are (e.g., marital status—single and never married, married, separated, divorced, widowed). If, however, you are not sure that all categories have been included in your coding scheme, then consider including a code for "other." Just be sure that your "other" code does not contain a substantial portion of your data because that would limit your ability to interpret the item. There are also times when combinations of codes are necessary, and this is particularly true with multiple response sets (items for which a respondent can choose more than one response).

4. *Consider whether an item has only one valid category or whether multiple categories can be used.* Because information can be complex, not every item you collect will have a clear, single category to use. Indeed, when you are not sure that a single category response is likely, it makes sense to use a multiple response item with instructions to "check off the above that apply." In these cases you need to code each possible response category as a "not checked" or "checked" answer. Thus, what appears to be a single item turns into multiple items, each representing a single choice. You can then decide whether to create combined item codes, recode the data into different variables after you have it in your statistical program, or use your program's multiple response analysis capabilities.

5. *Code items in a logical way.* No matter what shape your original information is in, you can make matters worse by using poor coding practices. All coding should be constructed in the most logical manner possible. For instance, if you are recording whether a police stop resulted in an arrest, your possible categories are "yes" and "no" (a dichotomy). However, if you assigned "0" to yes and "1" to no, there is a high likelihood you or someone else coding the data will make a mistake at some point. A zero is more logically used for "no"; to use it for something that doesn't mean no is illogical. Your coding should be "0" for no and "1" for yes. It is possible to compound such errors by having variables with the same response types coded differently (e.g., zero for yes one time and 1 for yes another, or even 1 for yes and then 2 for yes on the next variable)—code all variables with

the same response types the same way. In addition, with variable responses with more than two categories, you should determine the most logical sequence of numbering the responses. Don't forget that scale variables (at least ordinal level information) need to have their responses coded in order, with the smallest numbers at the low end and the largest numbers coded at the high end.

6. *Have a code for missing information.* There are often cases with items for which information is missing. For instance, if you ask about income on a survey, people sometimes purposefully do not answer. Therefore, you need to find a consistent scheme for coding missing information. A common practice is to use the number "9" for missing data. If there are *real* codes for the variable, then you obviously don't want to duplicate the number, and you must choose something else. One way to do this is to use one digit more than necessary for coding if a 9 represents an actual category. For instance, if all numbers between zero and 9 have already been used, then a "99" could be used to represent missing responses. It can also be useful to have two (or more) different missing codes, depending on the value of knowing exactly how something is missing. A case with a missing piece of information on an item can be a substantially different thing than a case with no information on any item (this is the difference between someone who answers a questionnaire but does not provide an answer for an item and someone who refuses to answer the questionnaire). There are other instances in which we expect an item to be missing as, for example, in the case of an item following a filter question with instructions "if the response is 'no,' please skip the next question." Consider having a special missing code for this.

7. *Don't create codes that are either difficult to remember or difficult to enter.* The "bottom line" when coding is not to do anything that would facilitate making errors. The two major reasons for making errors while entering data are having a numbering scheme that is difficult to remember without looking at the codebook again and again or using a sequence of numbers that are conducive to making typing mistakes. In the former, you can imagine the difficulty created by having a dozen or more categories, particularly combinations from a multiple response set item. In the latter instance, numbers are usually entered in the numeric keypad area of a keyboard, and certain sequences are mistake prone. Consider the numeric keypad for a minute. After getting used to entering numbers, there is the tendency to work as if you were a "touch typist" or enter numbers without looking. It is better to use a sequence of numbers, such as 1 through 3, on the same line rather than switching lines (0, 1, 2) because of the effect of lifting fingers off the keypad. The farther you have to move your fingers the greater is the likelihood of making a data entry mistake.

Statement of Hypotheses or Research Questions

While mostly pertinent to empirical theses, the statement of hypotheses is critical to your description of research. This essentially lays out the logical detail of your methodological model, why you used the variables you did (the data you collect), and how you will know what you have found with your analysis. There is another way to do the same thing by using "research questions," but it requires the ability to create a logical flow *as you do your analysis* rather than beforehand. As a result, it is usually easier to create hypotheses.

So what is a hypothesis? You have already stated at least one general hypothesis or proposition in your introductory chapter and possibly at the end of your conclusions chapter. Now it is time to focus on a much more specific form: the operational hypothesis. This hypothesis is a statement of the presumed relationship between two or more variables. For our purposes, let's keep the statement to two variables. The earlier hypotheses you used were "general" or "theoretical" or "conceptual" hypotheses; that is, they weren't specific enough to test. The job of testing falls to operational hypotheses.

The theoretical hypothesis we used as an example in the chapter on making problem statements was "Males are likely to receive more severe sanctions in criminal justice processing." If we have an available data set with processing variables, we would define "criminal justice processing" by using one of the variables in the data set. Assuming that there is a variable with information on the decision by the prosecutor to charge an offense (or not), we would say,

H_{A1}: *Males are more likely to be charged by the prosecutor with an offense than females.*

Note that this operationalizes criminal justice processing by using a variable with information about the charge decision by the prosecutor. The hypothesis also does *not* say that "greater numbers of males are charged than females." This is because we are not interested in comparing the numbers themselves—that is simply a product of the sample sizes of males and females—but instead we want to compare the relative likelihood of males and females being charged.

The hypothesis also does not specify which offenses are being charged and, indeed, uses all of them. If that were of concern and sufficient data existed, you might change the hypothesis to read "charged with a burglary." It is also likely that you will have more than one hypothesis or will have subsets of hypotheses. For example, the addition of burglary could actually be a subset hypothesis:

H_{A2}: *Males are more likely to be charged by the prosecutor with a burglary than females.*

Another concern exists because it occurs so often in theses. The fact is that you cannot test a null hypothesis: the statement of no difference or no relationship. That is because the random error probability distributions used with inferential statistics are based on concept of no real difference (i.e., variations are merely the product of random sampling error). You will always have to state an alternative hypothesis—and the best way is to not only say one variable will affect another, but also to point out the direction in which that effect occurs (otherwise called a "one-tailed hypothesis"). If your thesis chair or a committee member insists you phrase a null hypothesis, then by all means do so; but you must propose an alternative to test. Box 8-2 demonstrates the wording used for two-tailed and one-tailed hypotheses.

BOX 8-2 BOX HOW TO PHRASE HYPOTHESES

Two-tailed (nondirectional) hypotheses:
> *(the independent variable)* affects *(the dependent variable)*.
>> Example 1: Gender affects participation in marijuana smoking.
>> Example 2: Grades affect delinquent behavior.

One-tailed (directional) hypotheses:
> As *(the independent variable)* increases/decreases, the likelihood of *(the dependent variable)* increases/decreases.
> Example: As grades decrease, the likelihood of delinquent behavior increases.
>> This can also be phrased as: Higher grades decrease delinquent behavior.
> Example: Males are more likely to participate in marijuana smoking. or, Males have higher rates of participation in marijuana smoking.

Methodology for Collecting Data

As we mentioned earlier, every type of thesis has a methodology, even if it is nothing more than a documentation of the logic you used to determine what constitutes evidence for a theoretical position. The key to writing a description of your method of collecting data is to include detail. You want to say what you did and why you did it. Include discussions about:

- Which method you chose
- Why you chose that method (what were the advantages of this particular method?)
- How you structured the research process (the steps involved)
- The instruments you used or created
- How you determined those instruments were appropriate instruments
- (If secondary data) the process by which you gained access to the data
- Exactly how you collected the data
- Any training or instructions involved in collecting the data
- Your coding process
- How you determined the data were reliable

We examine two samples of the methodology discussion. The first one is perhaps at the top end of sophistication for a thesis and almost approaches a doctoral dissertation. The second is similar to many theses. We can easily imagine that, while the authors of these theses participated in the construction of the survey, both were actually products of being a graduate research assistant for one of the professors in the program.

BOX 8-3 QUANTITATIVE METHODOLOGY EXAMPLE: SYSTEMATIC
REVIEW

In this example, a student used a **systematic review** to study the
response rates for surveys to police officials over the last twenty years.
He not only describes his methodology but also anticipating a reader's
question, he goes on to explain why it is not a meta-analysis, a more
common technique for analyzing groups of studies.

Systematic review is of particular value in bringing together a
number of separately conducted studies, sometimes with conflicting findings and synthesizing their results for the evaluation of
new or existing practices.

To paraphrase Cooper and Hedges (1994), systematic reviews
can be a valid and reliable approach for avoiding the bias of single studies that are specific to a time, sample, and context and
utilize methods that are often of questionable quality.

This approach is referred to as a systematic review rather than
a meta-analysis because while it synthesizes the results of a number of smaller studies, it does not statistically combine the results
into a single summary estimate as would be the case using meta-
analysis. Though it does not require the rigorous quantitative methods applied in true meta-analysis, it uses scientific tools to summarize, appraise, and communicate the results and implications of
otherwise unmanageable quantities of research. (Legg, 2004, 16)

EXAMPLE 1

As the first example, we'll look at a methodology write-up of the same parole recidivism prediction study we used in describing sampling procedures.
We'll do this piece by piece to see how the different issues were treated. First,
here's what was written about the method chosen and the instrument.

A determination was made that the best approach was to use existing information from agency and prison records, both in electronic and paper format.
The time required to interview parolees and collect data firsthand, particularly
for the number of cases involved was deemed prohibitive. Thus, an instrument
was constructed to guide data collection, with the variables developed from
multiple sources. First, the predictive variables located in an earlier study were
incorporated. Second, items identified earlier in the classification report from
various research findings throughout the United States and Canada over the
past 20 years were used. Third, items suggested through interviews with parole
agents and parole administrators were included. Lastly, the project staff suggested possible items. All items were originally incorporated into the data collection instrument and approaches to their measurement were refined over a
period of six months. Of the original set of items, a majority were eliminated for
one or more of the following reasons: they were not applicable to the state's parole practices, any available information was likely to be unreliable and, finally,

the information in the closed case files used for the sample was either unavailable or unreliable and there was no alternative in electronic databases.

After eliminating a large number of variables for the reasons above, a final cut took place in the training session for coders. As part of the training, coders (knowledgeable senior parole agents and supervisors) were asked to examine all items for potential unreliability and unavailability in the closed case files. At that point, several closed case files were examined and all items on the instrument were reviewed one-by-one. This process led to the discarding of several more items, including two of the critical predictive variables. Those two variables (previous parole violations and inmate classification at release from prison) were subsequently collected in a separate search of automated databases (along with a few other variables deemed important). The final instrument, then, was created in a dynamic process that involved parole agents, project staff, research staff and parole administrators.

This tells us that the data are from secondary sources, with a major part of the data collected by culling through parolee case files. The variables in the study were derived from the literature, previous research, and experiences relevant to that particular state's parole agents. In addition, we now know care was taken to ensure the variables in the data collection instrument would be available and reliable. There is information about who the people were who collected and coded the data, and how variables were retained or removed from the study. In general, the description helps a reader feel more comfortable that the process of creating the instrument was a good one.

At this point, the instrument might be further described. It would also be reasonable to say how it was used and in what format.

Two versions of the instrument were constructed: a paper instrument and a computer program. The paper version was used for approximately the first month of coding and in instances where the coders, for various reasons, were not at the coding sites (see Appendix A for the paper version). The computerized version was used during the last two months of coding. All data were ultimately placed into the computerized version, either by coders or by the research staff. The computer program was specifically written for the project, based on a web-server/browser framework installed on all desktop computers at the two coding sites and all computers at the research center. The essence of the programming was to install server software running on a Windows 95 platform. A data-collection instrument was programmed in HTML and paralleled the image of the paper instrument. Once data were entered into the instrument a submit command sent the information to a compiler that produced a comma-delimited ASCII file. These files were subsequently compiled into multiple-case files and retrieved into the SPSS statistical package for analysis.

Let's now look at some coding information:

Coders were all senior parole agents or higher, with years of experience in reading parolee files. Each coder underwent one week of training on the data collection instrument, in both paper and computerized versions. Training consisted of a discussion of the instruments, with a thorough review of the individual items on the instruments. The interpretation of each item was covered and, where there were possible alternative interpretations, a standardized approach was developed. A codebook was provided each coder and modifications were made so that all item interpretations were also contained in the codebook. Once the coders had begun work, instructions were given that all subsequent interpretational problems should be discussed among the group and, after a collective solution was achieved, the coding interpretation would be documented in the codebooks. After notifying the research staff, a modified codebook was created and provided to the coding groups. A final task in the week of training was the completion of a coding reliability form. The form contained seven items that, on the basis of previous discussion, were deemed most likely to cause interpretational problems. Eleven people (eight coders, one alternate coder, and two project members who also did coding) completed the reliability form. Results were that three codes were divergent of the 77 possible, for an overall reliability score of .96. In addition, at the end of the three months of coding, all coders were debriefed and coding decisions were discussed. Any divergences were either incorporated into the definitions of the variables or, where possible, recoded to meet the original coding requirements.

Your reaction at this point is probably "Wow, I could never get all this done; this one even used very expensive people for three months to do the coding." You would be correct—except that sometimes state agencies come looking for researchers to oversee and design research for something the agency already wants to do. The graduate student here participated in the research, but much of the design was created by her professors. Regardless, the research was used by the graduate student for her thesis, and she had to report the methodology. Now let's turn to another example of a methodology discussion, this time a bit less complex.

EXAMPLE 2

Our second example of writing a methodology description comes from research designed to test the effect of people's characteristics on how much trust they feel they can place in major participants in a criminal trial. This time a mailed survey was used.

An instrument was developed from previously-constructed questions concerning criminal justice issues, jury and trial experience and opinions, multiple scales (social bonding scale, Srole's anomia scale, and Thurstone's scale on punitive attitudes toward criminals) and demographic characteristics. These questions were used in order to eliminate the difficulty of both constructing and determining the reliability and validity of new measurements of important items. A mailed questionnaire format was used because a random list of names and addresses was readily available from state driver's license listings and the estimated cost of mailing was far less than that of conducting interviews, either in person or by phone. In addition, survey methodology is particularly advantageous when attitudes and opinions are being requested.

From this discussion, we know that a reasonably appropriate methodology was used for measuring opinions and attitudes and that the methodology was more cost-effective than some other alternatives. The questions on the instrument were derived from other instruments and standard, readily available scales.

Now let's look at the continuation of the survey write-up explaining the survey procedure and response.

The sample contained 2,000 individuals who were mailed an introductory letter and, one week later, a questionnaire package with a cover letter, a return

BOX 8-4 QUANTITATIVE METHODOLOGY EXAMPLE:
UNSTRUCTURED INTERVIEW

This student included an interview with an expert on her topic area, which was hospital emergency preparedness planning. Her goal was to review plans, determine common elements, compare them to models of planning in other areas, and create a model for hospitals to use. In order to "ground" her work in practical considerations, she used the interview as a way to reflect on theoretical versus practical concerns and modify her final model accordingly. The following was her methodological plan for the interview:

1. Explain the need to develop information on the practical side of planning (i.e., how plans need to be adapted to real world contingencies).
2. For this purpose, interview a hospital security director with many years of experience.
3. Discuss the details of the interview process
   a. Why was this person selected (details about the person).
   b. How was the interview constructed?
      i. Was there a preconstructed instrument from which to ask questions from?
      ii. Was there an unstructured interview with no instrument?
      iii. Were there some preconstructed questions and the rest of the interview was unstructured?
   c. How long did the interview take?
   d. Were there any difficulties during the interview
   e. How was information recorded?
   f. Is it possible that recording influenced responses—if so, how?
   g. How were the interview results used to make sense of the topic?
      i. Were responses placed in categories?
      ii. Were responses related to previous points of interest?
4. How was the reliability and validity issue dealt with?
   a. Was the information valid?
   b. Would you get the same answers again?
   c. Would these results apply to all hospitals or only a certain type?
5. Present the questions asked (or if there were no prepared questions, structure the questions and responses by important topics and areas) and the responses under those questions/areas.
6. Interpret the answers and what they mean to the topic, specifically how this information might affect the elements in the model plan (or the plan to be proposed).
7. Discuss the limitations of the information and the interview process (what are the potential problems with the materials?).

envelope and a 12-page questionnaire. Those who did not respond within two weeks received a followup letter and, if there was still no response, a second questionnaire package was mailed a week later. A fifth and final letter was mailed to those who had not responded within 10 days of the mailing date of the second questionnaire. This procedure resulted in 1389 usable responses, and an adjusted return rate of 72 percent was achieved by subtracting deceased and nonforwardables from the original sample. The final distributions for gender, race and age approximated the state's census estimates for adults, aged 17 and over.

This tells us the original sample size (which could have been discussed earlier in greater detail), the details of conducting the mailed survey, and the size of the instrument. We also know the final response rate and how some of the common demographics stacked up against the population (census figures). This tells us that the responses to the questionnaire are usable—enough people responded and the ones who did appear to be representative of the population.

One of the critical groups for this study was "jury-eligible" respondents, because only that group can be analyzed if one is focusing on the opinions and attitudes of potential jurors.

From this sample individuals eligible for jury duty in their hometowns were located by asking questions about voter registration and property ownership, the two common jury pool lists used in the state. People who responded affirmatively to either question were placed in the jury-eligible group. A few respondents were added to this group who reported being summoned for jury duty even though they had neither registered to vote nor owned local real estate. The final jury-eligible group totaled 1096 persons.

Thus, we discover the definition of "eligible" was a respondent who either registered to vote or held local property ownership, with a few more respondents added who reported being previously summoned to jury duty. In addition, the number of these respondents is reported, and we can judge the sample size (almost 1,100) large enough for most analyses.

Variables Used in the Analysis and Their Description

From here, one would normally turn to a description of the variables to be used in the analysis, and, of course, those are derived from the hypotheses you would have already stated. Your chair and committee members might have preferences about how you do this, so ask before you begin writing this area. Some commonalities are that you should describe how you measured:

- The dependent variable, or variables, from your hypotheses
- The independent variable, or variables, from your hypotheses
- Any control variables you intend to include to better understand any relationships

It is common to describe these variables in the order above, however, description can be two things.

First, the simplest form of describing the variables could merely "lift" the information relating to each variable from your codebook. You can even state a question directly from a questionnaire or interview, or other data collection instrument. Here is a rather lengthy example from the jury thesis using a mailed survey questionnaire:

Dependent variable: Trust in prosecutors. The questionnaire contained nine questions under one general statement. That statement read as follows: "The media (TV, newspapers, radio) give us a picture of court cases as a struggle between opposing sides. Thinking about court cases in general, how do you feel about the TRUST you can place in each of these individuals during a trial? Please rate on a scale of 0 (would not trust at all) to 10 (would trust completely) and place an 'X' in the box representing the number of your choice." Each individual item contained the numbers 0 to 10 with a check-box below each number. "The prosecutor" was the third named individual in the list and answers on the 0 to 10 scale constitute the measurement of the dependent variable.

A variation of this "lifting" a question can be illustrated by an even more complex discussion that was required to define the dependent variable for the parole study. Because the purpose was to determine who would be reincarcerated while on parole, an item in the codebook example in Box 8-1 was used and explained. The problem was that there was no exact and simple approach to reincarceration.

Dependent variable: Reincarceration. This was defined as 0 = no reincarceration and 1 = reincarceration. The two values for the variable were created from an item measuring "Parole result at 12 months." The critical factor was to determine what constituted reincarceration, which was defined as item codes 2 (Returned to custody due to technical violation), 3 (Return to custody due to new offense), 4 (Parole violation and given new prison term), and 7 (Discharge due to incarceration in other state). No reincarceration was defined as item code "1" (No return to custody—still on parole). Parolees with all other codes (5, 6, 8 and 9) were removed from the analysis.

Thus, it took several categories of answers to the question to define the dependent variable. Further, we can see that problem cases (those without clear information on their reincarceration status, or without at least 12 months' parole experience) were resolved by omitting them from the analysis.

A simple example of defining an dependent, independent, and control variable would appear like this:

Dependent variable: Victimization. This was defined as answers to the question "Have you ever been a victim of crime during your lifetime" with answers of 0 = no and 1 = yes.

Independent variable: Gender. Defined as 0 = female and 1 = male.

Control variable: Age. Defined as years of age from answers to the question "How many years old are you, as of your last birthday?"

The second approach is not only to define the variable, but also to note its level of measurement and even report the univariate statistics on its distribution. To demonstrate this, we use the simple example above with just the dependent and independent variables and change the control variable to a 0 to 10 scale item (age would require too much space for the large frequency distribution).

Dependent variable: Victimization. This was defined as answers to the question "Have you ever been a victim of crime during your lifetime" with answers of 0 = no and 1 = yes. The level of measurement is nominal, but can be treated as ordinal (ranked) or interval because of the no/yes dichotomy (Fox, 1997).

Nonvictims comprised 35.7 percent of all cases in the data, with 64.3 percent of the respondents being victimized in their lifetimes.

Independent variable: Gender. Defined as 0 = female and 1 = male. This variable is also nominal level, with extension to ordinal and interval levels as a dichotomy representing "maleness" or "femaleness," depending on the direction chosen. Fifty-two percent of the sample were females and 48 percent were males.

Control variable: Nightime activity. This variable is measured by the question "How frequently are you away from your home at night (after 9:00 PM)?" with responses on a 0 (never) to 10 (every night) scale. The variable can be treated as interval level measurement. The mean response is 4.18 with a standard deviation of 2.4 and both the median and the modal responses are 5, suggesting most respondents are occasionally away from their homes at night (see Table 8-4). By far the bulk (almost 80 percent) of the respondents are never to occasionally away from their homes. Only about 3 percent are always out at night.

As you can see, this second approach provides information that is directly pertinent to understanding the variables. However, your chair may want you to put all univariate descriptions in the analysis chapter. If so, it should in be that chapter's first section before you really get into analytical concerns.

General Statistical Models to Be Applied

Since analysis was just mentioned, it makes sense that after you define your variables you would want to say what you plan to do with them. That plan of action is your analysis. It should contain the following three areas:

TABLE 8-4: RESPONSES TO FREQUENCY OF BEING AWAY FROM HOME AT NIGHT

	Frequency	Percent	Cumulative Percent
Never	114	10.3	10.3
1	51	4.6	14.9
2	119	10.8	25.7
3	120	10.9	36.5
4	82	7.4	43.9
5	396	35.9	79.8
6	68	6.1	86.0
7	64	5.8	91.7
8	46	4.2	95.9
9	13	1.2	97.1
Every night	32	2.9	100.0
Total	1,105	100.00	

- The logical approach you will take
- The analytical methods you will use
- The reason for using those analytical methods

These areas should sufficiently explain why you are doing this particular analysis. Remember that this is why you collected the data in the first place: you need to answer the issue or problem you originally proposed. Therefore, this is the section in which you convince the reader you have a good plan to develop that answer.

In reality, the summary of your review of the literature should have provided a good rationale for what needed to be examined and even how to do that examination. If this is true, then you already have your plan of analysis outlined, and the reader will be familiar with it. It is also possible to have a very short description of your analysis if the approach is a standard one with well-known statistical techniques.

Any analysis should move from simple to complex. The first part of your analysis should be a careful examination of the variables. Even if you have already done this in the methodology chapter—which we recommend—there is sometimes a follow-on in the analysis chapter. This would occur when your planned statistical tests require certain assumptions about the shape of the variable distributions. For instance, parametric tests routinely assume normally distributed data, and you might examine the variable distributions to see if they support the analysis you have planned. The second part should be the elementary bivariate analyses to test the initial or preliminary hypotheses. The following part, or parts, depending on how thorough your design is, attempts to control for factors that might affect the initial results. So, you might specify that you will first examine the univariate distributions, then proceed to the tests of basic hypotheses, follow-up with tests of any subhypotheses, and, finally, control for any variables that might affect the bivariate relationships.

Here is an example from one of the previous parole recidivism studies.

> The success on parole variable was measured as either "fail" (reincarcerated) or "success" (remained on parole) for a period of twelve months following release. Because the issue is to predict which parolees will succeed, the analysis will begin with a series of bivariate tables pairing each of the potential predictor variables (gang membership, prison disciplinary actions, age at first arrest, age at release from prison, and type of offense) with the dependent variable. All predictor variables have five or fewer categories representing order, therefore ordinal level statistics will be used to determine whether any of these variables have a statistically significant effect and, if so, the strength of the relationship. The standard alpha level of .05 will be used to define statistical significance. Rather than apply separate inferential and correlational tests, the analyses to follow will follow a standard procedure of using the Somers' d correlational test and its associated estimates of probability, as reported by the SPSS statistical analysis program. Somers' d is deemed a good choice for ordinal data when there are ties caused by variables with few categories (Williams, 2006).
>
> Following these analysis, all significant variables will be examined in a multivariate analysis so that the effect of all predictors can be controlled. This will allow a determination of the most important predictors of parolee success.

The statistic to be used for this purpose is logistic regression (Hosmer and Lemeshow, 2000) which is a statistical technique for a dichotomous (two-value) dependent variable. It provides an estimate of the "strength" of several variables in determining whether success or failure can be predicted. Thus, it will serve the purpose of this thesis, which is identifying the best predictors of parole success.

Another example of an analysis plan, more closely allied with the typical thesis, is taken from a thesis that tests the basic hypothesis that police officers are more likely to use force in an arrest if the arrestee is a minority member.

> The basic hypothesis will first be examined by a bivariate table using race and use of force variables. Because the independent variable, race, is measured at the nominal level, the Chi-square test will be performed to determine if there is a significant relationship. A significant relationship will be defined as a probability of .05 or smaller. The Chi-square test is a popular one and has been in use for almost a century.
>
> Following this test, the three control variables will be introduced and independent Chi-square tests will be calculated (using the SPSS statistical program) for each "layer" of the control variable. A layer of a control variable represents a test of the relationship between race and use of force for only one of the categories in the control variable. For example, the control variable time-of-day is categorized into day and night. A Chi-square test will be conducted for the race/force relationship for all cases that occurred during the day, then a separate test will be conducted for night cases. Comparing the two test results will enable the researcher to determine whether time of day affects the basic relationship.

As you can see, the analysis plan does not necessarily have to be a long one or a complex one. It just needs to be logical and one that will (mostly) provide an answer to your question. The reason an analysis typically moves from bivariate to multivariate—even if just for a "layered" table—is that bivariate relationships rarely tell us much and frequently disappear when other variables are introduced. The world is just too complex for simple relationships to be very helpful in answering most of our questions.

You also shouldn't panic at the explanation needed for the statistical tests. Your chair or a member of your committee can provide guidance and help, just ask. There are also many books and texts on statistics—just find one that provides what you need (Sage Publications has an excellent series known as the "little green books"). In many cases you don't have to do much and can simply state what you plan to use.

METHODOLOGICAL LIMITATIONS

All forms of measurement and analysis have limitations. This does not mean that we should abandon our attempts to conduct a study; instead we should attempt to compensate for the weaknesses in any empirical endeavor and/or develop ways to minimize their effects on the outcome. The key to writing this section is to acknowledge limitations inherent in your methodology and to explain how you can and will adjust to those potential problems. It is even conceivable that you will have methodological limitations

BOX 8-5 AN EXAMPLE OF ADDRESSING AND MINIMIZING THE EFFECT OF THE LIMITATIONS IN A LEGAL THESIS

For a thesis on the legal issues involved with police engaged in off-duty employment, the student explained the research limitations with careful language that enforced the point that one cannot guarantee that some pertinent case, somewhere, sometime, that she did not find, even in a conscientious search, has not been rendered. She explains

> Validating the law is normally the last step in legal research. Many people use Shepard's citators, KeyCite, or GlobalCite to make sure that the law is still good and has not been overturned or criticized by a subsequent court case. The research contained in this paper, for the most part, has not been entirely validated. The interest of the paper focuses on how various courts initially treated the issues of police extra employment and how various issues were defined and applied. (Krizan, p. 37).

She goes on to say that it is possible she has not included some less comprehensive issues and that she purposefully chose to focus on only the most commonly raised. She cautioned that administrators looking for updated guidance should examine the most recent Attorney General Opinions. She also adds a nice caveat about the scholarly, and hence not advisory, intent of the work.

> Lastly, nothing in this thesis should be construed as legal advice but rather an academic analysis of the various substantive legal issues for discussion and assessment of their potential impact and effects on management decisions and policies. This thesis should be utilized only as a guide to the preliminary legal research on the relevant legal issues of off-duty police employment.

from a number of various facets of your study, for example, if you use a secondary data set collected from a telephone survey. You then will have the limitations that come with the use of secondary data, as well as those that are inherited from the telephone survey process.

Acknowledging Your General Limitations

It is best to look through the literature to see if and how others have encountered and addressed the same difficulties in each of the areas for which you have limitations. A search of related research should clarify whether there is a standard way to address the limitations or whether there are several approaches that you can evaluate for their utility in your specific project. There is an expectation that you would either be able to take these same actions, explain why you have not, or detail why you have chosen alternate means to deal with each limitation.

In some cases, there is no remedy for a limitation. For example, even a relatively large prison data set may not have enough female inmates to allow for an analysis of females to see if they are somehow different from males. In these cases, the limitation is still raised, but with the understanding that this limitation will be considered again when it comes time to evaluate your findings and perhaps place some restrictions on your eventual interpretation of the outcomes. That is why there may be a need for you to raise limitations again in the final section of your thesis—usually in a section discussing your interpretation of the conclusions to be drawn from your analysis. At that time you do not need to rehash all of the methodological limitations and ways you adjusted for them, but what you may need to do is address circumstances throughout the research, causing you to restrict the generalizability of your conclusions or use caution in stating the implications of your research.

As described in Chapter Three, there are possible limitations to the use of secondary data that must be referenced in your methodology chapter. Use of that list and the corresponding advantages might show that the advantages outweigh the disadvantages for your specific subject. Look at this example:

> In some situations the use of secondary data can be considered a threat to the study's reliability (Hyman, 1972; Bailey, 1994). However, the form of secondary data used here, institutional records, has developed a reputation for greater accuracy, a savings of time and money, an allowance for larger samples, and the provision of continuity (Reidel, 1999; Bailey, 1994). According to Weiss (1972, p. 55), "With the coming of age of computers and the change in perspective from file cards to data banks and information systems, institutional records have a better chance of gaining top-level attention and being upgraded."
>
> The use of secondary data is often appropriate in situations where the variables are of a demographic nature (Kidder, 1981) or reflect steps in clientele processing (Weiss, 1996) both of which are characteristic of this study. In this case, the data provided information on the activities of organizations (both the prison and the detainer placing agency) at one point in time. Also, since these data are readily available to staff on the computer throughout the inmate's incarceration, they may be corrected and monitored for accuracy. Other justification includes the fact that an alternate source for these data or an alternate method of retrieval was neither practical nor obvious (Bailey, 1994).

An often cited disadvantage to secondary data is that the data themselves, how they are gathered, and what they actually reflect are not readily understood by the secondary user. Consider the researcher's resolution of the problem:

> The researcher in this instance had spent the last year working with the inmate files in the state's Department of Corrections where the investigation of these records was an integral part of the job. Therefore, the processes used, the coding of information, and the meaning of the data categories were familiar to the researcher.

With this information, the writer explains not only what the potential limitations are for the use of the secondary data, but also how those have been addressed and minimized in the research she conducted.

The most common data sets for secondary analysis used in criminal justice and criminology (discussed in Chapter Three) are Uniform Crime Reports, The National Crime Victimization Survey, U.S. Census Data, and some large surveys such as the National Youth Survey, and various government drug surveys such as the Drug Use Forecasting data and the Arrestee Drug Use Monitoring data. Many researchers are using these for multiple purposes. Unfortunately, this is also a disadvantage. The literature is replete with studies using exactly the same national data, on exactly the same issue, with perhaps a very minor twist. Analyses of the same data will produce the same result, time after time. This is also true of data from a few "classic" studies that have been overused.

While the advantages of national representation and sample sizes sufficient for more sophisticated statistical analyses are important ones, not every issue worthy of a thesis has such data readily available. Smaller and geographically isolated data sets can be located in some instances and, literally, represent the only choices in available data. One uses them, but with caution and full understanding of the limitations. The advantage, of course, is that without these small data sets there would be no investigation of the issue.

Specific Limitations in Your Data

Here is an example of a specific limitation, and an explanation, from the earlier example of the thesis examining trust in courtroom participants.

> A possible issue is the definition of trust present in the questionnaire. There were no other definitions or instructions beyond those above. This was done intentionally because of concerns that increasing the length of the already long instructions might result in unreliable answers. While trust may have different meanings to people, those meanings likely share enough similarity to justify using the results as a generalized measure of bias for or against courtroom participants.

This example was based on a methodological design that included primary data collection via survey (i.e., the researcher actually developed the measure and collected the data). If this approach still results in a discussion of limitations, imagine how pervasive the same problem with secondary data might be.

Any user of secondary data must use variables based on the original researcher's definitions and source of data collection. Therefore, it is virtually impossible to get exactly what you want as a measurement of the variables for *your* study. In fact, most secondary data users rely on variables that "come close" to what they have in mind. Given that you will have multiple variables you want to use, even the search for a good data set is limited to those providing some approximation of your preferred variables. Thus, a specific limitation you will need to handle is your choice of variables used as a "proxy" for the real ones you had in mind. This requires justifying the choices and providing a rationale for their use in your analyses.

Other common specific limitations involve samples that turn out to be minimally representative of your desired population, variables with extensive amounts of missing data, unavailability of one or more important variables (suggested from your literature review), and data distributions failing to meet the assumptions of your preferred statistical techniques. All of these, and other problems, should be noted and some attempt made to explain why you should continue with the analyses. This defense is not as difficult as it might sound.

Defending Your Methodology

Part of your discussion of limitations is the defense of problems noted earlier. This means that you will also have to do some research on the method itself. There are many good textbooks and journal articles for this purpose, and some are listed at the end of the chapter. As you conduct your research on the method you are about to employ, you can use the results to summarize the arguments that can be made in support of your methodology. As one student (Schubert, 1999) explained

> One of the key considerations that emerged in the beginning of this study was the type of methodology most appropriate for gaining meaningful information about the legal community's perception of DNA evidence and jurors' understanding of its results. In order to support the argument for a more qualitative approach, a brief demonstration of the current discussion surrounding qualitative and quantitative methods, as they are applied in the social sciences, provides some useful insights. For the purpose of this study, unstructured, informal interviews that are based on ideas of ethnographic research were best suited to engage with a highly specialized target population in order to discuss a very complex topic. Moreover, my personal interaction with the judges, prosecutors and attorneys, as well as with DNA experts allowed for a deeper understanding of their roles and experiences with DNA trials. Subsequently, this chapter will outline some of my experiences with members of the legal community in Flagstaff and Phoenix. (p. 60)

In this example, the student identified her method as "unstructured, informal interviews" and argued that, because of her highly specialized population target (court personnel involved in DNA trials) and the complexity of the topic (DNA evidence and its legal applications), her method was justified. She went on to explain that a more general survey of the legal community would likely produce many opinions on the matter, but few from professionals who had specifically been involved in such litigation. She explains that the response rate for a survey, "even if mailed to criminal law specialists, can be expected to be low and would most likely include opinions not based on knowledge and experience." As far as the complexity issue is concerned, she defends the open-ended, informal nature of her unstructured interviews as enriching the context of the information. It gave participants "an opportunity to elaborate on their subjective experiences, which included anecdotes of trials involving DNA evidence, relationships with experts and clients, personal struggles with regulations and legislation, as well as experiences with members of the scientific community." She further allows that "this type of storytelling provided for a more in-depth understanding of how different members in the legal community experienced DNA litigation and how their experience formed their attitudes and opinions, especially in regards to jurors' understanding the evidence" (Schubert, 1999, p. 63).

As a word of caution here, there are many types of study and issues for which this type of method, particularly the use of anecdotes and "storytelling" would not be considered appropriate. This case, however, is an excellent example of a good fit. The actual use of DNA in court was very new when Schubert began, and most smaller jurisdictions had no previous experience with the topic. With the researcher acting as an interpreter for scientific and legal information that would otherwise perhaps be less meaningful for a criminal justice audience, she has addressed a gap in the literature. For what she wanted to know, and the possibility of gaining specific useful information for the field on the use of DNA in court, this was the right approach. Thus, any new, cutting-edge technology or legal procedure may be suitable for this type of inquiry, rather than those topics for which a large database of cases and studies may be accumulated. The topic of DNA evidence today would probably not be studied the same way.

SUMMARY

The methodology chapter is viewed by students about to write a thesis as one of the most difficult ones. In fact, in struggling with the writing of the literature review and methodology chapters, many students give up. Don't let this happen to you. If you follow the guidelines and examples given, the problem won't be writing enough to develop a chapter—instead, the problem tends to be too much writing. Use the outline presented here, consult with your chair and committee members, provide frequent drafts of what you are writing, and you'll do fine.

If you are still writing the prospectus, remember that you don't have to include everything here. Coverage of the main points will probably be sufficient. The full detail can wait until you are working on the thesis itself.

REFERENCES

ALLISON, P. D. (2001). *Missing data* (Sage Quantitative Applications in the Social Sciences Series). Newbury Park, CA: Sage.

BAILEY, K. (1994). *Methods of social research,* 4th Ed. Glenco, IL: Free Press.

BLACK, J. , and Champion, D. (1976). *Methods and issues in social research.* Philadelphia: John Wiley & Sons.

COOPER, H., and Hedges, L. (1994). *The handbook of research synthesis.* New York: Russell Sage.

KRIZAN, V. (2004). *Legal issues of police off-duty employment.* Houston, TX: Unpublished thesis, University of Houston-Downtown.

LEGG, J. (2004). *A systematic review of research surveying police administrators between 1980 and 2003.* Houston, TX: Unpublished thesis, University of Houston-Downtown.

LIPSEY, M., and WILSON, D. (2000). *Practical meta-analysis* (Sage Applied Social Research Methods Series, Volume 49). Newbury Park, CA: Sage.

McSHANE, M. D., Williams, F. P., III, and Dolny, H. M. (2002). Do standard risk prediction instruments apply to female parolees? *Women and Criminal Justice* 13, 163–182.

REIDEL, M. (1999). *Research strategies for secondary data: A perspective for criminology and criminal justice.* Newbury Park, CA: Sage.

SCHUBERT, C. (1999). *Unwinding the double helix: DNA evidence in criminal trials.* Flagstaff, AZ: Unpublished thesis, Northern Arizona University.

WEISS, C. (1972). *Evaluation.* Englewood Cliffs, NJ: Prentice Hall.

WEISS, C. (1996). *Evaluation,* 2d ed. Englewood Cliffs, NJ: Prentice Hall.

9

THE PROSPECTUS AND THE PROSPECTUS DEFENSE

The purpose of the prospectus itself has been discussed in Chapter 1. While most students understand the need for a written proposal and the approval of that proposal by all members of the committee, some are intimidated by the "defense process." There are several good reasons for a public, oral defense, as nerve-wracking as that event may seem. It is not simply the continuation of some old tradition in which faculty torment students. The prospectus defense is an important vehicle to protect both the student and the committee against unnecessary and time-consuming misunderstandings down the road. A good prospectus defense will accomplish the following:

1. *Agreement on the topic, issues, method, and other related research for the work.* The full scope of the work is settled—from here the topic should certainly not become broader and, normally, it won't get narrower. The prospectus is an official document. In some universities it is kept as a record, as is the paperwork acknowledging the completion of the prospectus defense. Moreover, you *want* such a record. There have been rare, and unfortunate, events where the student disappears for a couple of years and during that time the entire committee has moved to other universities or retired. Only a formal record saves the student from starting over. Much less rare is the committee member who "forgets" what has been agreed upon and continues to request work on an issue, methodological approach, or analysis that is clearly outside of

the approved prospectus. An official copy of the prospectus can be used as a "reminder" of what had been agreed to.

2. *The provision of a forum for informing other members of the university community of the type of research being conducted by the department or college.* Part of the prestige of the master's degree and the thesis itself is that the work is deemed reputable and that it conforms to the academic expectations of the university. An open, public forum is a means for ensuring that accountability and, hence, the reputation of the degree you hold.

3. *The opportunity to demonstrate the thesis process as an example for new and upcoming thesis students.* Here, potential thesis students will be able to watch and learn about the development of a research proposal. Though you may feel like a guinea pig, the optimal thesis program will have allowed students to attend an earlier prospectus defense before it is their turn to present. It is important that you view students in the audience as sympathetic future defendees and realize the value of your role in their education as you, too, may have benefitted from those who came before you. Consequently, you should encourage others to attend your presentation and not try to discourage their presence. In most cases, students see that the defense is a very practical task and then can imagine how they might proceed in their own work. Understanding the process of proposing and writing up research, in whatever form it might take, is critical to structuring one's issue. So, make a pot of coffee and invite your fellow students.

SETTING A DATE

By following a timetable or schedule similar to the one outlined earlier in Chapter One, you should have received feedback in a systematic manner that is dessigned to minimize confusion and frustration and keep you on track toward each progressive goal. As you prepare for your prospectus defense, continue to circulate your draft, first to your chair, and, then, after making the necessary corrections, to your other committee members for their feedback. Be sure to address all of the edits and concerns, and go back and discuss any problems you may have in complying with their suggestions. You want to resolve as many issues as possible prior to the defense.

Most students are nervous about the prospectus defense. Thus it is important to keep the outcome in proper perspective. In some universities the prospectus defense may be resolved as "passed," "failed," or "passed with modifications to be made." In the latter case, these modifications are usually revisions that are worked informally through the committee and chair following the defense. Ordinarily the committee will not proceed to the prospectus defense phase unless the work is suitable for passing. It is only under rare or unpredicted circumstances that a defense will not be successful. In such cases, however, the defense will simply be rescheduled for a later date and in most cases is successful at that time as the issues are addressed and resolved.

Overall it is important to schedule a prospectus defense at a time that is comfortable for your committee members. Even though you might not be initially aware of them, there are multiple events that affect faculty in scheduling their time. The beginning and end of academic terms (quarters, semester, trimesters) are problematic because of the many demands on faculty time during those periods. In addition, be aware of the midterm examination period, advising periods, holidays, and conferences that faculty might be attending. Most faculty are not under contract over the summer, so that, too, is a difficult time for scheduling a defense. Keep in mind that even though you might be able to get your committee to meet during these times, they remain poor choices because of a potential lack of attention to your prospectus. Your best bet for having a good defense and a minimum of conflicts is to schedule a time when your committee members can focus on *your* work, rather than be preoccupied with competing needs.

There is an optimal date that allows you to have a competent understanding of your topic and your proposed research strategy, and to be prepared to present the material. This means that you can easily explain what you are doing and why you are doing it, as well as why you are not using alternative methods. You should be able to demonstrate that you are aware of the benefits as well as the limitations of your study. Recognizing that you are ready to proceed with the prospectus defense is as important as making sure that you are not waiting too long. As mentioned earlier, problems may arise if you are too far along in the study; the most serious of these include the risk of having committee members seek changes that negate work you have already completed.

As a final reminder about when to schedule the defense, remember that you cannot defend the prospectus and then complete the thesis over the next couple of weeks. Be sure to give yourself, and your committee, plenty of time to complete the entire process, and you will have far fewer headaches.

THE PROSPECTUS DOCUMENT

The prospectus document that you develop will be the result of consultation with your committee chair and other members. It is often best to seek out prospecti that other students in your department have completed in order to have a better idea of what is expected. If possible, look for examples previously supervised by your chair. That way you can be familiar with the style and type of documents that have been successfully defended. Half the work is the document you prepare, the other is the presentation.

Depending on the type of research design you have selected, the materials included in your prospectus document may vary. Most will require a title page, similar to the example in Box 9-1. If you are doing a legal research piece, you may include a reference list of court cases that will be involved and a description of the major legal principles to be discussed. If you are using an existing data set, recovery of that data and a list of the variables and

Learning to Use a Meerschaum Pipe: A Recidivism Prevention Program in a Minimum Security Prison

A Prospectus Presented to the Faculty of
The Department of Criminal Justice
Smokin' University of Bavaria

In Partial Fulfillment of Requirements for the
Master's Degree in Criminal Justice

James A. Tobacconist
December 2004

a description of their formats would be important. In preparing for a content analysis of the notebooks kept by DWI offenders, Susan carefully reviewed several different notebooks, which she had already acquired from the court, to ensure that her projection of the length of time each would take to analyze, and thus the number that would be reasonable to review in her study, would be accurate. She also included a permission letter from the court. For a survey of agency personnel, you would include a copy of the instrument, a letter of agreement to participate from the agency, and perhaps even your IRB/human subjects approval.

While some might argue that you should defend your prospectus before you go to the university committee, so that your design is finalized and approved by your committee, others would see the IRB approval as fundamental to proceeding with your prospectus defense. In departments where prospectus defenses are viewed as more preliminary and shaping in their activity, they may want to only send a finalized and defended prospectus proposal to the University Review Committee. However, in university settings where the IRB notoriously attempts to shape, change, and direct questionnaires and interview procedures, their approval prior to the prospectus defense may be more expedient. All in all, where full human subjects reviews are anticipated, it is best to have a thesis committee that is flexible, tolerant, and good natured.

There is no standardized approach to the actual content and length of a prospectus. Your department may have certain requirements but, even then, certain faculty are likely to diverge from them. On the whole, there are two versions of what may be expected as content: a thesislike approach and an independent document approach. The versions differ primarily as a product of faculty perception of how important the prospectus is, vis-à-vis the thesis itself. Neither approach is inherently preferable, and the decision of which to use is governed by the combined preferences of the department, the committee chair, and, in the best situations, the student.

Content of a Thesislike Approach

Faculty, or departments, who prefer the thesislike approach to prospectus content generally are concerned with the utility of the prospectus document. They encourage students to maximize their efforts in writing the thesis. As a result, the prospectus is viewed as being synonymous with the first three chapters of the thesis itself (the three chapters are the introduction, review of literature, and methodology). The actual chapter structure might not be required, but most of the content and length associated with the thesis chapters is similar—usually something on the order of forty pages of total text. Differences, if any, might be found in a slightly shortened review of the literature and a methodology section without a full explanation of the variables (assuming an empirical thesis). Because the writing of this version obviously takes longer to complete, chairs will have students who take longer to get to the prospectus defense. In addition, committee members should be working closely with students, and most issues would be ironed out prior to the defense. It even may be the case that data are already in hand, and minor data analysis has occurred prior to the defense. While more difficult on the front end, the advantage of such an approach is that the writing of the thesis does not take as long.

The Content of an Independent Document Prospectus

Departments and/or faculty with this approach tend to view the prospectus as a formal requirement in which the document itself has little direct application to the thesis. The prospectus defense, then, is more of a "get them on their way" ceremony with a much shorter time to committee approval of the thesis topic. This does not mean that the student can be lax in the presentation or details of what they intend to do for the thesis; it just means that the document itself is a short version of the thesislike approach discussed earlier. Most, if not all, of the same elements are in both prospecti. The length, however, tends to be more on the order of six to twelve pages, and the detail is substantially less. It succinctly puts forth your topic, the problems and issues involved, hypotheses or research questions you intend to investigate, and the methodology you intend to use. The literature review is sufficient to illustrate that you are aware of the major issues, yet it does not have anywhere near the comprehensiveness and detail of the problem statement or literature review chapters of the thesis proper. Rarely would a prospectus defense under this approach include an IRB approval, and it is likely that data are not yet available or collected.

GENERAL ELEMENTS FOUND IN ALL PROSPECTUS FORMATS

Regardless of approach and length, virtually all prospecti have certain common elements. Though they are similar to the elements in the various thesis chapters, there will be usually be differences in amount of detail and comprehensiveness. We suggest the following headings (particularly for the independent document approach discussed) and coverage for any prospectus.

1. *The introductory problem statement:* Discuss the broad problem under which your specific topic lies, and narrow the discussion down to your topic. A review of the literature on the *general* problem would be appropriate here, but do not include specific research on the problem.
2. *Literature review:* This is the area in which you briefly (or thoroughly, depending on the prospectus type) review the literature directly pertinent to your own topic. In most cases this will primarily be empirical literature, but be sure to cover the theoretical and conceptual literature as well. You do not have to cover all the literature in the prospectus but review enough to demonstrate you are cognizant of the issues and

problems surrounding your topic. Don't forget to summarize and draw lessons from the literature.

3. *Statement of the problem:* Refine the topic discussed in the introductory problem statement by restating the problem to be addressed in your thesis in a short, clear, and concise manner. If hypotheses or research questions are appropriate, these should be stated here. Be very explicit in your statements. Keep in mind that your committee has to know *exactly* what you intend to do, or there will be misinterpretations and misunderstanding down the line that will delay your completion. It also may be helpful to the committee to state what is *not* included in your study (i.e., what you are not going to do) if the scope could easily be broadened or misconstrued.

4. *Methodology:* Discuss the way in which you plan to pursue your study, and justify all choices. Sketch an outline of your method and mode of analysis. State the test instruments you will employ and the mode of analysis (e.g., which statistical tools or logical model). Even a theoretical work has a methodology and analytical mode—describe it. Specify what data you intend to use and whether you will collect the data yourself or use secondary data.

5. *Availability of data:* Comment on the data source and its anticipated availability. If you have ready access, or need assistance in gaining access, note that here. If yours is not an empirically driven data project, discuss the availability of whatever materials you will need to accomplish the work.

6. *Limitations of the study:* Comment on expected specific limitations: sample, time and money, available instruments and scales, and so forth. What are the reasonable timelines of the study, when will the data be available for analysis, and when do you expect to finish? One effective method is also to state what you are *not* doing (i.e., what data are you not collecting, what is not being tested, what conceptualizations of your variables are not included); in short, how is your study restricted? Note that you have already discussed the limitations surrounding your topic itself in the statement of the problem—do not repeat that here.

THE PRESENTATION

Most committees do not want you simply reading from your prospectus. The presentation is more than what is in that document. It is your opportunity to convince your academic committee and everyone else that your research is important, should be done, and that you are the person to do it in the manner in which you are prepared to do it. Moreover, you need to exhibit a degree of mastery over the material.

Though your chair will dictate his or her expectations for the prospectus defense, an example of a model for the presentation can be diagrammed as in Box 9-2. This indicates that your discussion may start broadly in terms

THE TRIANGLE OF ABSTRACTION—SUCCESSIVE NARROWING OF YOUR TOPIC

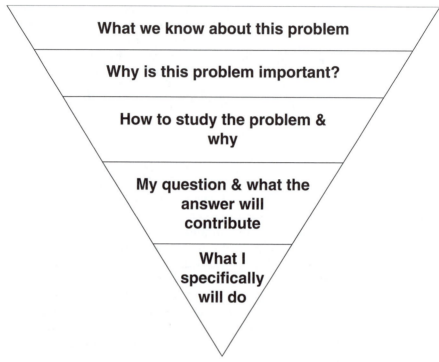

of the issue or problem and then narrow to your particular research question and the investigative process you will use—thus the shape of the inverted triangle and questions/issues from larger to smaller.

As you can see from the order of topics in the box, you can apportion your time according to the material that you have, in this order, so that you start broadly and finish narrowly focusing on your research methods or your study design. Usually a standard prospectus defense lasts about an hour, including time left at the end for discussion and questions. In most cases, the format will be as follows:

- Introduction by the chair (5 minutes).
- Student presentation of prospectus (20–25 minutes).
- Questions by committee (15 minutes or so).
- May be opened up to questions from audience (15 minutes or so).
- All but committee are excused so that members may deliberate.
- Student is called back into the defense room for results.
- Any further discussion related to revisions or plans.

It is not unusual to have some issues come up that need to be worked out and decisions that have to be made. These normally concern the course of the research, details about the methodology, potential broadness of the research topic, and so on. As this may be the first time that the whole committee has come together face to face, it is not unusual for many thoughts and ideas to be shared. Committee members may focus very intently on this work in a way that may seem unnerving. This is normal!

While your emotional reaction may be an unsettling "WOW, why didn't everybody mention these things before," it is important to realize that this is not uncommon. Academics getting together tend to come up with insights and comments that, during a busy semester, they may not have generated by themselves. In reality, the best of prospectus defenses results in the committee thinking together about your specific issue and developing a high-quality, tight approach to it. The prospectus defense is the place to have any of these new ideas or issues, comments or critiques discussed and resolved. By getting the group to agree on these issues while seated together at this time, you are then able to go back to work assured that you are on the right track and that there is less chance that anything new will arise beyond that point to jeopardize your progress. So, use this opportunity to get clarification, make sure no member has any further concerns or requests, and make clear notes for yourself as to what was said and what it all meant.

CONSIDERATIONS IN PREPARATION FOR THE PROSPECTUS DEFENSE

There are a number of things you might do to prepare for a prospectus defense, other than writing the document itself. Such preparation may prove to be invaluable to either your ability to meet expectations, get your point across clearly, or make sense of requests made during the defense.

1. Consult with your chair on the format for the prospectus defense, the degree of formality, the elements to be covered, the equipment and format you have chosen for the presentation, any handouts they expect you to distribute, and the time frame they would like to use.
2. If you plan on doing a PowerPoint presentation, make sure that it is completely prepared ahead in at least enough time for your chair to review and edit. Arrive enough ahead of time at the location of the defense to ensure that all the necessary equipment is available, working, and completely compatible with the format you have chosen. A dry run is prudent.
3. Arrange ahead to have a note taker during the defense. This could be a friend or fellow student. Because so many ideas may be raised and so much advice given, it may be very hard to remember everything that you need to. An impartial note taker may make it easier for you to recall what was said by who and specifically what was asked of you during the process.
4. Bring clean copies of your prospectus document if you have not already given your professors the most recent copy that you will be

working from that day. It is awkward and undesirable to have multiple, prior copies circulating when you are in the defense process, and this only adds to potential confusion. Thus, before beginning your defense, make sure that each member has the most recent version and understands that this is the copy you will be defending from.

Following the defense, in the next day or so, you may want to meet with your chair or correspond with your committee members to ensure that you correctly interpreted the directions and suggestions you were given during the defense. In a summary fashion, reflect back their comments and your understanding of them for confirmation. This way, having had some time to think about what was proposed and everything that was said, your committee may want to adjust some earlier expectations or comments.

WHAT TO DO AND WHAT NOT TO DO

One of the most helpful plans you can make is to chose a format and presentation style that is consistent with your personal strengths and abilities. This is not the time to experiment with new techniques or technologies, nor to see if you are proficient in extemporaneous commentary. Many students learn the lessons described in this chapter the hard way.

For example, Brian was competent and confident with PowerPoint presentations, but he made the mistake of letting a friend talk him into using a remote control at his prospectus defense. At first, the computer wouldn't recognize the remote, resulting in ten minutes of fiddling with the operating system. Then after it began working, Brian wasn't familiar with the buttons, advanced slides when he didn't intend to and had to back up frequently, at one point even restarting his presentation. Finally, the entire episode broke down Brian's composure, and he was nervous through the entire presentation, resulting in misstatements and the inability to think on his feet.

Roberto didn't try any new technology for his presentation, and he also was comfortable with PowerPoint presentations. His problem was failing to connect his laptop to the LCD projector and checking out the equipment prior to the start of the defense. The projector refused to recognize the video signal from his laptop, and it took almost fifteen minutes to make it work. Meanwhile, the committee was growing impatient, and Roberto was growing ever more flustered. By the time the projector finally worked, Roberto was a proverbial basket case.

Max tried to inject humor into his presentation with unscripted "small talk" and, in not paying attention to what he was saying, joked that "none of this was a very serious matter anyhow since there was always error in research." The committee was not amused. And last but not least there was Janice who knew that she would not be comfortable with PowerPoint, so she opted for transparencies and the overhead projector with which she was more experienced. Her presentation was going smoothly until the bulb burned out, and there was no replacement to be found. She had to continue without it, which could readily be smoothed out except that it made her more nervous, which made her talk faster and her presentation suffered.

All these examples are provided not to frighten you but to simply illustrate that unforseen circumstances can occur. And even if things do go wrong, your committee is likely to be kind and forgiving as we have all been in your shoes at one time or another. Still, it is best to rehearse and prepare in order to minimize the risks involved in unfamiliar practices.

What to Do

- Do listen carefully to your chair when she or he makes suggestions. Most likely, they are the product of experience and will make your thesis go more smoothly.
- Do discuss your thesis ideas and as much detail as you can develop with your committee members before the defense.
- Do heed the concerns of all committee members and attempt to resolve them.

What Not to Do

- Do not create an instrument and collect data prior to the defense (you run the risk of wasting time spent on the effort).
- Do not read from papers, notes, overheads, or PowerPoint slides. Present your materials as if you know them intimately (you should).

Below you will find a list of some popular press guides to improving oral presentations and PowerPoint techniques and the types of information they cover. Some of these resources will be available in your library or can be ordered online. Many are under $20, and more recent and revised editions may now be available to you.

BAJAJ, G. (2005). *Cutting edge powerpoint for dummies.* Hoboken, NJ: For Dummies (Wiley).

DIRESTA, D. (1998). *Knockout presentations: How to deliver your message with power, punch, and pizzaz.* Madison, WI: Chandler House Press.

ESPOSITO, J. E. (2000). *In the spotlight: Overcome your fear of public speaking and performing.* Southington, CT: Strong Books.

LEECH, T. (2004). *How to prepare, stage and deliver winning presentations.* 3d Ed. New York: American Management Association.

LOWE, D. (2003). *PowerPoint 2003 for dummies.* Hoboken, NJ: For Dummies (Wiley).

NEGRINO, T. (2004). *Creating a presentation in PowerPoint: Visual quickproject guide.* Berkeley, CA: Peachpit Press.

WALKER, T. J. (2003). *How to create more effective powerpoint presentations.* New York: Media Training Worldwide.

WEMPEN, F. (2004). *PowerPoint advanced presentation techniques.* Hoboken, NJ: John Wiley.

SUMMARY: THE PROSPECTUS MILESTONE

A positive mind-set and a realistic perspective is the key to a stress-free prospectus defense. As Amie recalls, "The defense is not about defending yourself or your intelligence, but about working within a cooperative academic environment to not only demonstrate your current knowledge and abilities, but also about the continuing learning process."

Being prepared is one of the best ways to ensure that your prospectus defense goes smoothly. You should arrive at the room where your defense is scheduled ahead of time to ensure that the layout is properly arranged. Bring your work in multiple formats (CD, USB memory stick, diskette, Zip diskette, etc.). Locate outlets, extension cords, lighting switches, a podium, a glass of water, or any other materials that will be needed during your presentation. Make sure that wireless connections are as expected and that you have the number of USB ports for all of the drives you may need to utilize. Demonstrating you are organized and in control not only bodes well for your final thesis, but also reflects your mastery of graduate level skills.

The prospectus defense is a major milestone in the thesis process and its accomplishment will no doubt give you a sense of the "light at the end of the tunnel." Enjoy the moment, it is well deserved.

Section Three

ANALYZING INFORMATION AND DRAWING CONCLUSIONS

Before you begin your final chapters, check with your chair and committee for advice on what type of chapters and chapter organization would best fit your work. They will be able to guide you in determining which elements would be most appropriate in displaying your analysis or discussing your findings.

Traditionally, the last part of the thesis contains two major chapters: the analysis chapter and the conclusions chapter (both can be split into multiple chapters, depending on your needs). While the first three chapters (assuming the traditional chapter structure we have already discussed) can mostly be written before any data are collected, the final chapters are the essence of your analytical work. This is where you display your ability to search through information (data), organize it and set up logical questions to be answered, bring analytical techniques to bear on these questions, and make sense of your results. In short, this part of the thesis is the crux of the research—the reason you are doing the work to begin with.

The material in Chapter Ten provides an outline for writing up an analysis. Using a simple-to-more-complex organizing scheme, there are illustrations and examples of how you begin an analysis and follow through to answer your research questions. In particular, there are examples of what you might include in tables and the way in which they can be formatted. There are also sample write-ups of how you describe various parts of the analysis and what you need to say when hypotheses are tested.

While not all forms of analysis can be included and the focus is primarily on empirical theses, the chapter will provide a good sense of the style and format involved in analytical work.

Chapter Eleven outlines some suggestions for addressing the final part of your thesis which usually contains items such as summary of the work, summary of the findings, discussion, conclusions, policy implications, limitations of the findings, and concerns for future research. As the different elements indicate, you may be asked to do a summary of the findings or results rather than a summary of the study itself. In shorter works, a summary may not be needed, but, where there is a great deal of statistical analysis, you may be asked to put a summary of the findings either at the end of the analysis chapter or in the beginning of your conclusions chapters.

Whether it is done in one chapter or multiple chapters, the discussion and conclusions is arguably the most important part of the thesis. It is also often one of the toughest for students to master because it is, finally, the one place where you can suggest, argue, speculate, and, to some extent, go out on a limb about what the research means—that is, its significance. There is a fine art to this technique, and one must approach it with evidence, logic, careful language and the scientific principle of inference.

10

ANALYZING
AND PRESENTING
YOUR DATA
AND FINDINGS

The analysis of your data is a critical part of the thesis. It should be informed by the hypotheses you have created and the analysis plan already described in the methodology chapter. Thus, an analysis chapter has three goals:

- Focus the data on your problem.
- Conduct a logical analysis designed to examine your problem.
- Describe the results.

Even if you have a nonempirical thesis, you still have the task of creating a clear and logical description of your theoretical propositions, legal analysis, or historical events. Moreover, you should come to the results in a way that suggests someone else examining the same problem would be likely to arrive at the same conclusions.

The analysis chapter can begin with a restatement of the purpose of the thesis and a brief summary of the analysis plan. After that you begin the analysis itself. In an empirical thesis, you may start with univariate descriptions of your variables (if your thesis chair didn't want this in the methodology chapter). For a discussion and examples of this, see Chapter Eight. Most theses will begin with a bivariate analysis, though. The usual approach is to complete all bivariate analyses according to the logical order set up by your hypotheses or research questions and then begin multivariate analyses. In some instances, you might have bivariate subhypotheses to follow before moving to multivariate.

In all of this, you must describe the results you find. While you will present results in tables, a key maxim is to never let the tables describe the results for you. *Always* discuss what is presented in the tables. A second maxim is to describe and interpret but not thoroughly discuss and draw conclusions. That belongs in the conclusions chapter.

As with the methodology chapter, we now focus on the approach an empirical thesis will take to analysis.

BIVARIATE STATISTICAL ANALYSIS

You want to begin your bivariate analyses in the same order presented by your hypotheses, primarily because you had a logical reason for that

BOX 10-1 HOW DO YOU INTERPRET MEASURES OF ASSOCIATION?

There are three forms of measures of association or correlations:
- PRE measures (Lambda, Uncertainty Coefficient, Gamma, Somers' d),
- Indirect PRE measures (Phi, Spearman's Rho, Pearson's r)
- Non-PRE measures (Cramer's V, Contingency Coefficient, Tau)

All PRE and indirect-PRE measures range from 0 to 1.0 ($\pm$1.0, if at least ordinal).

If at all possible, avoid non-PRE measures.

PRE measures are interpreted as follows:

1. Use the correlational value directly
2. Choose the "asymmetrical" version if you have independent and dependent variables (assuming you have this version available—if not, you would prefer a statistic that does this).
3. State (fill in the underlined words as appropriate for your study) that "(the independent variable) accounts for (correlational value X 100) percent of the variance in (dependent variable). Or, "income accounts for 14 percent of the variance in the delinquency rate."
4. If you have a one-tailed hypothesis (direction), you need to add direction to the statement above: "with an increase/decrease in income resulting in an increase/decrease in the delinquency rate." Whether you use the term "increase" or "decrease" depends on what you predicted.

Indirect PRE measures are simply *squared* to get the proportion of explained variance. After doing that, you follow the model above.

The results of most non-PRE measures can't be compared without having identical circumstances for the relationships you are trying to compare (a *very* rare situation) and even then still may not range from 0 to $\pm$1.0.

order. To reify that approach, it is best to start with a restatement of the first hypothesis and then follow with a test of that approach. In some instances, you can do multiple bivariate tests if the level of measurement of the variable is interval and permits both a continuous and collapsed (tabular) version of the independent and/or dependent variables. Assuming that is possible, a good approach is to do the continuous test first and then the collapsed version. The logic behind this is the continuous version (such as a t-test, analysis of variance, or perhaps a Pearson's r with associated probability) is the "real" test. A collapsed version (such as taking income and recoding it into three categories) is more of an exploration to see if a relationship exists for groups of people rather than individuals (the continuous test).

Less Complex

An example of a simpler version bivariate analysis is seen below. Alexis was interested in testing whether criminal victimization affected fear of crime. She used a standard measure of fear of crime and looked at victimization for any type of crime during the past year. Her write-up of the first part of the analysis looked like this:

> The primary hypothesis was: Victimization by any type of crime will increase an individual's fear of crime. Looking at Table 4-1, it is evident that those who have been a victim of crime during the past year are somewhat more likely to answer that they are afraid to walk within four blocks of their home at night than those who have not been a victim of crime. The difference between the "yes" responses of the two groups is approximately 16.5 percent in favor of victims. Similarly, those who have not been a victim of crime were 12.3 percent more likely to answer "no." The direction of the hypothesis is supported. The Chi-square value was 18.609 with 2 degrees of freedom and a one-tailed probability of $\leq .001$. A probability of this size is statistically significant, therefore the alternative hypothesis is accepted and the null rejected. Victimization affects fear of crime and those who are victimized exhibit more fear of crime.

TABLE 4-1: EFFECT OF VICTIMIZATION ON FEAR OF CRIME

			Afraid to walk four blocks from your home at night?			
			NO	MAYBE	YES	Total
Victim of crime during past year?	No	N	93	115	142	350
		%	26.6%	32.9%	40.6%	100.0%
	Yes	N	33	66	132	231
		%	14.3%	28.6%	57.1%	100.0%
Total		N	126	181	274	581
		%	21.7%	31.2%	47.2%	100.0%

The important parts of this example are that the hypothesis was stated so that it was clear what was being tested, the direction of the hypothesis was kept in mind, the percentages in the relevant table cells were examined, and, finally, the result of the Chi-square test was reported. Alexis even noted that she accepted the alternative hypothesis on the basis of a statistically significant result. While she reported the statistical results in the text, it is also acceptable to record the statistical information either as a footnote under the table or as a separate table. Some would also report a measure of association so as to note the strength of the relationship. If that is desired (and it is not a bad idea because any test of significance is affected by sample size as well as a relationship between the variables), then an appropriate test is reported directly after a significant result. If the result is not significant, there is no reason to report a correlation. Assuming a correlation is desired, Alexis's final statement might have been:

> The uncertainty coefficient was used as a measure of association. A value of .016 indicates that victimization accounts for 1.6 percent of the variation in fear of crime, with an increase in victimization resulting in an increase in fear of crime.

You can see from this statement that a significant result does not necessarily mean the relationship is an important or meaningful one. Having 1.6 percent explained variance suggests that victimization does not affect fear of crime very much—there is more than 98 percent of fear left to be explained. This is the difference between statistical significance and substantive significance. Let's now look at a more complex version of a bivariate analysis.

More Complex

As an example of a dual bivariate analysis with both continuous and collapsed versions of the same variables, we'll use Jamie's thesis, which was focused on testing Travis Hirschi's social control theory. Jamie tested the four elements of the bond one by one against delinquency. We look at the write-up from his section on involvement (measured by the total amount of time spent weekly on school work, in extracurricular activities, and any employment). Delinquency was measured by an index created from a series of self-report items. Note that he does two analyses, one appropriate for the interval nature of his variables (using Pearson's r) and the other as a cross-tabulation (using Chi-square).

> Hypothesis 1 stated "Higher rates of involvement will lead to lower rates of delinquency." In order to test this hypothesis, a Pearson correlation was calculated between the composite involvement variable and the composite delinquency variable. The resulting correlation was $-.519$, with a probability of .001. Because the direction of the relationship was the predicted negative one and the correlation was statistically significant, the hypothesis is supported. Further, involvement explains almost 27 percent of the variance in delinquency.
>
> A crosstabulation of a collapsed version of the involvement/delinquency relationship was also conducted. To facilitate the analysis of the relationship,

both the involvement and delinquency variables were collapsed into three categories of low, medium and high. Each category is comprised of approximately one-third of the sample respondents. Those respondents in the upper third of involvement scores would be expected to be in the lower third of delinquency scores. Conversely, those in the lower third of involvement scores should be in the upper third of delinquency scores. As Table 4-5 demonstrates, that was indeed the case. Almost 51 percent of those with the lowest involvement scores were in the highest delinquency category. Similarly, 57.7% of the upper involvement group had delinquency scores in the lowest third. The direction of the relationships and the significant Chi-square probability ($\leq .001$) therefore continue to support the hypothesis. The strength of this relationship, using Somers' d (d $= -.381$), suggests that involvement accounts for 38.1% of the variance in delinquency, which is a moderately strong relationship.

In this example, Jamie actually did two bivariate tests. First, he looked at the relationship between two continuous variables, rates of involvement and rates of delinquency, using Pearson's correlation coefficient (r) to do that. Because there is no table associated with this test, all he had to do was report the correlation and probability level. Nonetheless, it was a complete bivariate test. Second, Jamie collapsed the variables to see if similarly situated juveniles would, as a group, demonstrate the same relationship. While the second bivariate analysis is not required, it provides another test of the hypothesis, and, if further analyses will be conducted using collapsed variables, it is an important step.

MULTIVARIATE ANALYSES

Controlling for Variables in Tables

While they might sound difficult or complex, multivariate analyses are not necessarily any more difficult to do than most bivariate analyses. The basic

TABLE 4-5: RELATIONSHIP OF INVOLVEMENT WITH SELF-REPORTED DELINQUENCY

			Amount of Self-Reported Delinquency			
			Low	Medium	High	Total
Involvement	Low	N	50	129	183	362
		%	13.8%	35.6%	50.6%	100.0%
	Medium	N	103	177	94	374
		%	27.5%	47.3%	25.1%	100.0%
	High	N	220	112	49	381
		%	57.7%	29.4%	12.9%	100.0%
Total		N	373	418	326	1117
		%	33.4%	37.4%	29.2%	100.0%

difference is that there are at least two variables in addition to the dependent variable. Once you look at a bivariate relationship, a natural question emerges: Is this relationship a real one or is it the product of another variable that affects both the independent and dependent variable? One way to look at this is that variable A and B might vary together because they are both caused by C. Another possibility is that multiple variables affect the dependent variable—something common in real life situations. There is even the likelihood that multiple independent variables "share" some of the same effect—as in the case where education and income, used as dependent variables, obviously are not measurements of two unique concepts. Multivariate statistics can assist in answering these questions for us. Sometimes, though, a multivariate analysis is just an elaboration created by adding another variable to a table.

Using Jamie's thesis testing social control theory, we have an example of adding an additional variable to a table. Because gender traditionally affects relationships between independent variables and delinquency or crime, it is commonly used as a control variable. Jamie described his results as follows:

> A follow-on analysis was conducted to determine if gender affected the relationship. Table 4-10, below, reports the results of this elaboration. As

TABLE 4-10:   RELATIONSHIP OF INVOLVEMENT WITH DELINQUENCY, CONTROLLING FOR GENDER

Gender of Respondent				Self-Reported Delinquency			
				Low	Medium	High	Total
Female	Involvement	Low	N	21	69	62	152
			%	13.8%	45.4%	40.8%	100.0%
		Medium	N	44	98	59	201
			%	21.9%	48.8%	29.4%	100.0%
		High	N	129	72	26	227
			%	56.8%	31.7%	11.5%	100.0%
	Total		N	194	239	147	580
			%	33.4%	41.2%	25.3%	100.0%
Male	Involvement	Low	N	29	60	121	210
			%	13.8%	28.6%	57.6%	100.0%
		Medium	N	59	80	35	174
			%	33.9%	46.0%	20.1%	100.0%
		High	N	91	40	23	154
			%	59.1%	26.0%	14.9%	100.0%
	Total		N	179	180	179	538
			%	33.3%	33.5%	33.3%	100.0%

the hypothesis predicts, those males who have higher involvement (the upper third) are more likely to have the lowest delinquency rates (lower third). Conversely, those with lower involvement are in the upper third of delinquency rates. Moreover, the results are statistically significant, with a chi-square probability $\leq .001$. Looking at females, the same general results occur, though the relationship is not quite as strong as with males (lower third involvement males = 57% as opposed to females with 41%). This result is also statistically significant, with a chi-square probability $\leq .001$. For hypothesis 1, the results indicate full support for the entire sample as well as for male and female subsamples. Further, using Somers' d as an appropriate test of association, the involvement/delinquency relationship is relatively strong for both females (d = $-.358$) and males (d = $-.411$). Thus, with females, involvement explains almost 36 percent of the variance in delinquency and, for males, slightly more than 41 percent. The results are consistent with a position that greater levels of involvement reduces self-reported delinquency.

In this example, gender is introduced as a third variable into the table—this is frequently referred to as "layering" a table. It is possible to add even more variables to a table, but the number of cells quickly creates very small cell sizes, so that is not an advisable procedure. If you notice, Table 4-10 is really two tables, one for females and one for males. Each one cross-tabulates the relationship between involvement and delinquency, but just for those cases in the table. In interpreting layered tables, don't forget that you are looking for the original bivariate relationship, not one with the new variable. Thus, you interpret it by saying, as above, that "for males, involvement affects delinquency." The statistical output should also provide a test of significance for *each* layer of the table (i.e., females and males), because we are not interested in the relationship across the entire set of layers—that is the original bivariate relationship.

As a technical note, calculating a typical inferential statistic (such as Chi-square) for each layer in the table is a bit problematic. There is something called an experiment-wise error rate where an alpha level of p = .05 applies to a *single* test, but when you do *multiple* tests, the .05 level no longer applies. The probability level of all of the tests being .05 or lower is actually higher than .05, so you make mistakes thinking a result is significant when it is really not. When you are only using only a few layers, though, the error is probably not too bad, and you can continue with the usual tabular statistics. If you have an interval level dependent variable and are using multiple t-tests, however, you definitely want to switch to an analysis of variance statistic rather than using multiple t-tests.

Controlling Variables Statistically

Most continuous variable (e.g., income, age) relationships cannot be viewed in a table but, rather, statistically. For instance, an attempt to examine the relationship between income levels and crime rates in large cities would be impossible to decipher in a table, even though you could construct one. Instead, statistics such as Pearson's r are used to see what effect an increment in one variable has on another. Fortunately, controlling for the effect of other variables on such relationships is a well-established practice. Pearson's r generalizes to regression, and there are several forms of regression capable of using multiple variables. Three of the major forms are partial regression (partial r), multiple regression (multiple R), and logistic regression (a form specially designed for binary, or dichotomous, dependent variables). We discuss those briefly below. The statistics text you used in your graduate course will probably have an elementary discussion of at least two of these. For a more thorough discussion of each of these techniques, browse through your library or pick up a copy of one of the books we mention in the chapter sections below.

REGRESSION

Partial Regression

This technique is conceptually simple. The name is derived from "partitioning" variance in the dependent variable by the effects of independent and control variables. For instance, assuming you are interested in the income and crime relationship, there are other factors that might influence the basic relationship, such as proportion of minority representation in a city and average educational level. Both are potentially related to income. On the other hand, if you are using income levels to explain crime rates, you don't want to be using the coeffect of other variables as part of your relationship with crime. Partial regression offers the opportunity to control for (partial out) the effect of both minority representation and education, leaving your basic income/crime relationship independent of those variables. The general effect is analogous to having the A→B relationship minus the effect of C and D variables. Statistical output generates a bivariate r (the original relationship) and a partial r (original relationship minus the effect of the control variables). Here's how this works.

Gina was interested in the effect of unemployment on crime rates. She was able to break out unemployment and crime rate data for zip code areas in her large city by using government databases. The Pearson's r for the unemployment and crime relationship was .0544 with a significant probability of .045. Realizing that unemployment is partially a product of the proportion of workers age eighteen to sixty-five, those not disabled, and educational level, Gina decided to control for the effect of those variables on her bivariate relationship. Her choice of a statistic to do this was partial correlation. She entered the independent, three controls, and dependent variables into a partial regression. The outcome is explained in the table.

Variable	Bivariate r with Crime Rate	Bivariate Prob.*	3rd Order Partial r with Crime Rate	Partial Prob.*
Independent:				
Unemployment rate	.0544	.045	.0424	.098
Controls:				
Workers 18–65	−.0130	.550		
Disabled	−.0418	.103		
Educational level	−.0848	.017		

*One-tailed probability.

The interpretation of the statistical output is that, controlling for three variables (3rd order partial), the relationship between unemployment rate and crime rate changes from .0544, which is statistically significant (p ≤ .05), to .0424. The partial r is no longer significant (p > .05), thus there is no relationship between unemployment and crime once the combined effect of variables representing workers, disabled, and educational level is removed from the original relationship. By the way, even the bivariate "significant" correlation is nothing to get excited about. To interpret r, you square Pearson's r (one of the few statistics that must be squared to get to a PRE approach) to get the proportion of variance "explained" in the dependent variable, and this one is only .0029, or less than 3/10s of one percent of the variance in crime rates. Gina's explanation for these results looked like this:

> The hypothesized relationship between unemployment rates and crime rates was that higher unemployment rates would result in higher crime rates (i.e., a positive relationship). The initial Pearson's r was .0544, and significant (p = .045). Thus, as expected, the relationship was positive. However, various factors potentially affect both unemployment rates and crime rates. Three of those factors, percentage of workers in the population, percentage of disabled in the population, and median educational level were used in a partial regression to get a better estimate of the independent effect of unemployment on crime. The partial r results are reported in Table 4-7. The third order partial r was .0424, a small decrease in the unemployment/crime relationship, but the resulting probability was no longer significant (p = .098). Therefore, controlling for the three variables, the expected effect of unemployment rates on crime rates disappears.

Exactly what gets included in a table of information on partial correlations is a product of preferences. Your chair, or a committee member, may want to see the bivariate relationships between each of the control variables and the independent variable. Third-order partials may also be requested for each of the control variables and the dependent variable, particularly if there is a sense that some other variables "explain" the dependent variable better than your independent variable. Check with your committee to see which pieces of information they prefer, or present them with a couple of variations and ask them to "approve" one for you. And remember, if you get confused by the statistical output, you can ask one of your committee members to help you.

Multiple Regression

If your task is to determine the effect on the dependent variable of a group of independent variables, then multiple regression (R) is usually the technique to use. This approach is very similar to partial regression, and can provide those results also, but focuses on the combined effect of variables. If you are testing multiple independent (or predictor) variables to see what works best, multiple regression is also a good tool to use. Say, for instance, you are interested in testing multiple theories of crime against each other and had only one variable for each theory. In that case you would first look at the bivariate relationships and determine which appeared to be "strongest." Then you would use multiple regression to enter all of the variables into the equation against the dependent variable. There should be two resulting products of interest: the multiple R and information on the individual variables. The R provides the total effect of all variables and, if squared, the proportion of variance you have explained. The individual variable information will tell you what each variable contributed to the entire R and whether it was a significant contribution. A "standardized correlation coefficient," or "Beta" is also available in the individual variable information. That tells you the partial effect of a one-unit increase in an independent variable on the dependent variable. Some researchers like to focus on that as a measure of "strength."

There is one caveat here, though: the variable with the strongest bivariate correlation is automatically entered first, then the one with the remaining largest correlation after removing the effect of the first, and so on. This is *not* the same as a partial correlation—if you want to know the independent effect of each variable you have to ask for partial correlations and then report those. Multiple R can also be used to enter groups of variables together as a block, or as if they were a single variable. This can be done in a stepwise, backward, or forward multiple regression. In these approaches, you can report the change in R-square after each one is entered in the model as the effect of that variable (similar to a partial *r*-square, but in reality a *part* correlation where only those variables in the model to that point are controlled for). We strongly suggest you read something about multiple regression before using this technique. On the web, the UCLA Academic Technology Services's SPSS Web Books are a good source of information for anyone using that statistical package (*http://www.ats.ucla.edu/stat/spss/webbooks/reg/default.htm*). Two inexpensive, but good, books are those by Allison (1998) and Berry and Feldman (1985).

Let's look at an example of stepwise multiple regression. Alicia was testing three criminological theories to see which one best explained bullying in school. She used measures representing social control, self-control, social learning, and anomie theories. Already having done the bivariate tests, she choose to do a stepwise multiple regression as a multivariate test and reported these results.

> Using a stepwise multiple regression, the four theoretical variables are examined for their effect on school bullying. This technique locates all significant variables, but enters them in the equation with bullying in order of their predictive importance. As opposed to the bivariate results, where all four of the theoretical variables were statistically significant, only two of the theoretical variables are significant in the model (Table 4-9). Those two, in order of their importance, were social learning (R of .156, R-square change = .024) and anomie (R of .156, R-square change = .017) for a total R-square of .042. Thus, at least as measured here, social learning and anomie theories do a better job of explaining school bullying than social control and self-control theories. The degree of explanation, however, is less than impressive at 4.2 percent of the variance in bullying. It seems that other variables, or perhaps better measures of the theoretical variables, are needed to better explain school bullying.

Logistic Regression

This technique is very similar to multiple regression, but it allows you to use a binary dependent variable (yes/no, success/failure) because of the way it treats the two extreme ends of an assumed continuum for a binary variable (the use of a natural logrithmic approach rather than a linear one). All you really need to know is that if you have a binary dependent variable and *either* continuous or categorical independent/control variables, you can probably use logistic regression. It is a bit more difficult to interpret than most forms of linear regression, but you can approximate the same information. A statistic called Neglekerke's R-square is almost the same as a multiple R-square. A form of regression coefficient similar to the slope (b) is also available. As with multiple regression, you will probably need to read about logistic regression before using it. A good web source is G. David Garson's web page: *http://www2.chass.ncsu.edu/garson/PA765/logistic.htm*. An inexpensive, good book written by Fred Pampel (2000) can be helpful. Another, but more difficult alternative, by David Hosmer and Stanley Lemeshow (2000) is almost

TABLE 4-9: MULTIPLE REGRESSION OF THEORETICAL VARIABLES WITH SCHOOL BULLYING

Step	Theoretical variables	R	R-Square Change	Beta for Final Model	Probability
1	Social learning	.156	.024	.156	.001
2	Anomie	.205	.042	.132	.001

the "bible" on logistic regression. The following example from the parole recidivism study mentioned earlier should help you in using and interpreting logistic regression.

While the bivariate analysis identified several variables significantly related to success of both males and females on parole, several of those are likely to be related to each other. The analysis below takes the four variables with the highest bivariate correlations from preceding analyses and enters them into two multivariate logistic regressions with parole success as the dependent variable. The two regressions are for females and males, respectively, as the basic research question is whether females have different predictors of parole success than males. The results (Table 4-12) show that all four variables serve as significant predictors for males, with 13.6 percent of the variation in success explained. Females, on the other hand, had only two significant predictors (number of prior arrests and parole release status). However, these two predictors produced 17.6 percent explained variation in success, which was higher than the four variables produced for males. The results for the two predictors were the same across both genders: having 4 or more prior arrests and having a previous parole violation were negatively related to success. For males, being 25 to 30 years old at parole release and being over age 25 were both negatively related to success. From these results, it appears that fewer predictors can be used to predict female recidivism.

TABLE 4-12: BINARY LOGISTIC REGRESSION FOR PREDICTOR VARIABLES AND PAROLE SUCCESS

Predictor and Category	Probability		R^1	
	Females	Males	Females	Males
Age at Release	.1721	.0098	.0000	−.0348
25 to 30	.1721	.0098	.0000	−.0348
Other	****	****	****	****
Age at First Arrest	.4172	.0000	.0000	.0828
Under 18	.2583	.0000	−.0000	−.0859
18 to 25	.2666	.0001	−.0000	−.0572
Over 25	****	****	****	****
Number of Prior Arrests	.0000	.0000	.1621	.1041
0 to 3	****	****	****	****
4 to 14	.0000	.0000	−.1682	−.0969
Over 14	.0002	.0000	−.1377	−.0951
Parole Release Status	.0002	.0000	−.1345	−.1636
New release	****	****	****	****
Parole violator	.0002	.0000	−.1345	−.1636
Constant	.0000	.0000		
Naglekerke R-Square			.176	.136

**** = Contrast category to which all other categories are compared.
Negative signs were assigned from the logit coefficients (b values in SPSS Output).

More statistical results than those discussed earlier are available from logistic regression to allow you to interpret relationships. When categorical variables are used, as in the example above, you can get odds ratios that explain the odds of each category increasing or decreasing the likelihood of being in the critical category of the dependent variable (parole success in the above example). A classification table is also available which provides information on the number of cases correctly classified in either of the two dependent variable categories. Use this latter information with care, as both the percentages correctly classified by using the predictors and the interpretation of those percentages depend on the original percentage split in the dependent variable.

HINTS FOR SPECIAL PARTS OF THE ANALYSIS CHAPTER

Creating Tables and Figures

There are a few guidelines for constructing tables. First, always create a title for the table that clearly indicates what it represents. Second, construct all similar tables in the same way. If you are doing cross-tabulation tables and have an independent variable, you can place them on the side (rows) or on the top (columns) but *do not* switch the location from table to table unless you *want* to make an interpretational mistake (or worse yet, cause one of your committee members to make an interpretational mistake). We personally like to see independent (or predictor) variables on the side of the table, thus creating the rows; but your chair or committee members may have specific preferences. You also need to remember to calculate percentages in a cross-tabulation table the correct way—with the independent variable—so that they total to 100 percent. Failure to do so can result in interpreting differences as real that are nothing more than subsample size differences. We once saw an entire "completed" thesis handed to committee members (this was the first time anyone but the chair had seen it) with all tables percentaged incorrectly. Unfortunately, that also meant that all interpretations were incorrect, and the analysis and conclusions had to be redone. There are enough slings and arrows of outrageous fortune in the thesis process; don't shoot yourself in the foot with your own arrow.

For all tables, of any type, show an example to your chair and then to your committee members. Let them approve what you are doing. This is particularly true of complex tables where there are multiple variables and multiple pieces of information. Graphs and figures are among those with the constructed image representing a high degree of preference. It is especially important to show these to your committee and get approval. Many graphs, particularly those based on data, don't contribute much information beyond that already in tables. Don't let a "pretty graph" get in your way if it really doesn't add information. Keep in mind that you have to describe, in the text, everything in a table, figure, or graph anyway.

Using Variable Names in Text or Tables

When referring to the variables in your analysis, use what they *mean* for their names. Some students have the urge to use the same variable name as the one in the data set they are using. For example, educational level may be listed in the dataset as "edlvl." *Do not* use the data set version; it is merely a product of the requirements of the statistical package you or someone else anticipated using. In the past, most variable names were limited to eight characters for technical reasons. Thus, everything was abbreviated. It was, and is, not uncommon to find variable names that are merely references to questions or items on an instrument (e.g., Q12a for question 12a).

It is not particularly helpful, and certainly not very clear, to say something like "EDLVL was significantly related to JVNLDEL." Or, in normal language, "Educational level was significantly related to juvenile delinquency." Even in the tables you will construct, do not use abbreviated data set variable names. Remember, the task is to be clear in what you are writing; if your writing isn't clear, then rewrite!

Writing Up Your Findings

One of the biggest mistakes in most thesis drafts is to create a vast number of tables and then say "the information can be found in Table 4-12." *Always* describe the important information from a table and interpret it. For two reasons, you never want readers to have to look at tables and interpret them without any assistance. First, it takes them away from the text itself and you lose continuity. Second, something you have seen after carefully examining the table may not be evident to readers taking a quick glance, and you risk not having them understand your interpretations.

Another mistake novice researchers commonly make is to engage in elaborate and speculative interpretations as they present the results of each analysis. Save this for your conclusions chapter; if you do it in the analysis chapter, you will find yourself struggling to write the conclusions chapter. Moreover, elaborate interpretations simply get in the way at this point. You are describing the results so everyone will know what they are, not defending an interpretation. This is particularly the case for qualitative research efforts. You want to accurately portray the situations, interactions, relationships, and in situ meanings—that will be more than enough content for a single chapter.

Finally, in writing up analytical results you need to be detailed. It is okay to repeat what is in the tables. Say precisely what test is being used, what (if any) problems are encountered, what the figures in the table mean, whether the results are statistically significant, and, if so, what the strength of the relationship is. Don't worry about sounding repetitive—just be accurate and detailed in your reportage.

Using Quotes from Interviews

There are two general approaches to using quotes from interviews in your data analysis. Which of the two you choose may be a style decision or a matter of personal preference. One is the very literal approach used by some ethnographers. They report verbatim what is said and answered including "hmmms" and "errrrrs" to give the reader an exact replica of the transcription. It is often done when the writer feels that exact manner of delivery, the need to prompt, and the speakers' indecisiveness are important pieces of information that lead us to better understanding of the subjects. As the following example shows, Camille (Gibson, 2002, p. 229) was able to capture the hesitancy and struggle in her young subjects conversations as well as the interviewers interjections to encourage their elaboration by use of the verbatim method.

R:	How many classes did you pass?
EVAN:	Aaammm everything except physics
R:	Oh, you passed everything except physics?
EVAN:	Yeah.
R:	What was the problem with physics?
EVAN:	It's like, ok. I don't think it's really hard. It's just, some of the concepts I don't understand.
R:	Unnhuh
EVEN:	And it's like, something like in other subjects I get the concepts but physics—it's like math and science mixed together.
R:	Ummhuh
EVAN:	So, it's kinda hard you know.

If it is appropriate, some interviewers will use tape recordings and transcription services to allow the degree of detail you see in the example dialogue. However, the cost of this method may make it less practical for some research projects. And, as you would anticipate, there are also situations where it may not be appropriate to tape an interview—such as with offenders who are less trusting or persons who may be disclosing knowledge of criminal events that you are treating as "confidential." This method then relies more on notes and recall and, in many instances, takes more license with what was said. Often there is some cleaning of the material for the sake of efficiency, especially when it is perceived that the point will not be altered and the value to the reader will not be diminished in the process. There is more selective cutting and pasting of the interview material, comments from different people might be strung together to address a point being discussed, and the prompting or clarifications of the interviewer may be removed. The quotes may be shorter and interrupted more often with narrative explanations to fill in context for the reader. Thus, the same conversation recorded by Camille might be presented as the following: "When asked about his failing grade in physics, Evan explained, 'I don't think it's really hard. It's just, some of the concepts I don't understand. . . . it's like math and science mixed together so it's kinda hard you know.'"

The advantage of this method is that it not only streamlines the material and may make it easier for the reader to get through but also makes it easier to focus on some subtle points, such as Evan saying "it's not hard" but then contradicting that in the subsequent statement with the fact that it *is* hard.

When presenting material from her interactions with the homeless, Judith culled through the many transcripted pages of comments offered by her subjects and organized their themes according to the issues suggested by the theorists she was critiquing. Thus, her questions and the answers were tied directly to the literature, which she had reviewed earlier. As she did, it is helpful to present the arguments to the reader in a systematic way so that they recognize previously discussed themes. For example, in the literature review chapter Judith summarizes work by Ferrell (2001, 2005) who argues that the homeless are forced out of the area of urban renewal by police; harassed, criminalized, and disadvantaged by the change. In interviewing her subjects, "Mary" and "Sally" she asks directly about this and provides their responses.

> Sally and Mary will agree that they have both benefitted from the "muker-de-mucks" moving back into the cities. "When Houston's downtown became vacant, there was only us homeless down here. No one had money and there were no fancy restaurants—which means there were no garbage cans filled with uneaten food. . . . Life is good down here . . . nobody bothers you, the law don't care whether we are dead or alive and I can sleep wherever and whenever I feel like it."

Judith then proceeds to introduce case after case of homeless individuals whom she personally interviewed and includes comments that let readers see the contradictions between their views and the allegations found in some of the literature. At this same time Judith also compares the similarities in her findings to another writer who earlier interviewed some homeless people in New York City.

> Bernard, one of Toth's (1993) tunnel dwellers, also comments on the availability of food after responding to the author's inquiry about eating arrangements, "They throw away the cream of the cream in New York, which makes scavenging relatively productive." (p. 103).

In this way, Judith has provided the reader with a clear picture of how her findings are supported by similar works in this area, but are disputed, to some degree, by theorists studying the issues more broadly.

SUMMARY

In writing an analysis chapter, whether it is a product of an empirical study, a theoretical and logical analysis, or a qualitative study, the key ingredient is detail. You want to describe everything you did very thoroughly and leave no doubts in the mind of readers about your analyzed "data." Make sure all similar parts of the analysis are standardized—that is, you have done them the same way. This is especially important in the case of tables found in an empirical study. Explain yourself whenever you think it might be necessary. But *don't* engage in explaining what it all means. Explanations and interpretations belong in the conclusions chapter, so let's go there now.

REFERENCES

ALLISON, P. (1998). *Multiple regression: A primer.* Newbury Park, CA: Pine Forge Press.

BERRY, W., and FELDMAN, S. (1985). *Multiple regression in practice.* Newbury Park, CA: Sage.

FERRELL, J. (2001). *Tearing down the streets : Adventures in urban anarchy.* New York: Palgrave Macmillan.

FERRELL, J. (2005). *Empire of scrounge: Inside the urban underground of dumpster diving, trash picking, and street scavenging.* New York: New York University Press.

GIBSON, C. (2002). *Being real. The student-teacher relationship and African-American male delinquency.* NY: LFB Scholarly.

HOSMER, D. W., Jr. and Lemeshow, S. (2000). *Applied logistic regression,* 2d ed. New York: Wiley-Interscience.

PAMPEL, F. (2000). *Logistic regression : A primer.* Newbury Park, CA: Sage.

TOTH, J. (1993). *The mole people: Life in the tunnels beneath New York City.* Chicago, IL: Chicago Review Press.

Conclusions, Implications, and Limitations

THE END VERSUS THE BEGINNING

Your writing at the end of the thesis has a different purpose and, consequently, a different tone than that in the initial chapters. One of the differences is the level or depth of explanation in which you engage. The background material and development used in the early chapters is not repeated here. Any summary or reference to the problem is not as broad here as it was initially. In the conclusions, your focus should be only on the more specific issue of the study.

For example, the following thesis undertakes the topic of patrol officer attitudes toward mandatory arrest for domestic battering. The broad-to-narrow approach used in the first chapter to arrive at the thesis topic is not necessary in the final chapter.

(Chapter 1) Problem Statement

While domestic battering has long been considered a social problem subject to various forms of intervention and prevention, only more recently have punitive and legal. . . . Statistics on domestic homicide show early patterns of violent interactions. . . .

Current prosecution trends, case tracking and criminal reporting have focused attention on. . . .

(In the Discussion and Conclusions Chapter)

Both media and the public put pressure on police to respond to domestic violence. . . . To date, police responses to domestic violence, particularly mandatory arrests, have shown specific positive effects when applied to certain demographic. . . . therefore, patrol officer attitudes toward the utility of arrest in domestic violence incidence are critical to the effective. . . .

As this example shows, the initial chapter has many of the statistics and facts that emphasize the size and scope of the problem and its importance today. In the final chapter the author simply directs the reader to that portion of the topic examined in the thesis and the specific issue chosen. The author does not need to return to the earlier discussion of domestic violence in general, but should immediately begin with the narrow focus of police responses to domestic violence.

In the next example, a thesis evaluating legislative responses to drunken driving demonstrates the same technique.

(Chapter 1) Problem Statement

Each year drunken driving accidents claim the lives of. . . . Insurance estimates are that drunken driving costs each American over $. . . . Advocate groups such as Mothers Against Drunk Driving. . . . A wide range of approaches from education to punishment. . . .

(In the Discussion and Conclusions Chapter)

Various legislative initiatives aimed at drunk driving have been explored with mixed results, often because of the difficulty in isolating effects of individual changes in statutes. Two of the most commonly pursued options have been. . . .

Understanding the tone and the purpose of the final chapter will make it easier to write. At all times you should consider that the reader has just recently been through the earlier discussions and only requires some final insights into what it all means. As much as possible avoid repeating material from your introduction, literature review, and analysis. At this point, you should be mapping out your final chapter with your chair. Depending on the nature of your research, and the preferences of your committee, any of the following sections may be part of your final chapter.

THE SUMMARY SECTION

In some cases, particularly where your document is long, consists of more than the usual number of chapters, or involves complex analyses, you may want to include a summary of your thesis in the final chapters. When the readers may have been distracted by multiple methodologies, conflicting findings, or shifts between several important issues, it may be worthwhile to very briefly (within two paragraphs or so) recap the problem, the previous approaches to the problem, your study and methodology, and the research focus. After that, a brief statement of your findings should capture only the most salient and meaningful of the outcomes. This becomes the launching point of your conclusions.

Examples from several different types of summaries are provided here. As the first one below demonstrates, your summary should only briefly highlight the major framework for the research, thus serving as a guide to the person who may skip to the end and only read the conclusions. In example one, Dey Zamora (2004, pp. 83–84) wrote:

SUMMARY OF THE STUDY AND RESULTS

The identification of key risk factors that may predict juvenile delinquency is necessary in order to develop techniques for best practices in prevention and intervention. Failure in academic achievement and juvenile delinquency have been found to co-occur and have also been labeled by several studies to be among the most common and influential factors that underlie the incidence of youth crime. It would be imperative then, that we explore the association and strength of the relationship between these two factors which was the objective of this study.

Using secondary data collected from county juvenile justice charter schools and the probation department, this researcher was able to develop 85 different variables that were used to measure the strength of the relationship between academic achievement and delinquency. The hypotheses analyzed here also introduced other common risk factors for delinquency including age, grade level, race and family income to see what role, if any, they played in that relationship.

The data provided evidence that low levels of academic achievement were related to high levels of involvement in juvenile delinquency. These findings were consistent with both the theory and the studies previously presented. Though these findings were not as strong as those in the literature, they did coincide with the concepts described in social control and anomie theories. Therefore, it can be assumed that frustrations encountered by juveniles who have difficulties in school often result in the lack of formation of bonds to the educational institution and therefore, a lack of legitimate opportunities that may lead to involvement in delinquency.

As this example indicates, Deyanira is able to explain her rationale for the study, what she did, and what she found, in three very succinct paragraphs. She is now able to concentrate on interpreting what her results mean and making suggestions for future research on this issue. At this point, she will begin to write in a much more "thinking out loud" mode. She can suggest what may now be needed, what the effects of implementation might be, and the costs and benefits of various approaches suggested by her findings. The rest of her writing will be much more "what if" in style, elaborating on the various possibilities—though the writer must be careful to defend her suggestions as being supported by her research, or by previous research, and having some obvious merit and logic to them.

In summary, then, the summary is a very specific component that simply and clearly reiterates for the reader what the study did and what the study found or did not find. It is only in the next sections, then, the discussion and conclusions that tell the reader what those findings mean.

THE DISCUSSION SECTION

The use of a discussion section usually signifies a broader, more general coverage of topics and issues raised by an in-depth study. It may be a good place to cover other issues that arose during the process of the research—those not directly related to policy or further research implications. Oftentimes this section is used with a theoretical thesis or one where the focus of the findings does not lend itself directly to policy, legislation, or agency administration. The use of a discussion section may also be appropriate when there were no clear findings from the research or mixed findings. The author may take the reader through some possible explanations for why the results leaned a certain way or failed to lean at all. In some cases, the author may want to discuss how limitations in the data affected the outcome, rather than in a separate section on "limitations of the findings." For example, in her discussion, Deirdre explained how the use of official crime statistics or census data may have impacted the outcome and how data gathered from other sources may be more useful for illustrating various theoretical constructs.

For his thesis John conducted a systematic review of the survey methodologies and response rates for questionnaires sent to police administrators over the past twenty years. In his final chapter, he commented on the lack of details about the way surveys were conducted so that readers could assess the viability of the various strategies relative to return rates. He explains (Legg, 2004, p. 36)

> Discovered in this systematic review was the exclusion of several of the variables critical to this analysis. For example, while virtually all provided the number of surveys distributed and the return rate, the specifics of the use of cover letters, letters of support, incentives were not mentioned. It can only be surmised that either during editing these variables were not considered central to the research at hand, and therefore were removed or they were not included by the author. It may be that while return rates are deemed essential, how they were obtained or enhanced is not considered critical. The appeal, therefore, to include complete and intact methodological procedures, at least in footnotes, would go a long way toward answering the many questions that still exist about improving survey response rates.

As you can see, John discusses some reasons why he may have encountered the difficulties that he did. His writing is detailed and thoughtful, carrying the reader through some possible explanations and some ideas about how these difficulties could be resolved.

THE CONCLUSIONS SECTION

Conclusions are not to be confused with a summary or a repetition of the findings or even discussions but are more generalized extrapolations from that material that guides the reader through what those findings mean. Writing conclusions is a creative process that calls for the author to think beyond just what was found and to suggest a range of possible and very honest interpretations of those findings.

At this point it may be appropriate to generalize how your findings compared with past research if you have not done so already in your summary. As Lois (Dewey, L. 2005, p. 65–66) wrote

> Previous literature on generational attitudes regarding jury service revealed that as citizens age and get better employment positions at a higher rate of pay and better benefits, they have more faith in the judicial system and report for jury service they had ignored at an earlier age. This study supports many of those findings as it is likely that greater household income results in more favorable attitudes toward jury service. This study also supports previous literature suggesting childcare is a contributing factor for citizens who do not report for jury duty.

In a historical thesis Jim is able to conclude that even though the jury's verdict of acquittal was particularly distressing for the family of the police chief gunned down in a crowded restaurant, it is perhaps not unlike other controversial trials. He tells us (Dewey, J. 2005, p. 61):

> There have always been examples of jury decisions which have, to say the least, been unexpected. Longtime Texas attorney Joe Shannon, Chief Prosecutor for the Tarrant County District Attorney's office advised against generalizing about what Texas juries are likely to believe. Still, he conceded admiration for a good lawyer's finely crafted narrative may be part of the state culture. Wealthy defendants, high-profile lawyers and Texas juries have teamed up for plenty of surprise verdicts over the years resulting in tabloid bonanzas and made-for-TV movies.

In some cases, the conclusions (i.e., what the findings mean) will lead the reader logically to the next section—the implications. The conclusions set the stage for what should then be done, or why we should expect that what you have been doing may or may not work.

Organizing your conclusions will help the reader focus on those specific outcomes you found to be most important for your study. For example, David elaborated on three major consequences (mission creep, mission distortion, and organizational lag) he found in police/probation officer partnerships and spent a few pages highlighting their characteristics and how to address them.

Making your conclusive statements clear is an important goal. Be prepared to state whether something had a positive or negative impact, whether variables were related, or whether attitudes or values had changed over the course of the study period. Be sure to tell the reader exactly what the findings mean, in as careful a language as you can. It is possible to be guarded and cautious in your wording without being obscure and confusing.

IMPLICATIONS FOR POLICY

Implications for policy can be either macro- or microlevel ones. Macrolevel implications would be things the government could do in general, such as laws that would affect everyone, or attempts to change attitudes, values, and priorities. Policy implications more on the microlevel would be localized effects, such as changes in agency procedures, budgeting, and staffing, or regulations and restrictions as suggested by your research. For example, a microlevel implication of a study on the use of mounted patrol officers in one police agency might be the restructuring of officer's shifts, a more centralized stable facility, or the use of single officer patrols. If employment of mounted patrol was found to be cost-effective and popular with the public, a macrolevel suggestion might be the implementation of mounted patrols in cities that had not considered them before, or their experimental use in a broader range of services such as new homeland security functions and traditional vehicle or bicycle patrol areas.

In the policy implications section of the thesis, you should draw specifically from your findings; do not suggest changes that are not directly implied by your results. The implications should be natural, and logical ideas should stem from your research. As a test of a potential logical implication, ask yourself, "Would this be obvious to an unbiased reader?" If the answer is "yes," then you have probably not engaged in overreach.

In the conclusion section of her thesis on the off-duty employment of police, Valerie (Krizan, 2004) argued that detailed, written, legally informed policies were necessary. More specifically, in her policy implications she discussed examples of what those policies might look like and what they would cover. Her outline of the section on policy implications looked like this:

Policy Implications

Model Policies on Extra Employment
Imposition of Sanctions on Officers who Violate Policy
Suggestions for Best Practices
  Prepare Detailed Off-Duty Policies
  Mandatory Extended Training
  Hold-Harmless and Indemnification Agreements
  Shared Liability Agreements
  Ongoing Agency Oversight
  Mandatory Alternative Dispute Resolution
  Proactive Involvement in Defensive Court Strategies
  Proposed Changes in Enabling Legislation and Tort Reform

Here, as in other parts of the final chapter, an author's careful choice of words is often the difference between reasonable findings and easily rejected ones. Authors should rely on words such as "may," "could be," and "in some cases" because they constitute accepted scholarly language and are more likely to stand up to challenge. Overstatement is dangerous in many ways. Examples of careful phrasing look like this (Eith, 2005, p. 139): "Middle schools may help to foster the student-school bond by reducing school enrollment." And "while schools may take a 'get tough' approach to discipline infractions, this may not be the most effectively policy to foster bonding among the students." Notice how the author uses terms like "may help," "may take," and "may not be the most effective." These terms, and others, help couch the findings in a suggestive sense that is more likely to draw debate and less likely to draw criticism.

Finally, writers must resist the urge to go beyond the limits of their study or suggest implications that are not a natural extension of the thesis findings. One of the ways to redirect discussion from conclusions implied in your particular work, and those that are not, is to include a section on how additional topics and related ideas may be handled in future research.

IMPLICATIONS FOR RESEARCH

In this section, you should be able to comment on additional research that would provide information relevant to the topic under discussion. This would be either by furthering the work begun here or, if the findings of the thesis did not seem to indicate a fruitful line of inquiry, directing the readers toward a different set of variables, methods, or analytical schemes to uncover potentially meaningful evidence. The implications for research could identify further elaboration of constructs involved in your research, the resolution of any unclear or conflicted areas identified in your analysis, or the use of larger, more inclusive data sets.

In this part of the thesis, writers often will point out deeper or more detailed analyses that only received cursory examination in their study. This was the case for Lorraine in her study of young parole violators, as she indicates (Samuels, 2001, p. 53–54):

> In this study, no differentiation was made between "types" of offenses except to label them new (i.e., not a violation) and violent. Therefore future research could look closely at types of offenses and to examine them by different age categories. It would be interesting to see whether the specific offenses committed after release by young offenders differs from older parolees.

Lorraine goes on to explain that critics of juvenile transfers to adult court often fear that youth learn and develop more advanced criminal skills from periods of incarceration. She suggests that this could be tested by analyzing offenses by age and varying periods of confinement through parole violation data. Thus, she is able to tie future research to current theoretical and policy-oriented arguments.

After discussing the various contributions to criminology made by a select group of early African American sociologists, Dalila (Mebane, 2002, p. 62) called for more integration of the work of these authors, as well as other African American theorists.

> The work of African American writers can easily be integrated into existing criminological theory while still preserving their unique features and contributions. The inclusion of this work will strengthen the impact of mainstream theory by demonstrating support across race and economic levels. . . . These theories

should be examined, evaluated and tested in the same manner as the mainstream theories.

While Dalila's recommendations for future research are quite broad, indicating changes in the way we have been conducting criminological research overall, some recommendations are very specific, as in the case below dealing with the education of juvenile offenders (Zamora, 2004, p. 90).

> Though many previous studies have answered questions about the relationship between academic achievement and delinquency, the focus should now be on the nuances of that relationship. Approaches should more closely examine juveniles who attend alternative schools versus regular schools, youth with incarcerated parents, those whose parents have had their parental rights terminated, or youth who were previously identified as "at risk."

LIMITATIONS OF THE INTERPRETATIONS AND IMPLICATIONS

Remarks about limitations of interpreting the research or drawing inferences from it should be brief. You are simply acknowledging potential sources of error or guarding from a reader's misunderstanding the significance of the work. In some cases you may simply make some generalized statements addressing the scope of the work in general, perhaps with a cautionary note that the work is preliminary or exploratory.

As David Murphy (2005, p. 164) wrote, "These findings, although preliminary and offered with the usual cautions and caveats, are intended to inform the decisions of line officers and policy-makers as they attempt to manage the challenges associated with the development of productive and professionally responsible working relationships between the police and probation officers."

You also could more specifically remind the reader that the methodological weaknesses discussed earlier (such as with sample size or data collection) would also have ramifications for the interpretation of findings. For instance, many theses are based on nonrandom samples and—at least somewhere in the work—readers should be cautioned about generalizing from the findings. Your chair will discuss with you the best place for such disclaimers.

Often your limitations will focus on the specific nature of your analyses and the fact that you did not examine all possible intervening or mitigating factors, nor should you have been expected to do so. In a study comparing the characteristics of inmates with high, low, and no disciplinary infractions, Gentry (1987, p. 63–64) explained, "This research is limited in that it does not account for the relationship between the inmate and correctional officer and ignores the situational factors surrounding each incident." His explanation considers that other factors may have accounted for the differences, even though the focus of his thesis was simply, and logically, that differences between the inmates accounted for differences in infraction rates. The author's comment was merely a way of saying that, while he or she has examined the most likely and direct possible influences and controlled for some of the external influences (by using one single prison unit at one point in time), there are still other factors that might change the results. This is not a negative reflection on the design used, nor the scope or breadth of the student's work, but instead a hallmark of scientific inquiry—nothing is ever "proven," and no research is never definitive.

THE BIG "SO WHAT?"

Arguably, your first and last chapters are the most important in the thesis. First, you must convince the reader that the study is a worthwhile endeavor. Second, you must be able to articulate your findings and convince the reader that they are meaningful. When you finish writing, you should be certain that you have addressed their skepticism or you might receive the infamous academic "so what?"

The organization of your ideas and the clarity of your writing are the most important features of the first and final chapters. Consequently, you will need to spend a considerable amount of time deciding exactly what it is you want to say and the best way to say it. While the tendency of many students is to simply rush through this last chapter and "get it over with," it is also important to remember that this is the one part of your thesis most likely to be read by others.

The construction of an outline for this last chapter is a valuable tool for the timely and meaningful completion of this chapter. By consulting with your committee on the anticipated contents of your conclusions and implications before you begin writing, you will save time in revisions later. Your committee members are likely to have more specific expectations for this chapter, relative to the others, so it is imperative that you know what those are at an early stage.

REFERENCES

Dewey, J. (2005). *The shooting of Deputy Chief William E. Murphy.* Houston, TX: Unpublished masters' thesis, University of Houston–Downtown.

Dewey, L. (2005). *Juror "no shows": Examining the lack of citizen response to jury summons and its effects on jury representativeness.* Houston, TX: Unpublished masters' thesis, University of Houston–Downtown.

Eith, C. A. (2005). *Delinquency, schools and the social bond.* New York: LFB Scholarly.

Gentry, H. M. (1987). *A comparison of the chronic rule violator, the occasional rule violator and non-violator in the Texas Department of Corrections.* Huntsville, TX: Unpublished masters' thesis, Sam Houston State University.

Krizan, V. (2004). *Legal issues of police off-duty employment.* Houston, TX: Unpublished masters' thesis, University of Houston–Downtown.

Legg, J. P. (2004). *A systematic review of research surveying police administrators between 1980 and 2003.* Houston, TX: Unpublished masters' thesis, University of Houston–Downtown.

Mebane, D. (2002). *Integrating African-American criminology.* Prairie View, TX: Unpublished masters' thesis, Prairie View A&M University.

MURPHY, D. (2005). *Making police-probation partnerships work.* New York: LFB Scholarly Publishing.

SAMUELS, L. (2001). *An analysis of young parolees in comparison to their parole cohorts.* Prairie View, TX: Unpublished masters' thesis, Prairie View A&M University.

ZAMORA, D. (2004). *Academic achievement and delinquency: A study of detained youth in Harris County.* Houston, TX: Unpublished masters' thesis, University of Houston–Downtown.

Section Four
THE FINAL DEFENSE AND BEYOND

The chapters in this section are practical ones. The focus is on helping the student to understand the final stages of the thesis process and best prepare for the thesis defense. In addition, there is life beyond the thesis for some students. As a result, we suggest ways to continue the work on a thesis into scholarly presentations, and even publication.

Chapter Twelve assists the student in finalizing the thesis document and preparing it for formal submission to the university. There are several additional elements that need to be constructed at this time, including a table of contents, an abstract, lists of tables, and a formal acknowledgments page, if you so desire.

This chapter also discusses some of the ways to best prepare for the defense. It offers a number of suggestions based on the type of research done, the strengths of the student, and the preferences of the committee. There are a number of small tasks to be done at this point to ready the document for submission. While the finishing touches are applied to your thesis, it is time to prepare for the final defense. Using many of the same strategies as in the prospectus defense and learning from that experience, it is possible to make this important presentation less stressful and more interesting for attendees.

Finally, in Chapter Thirteen, the student is given a brief orientation toward the use and continued development of the thesis research. Because the thesis is an academic work based in traditional formats, you will need to do revisions, edits, and reformatting in order to further develop your work toward a paper presentation or an article.

12

THE FINAL DOCUMENT AND THESIS DEFENSE

THE DOCUMENT

At the final stage of your thesis, you will no doubt be tired of reading the document and may find it difficult to detect errors due to your familiarity with the work. Taking some time away from the document may help you to come back with a fresh eye for the proofreading phase. As explained earlier, proofreading will either involve you making separate passes through the work looking for different types of errors and corrections or the willingness of your trusted academic peers to look over the thesis for you. Keep in mind that this document will become part of your college library's permanent collection and that in the years ahead many interested patrons may be reading through your work.

The last task for the thesis document is the preparation of the front material. Check with your committee for their expectations as to what should be included in the front material and any specifications they may have for the final preparation of the manuscript. Be aware that there may be deadlines for submission of the thesis prior to graduation, and time may be short. Therefore, careful preparation of the final copy of your thesis with attention to all of the format details is critical.

Proofreading Checklist

One of the best ways to deal with the more mundane parts of the thesis, and in particular proofreading, is to prepare a checklist of items that must be done. Some departments may have these already prepared, so ask your graduate coordinator if one exists. If not, try working from this list.

- Ensure that you have proper **line spacing** throughout. Usually that means three spaces after each section before the new subheading and two spaces after each new subheading. In some instances it is necessary to go in and manually override a setting for spacing in order to insert three lines where there are normally two. The sooner you have the correct spacing in place, the more accurate will be your corresponding page numbering.
- Check all **margins** to make sure they match the requirements for your university or department. Margins of 1.5 inches on all four sides of the page are common, but do not assume these dimensions are correct.
- Check to make sure that all legal cases, book titles, and legislative acts are **italicized**.
- Visit all **Web sites** one last time to guarantee that they are still valid.
- Read through once to verify that each citation listed in the text is also in the bibliography with the corresponding publication date, particularly where multiple works of a single author are used. Make sure that any use of et al. in your citations is filled in with the correct sequence of coauthors' names in the bibliography.
- Each **bibliographic reference** should be complete according to your style of citation, whether it be APA or any other style. This means that a book should not be missing the city of publication or a newspaper article should not be missing the entire day, month, and year the article appeared.
- **Check for widows and orphans**. Make sure that pages break where you intend them to using the printing format that you intend to use for your final version.
- **Read through each table** carefully checking for plus and minus signs and alignment of columns. Re-add numbers in the columns for correct totals, and make sure that the in-text reference to that table or figure is correct and includes the appropriate number. The most common system of **numbering tables and charts** is to have them numbered sequentially according to the chapter numbers. This means that the first table in Chapter 4 would be Table 4-1. The first figure in that chapter would be Figure 4-1. Using the chapter numbers as a reference helps to organize the materials in a way that is more easily adjusted in revisions, and it keeps the numbers from appearing too large.
- Ensure that **page numbering** is appropriate. Though you may have stored the chapters in separate files, you will need to go in and set page numbering to run consecutively. This is usually easiest if you simply embed the command to start numbering at a certain page number at the beginning of each file rather than attempt to create a superfile of the entire document (there is also a way to create chapter links in your word processor—if you want to do this, check the help index in your program). This will also make it easier to do any typographical edits after the defense and before your final printing on special paper.
- Finally, in almost all cases it is best to avoid the use of **running heads**. Running heads, as the American Psychological Association (APA) manual

will tell you, were created to avoid confusion, when years ago journal editors received hundreds of articles at once and may have had many papers spread over their desks. Unless your committee members have so many papers in the editing process that pages might get confused, there is little need for the level of identification a running head provides in a thesis.

The Abstract

The abstract will be placed in the very front of your manuscript after the title page and before your table of contents. Thus it will not have a page number, as page numbering does not begin until after the table of contents.

Unlike an abstract for an article that is usually about 200 words, your thesis abstract will be approximately one page (double spaced) or about 400–500 words. The tone is general and usually written in the past tense. The content should very succinctly cover the research issue, what you did and why, what you found, and what it means. Leave out specifics like those details that would require citations and, in most cases, any references to numerical findings. Remember the purpose of the abstract is to allow the reader (researcher) to skim through your thumbnail sketch to see if topic fits their search/needs. Thus, your synopsis should condense your findings for someone briefing all throughout the literature.

Page 000 demonstrates an effective abstract from Julie Coon (2007). Notice that it is brief, to the point, and captures the essence of the work.

Another example of an abstract is on page 000, this time from a study that examined the use of warrants of outstanding charges, or detainers, on prison inmates testing conflict theory.

Table of Contents

Your table of contents should be constructed to follow headings and subheadings throughout the work. The example on page 000 is the first page of Susan's table of contents. Note the tabs set in for subheadings and that all entries have page numbers set flush right with dot leaders.

Once you have assembled all of your headings, subheadings, and sub-subheadings in the table of contents, read through it carefully to make sure the order still seems logical and provides the best flow. This is the last time to make any decisions about restructuring the material. Sometimes the sequencing of the material is much easier to see when it is in this abbreviated table format. Go over your final version with your chair one last time to ensure that he or she is comfortable with your chronology as well.

Front Material

The front material is anything that precedes the first page of the text. This usually includes the title page, signature page, abstract, and acknowledgments. As a rule, only materials following the table of contents are numbered. Any

AN EXAMPLE OF AN ABSTRACT

ABSTRACT

Crime and violence in schools continues to concern the nation. Federally sponsored projects have examined school problems and described available security technologies. These studies have also suggested how security products should be used and their possible advantages and disadvantages. There has been a lack of information concerning what security technologies are being used and by what types of schools. This study uses a national sample of public schools to answer three major research questions: (1) What security technologies are most commonly used by schools? (2) What school and contextual level factors are associated with the level of security technology use? (3) Is security technology use in schools better explained by school problems or other factors? The results of this research suggest that there is variation in the level of security product use among schools. Marking/identifying school property, lighting, telephones, or duress alarms in classrooms, and burglar alarm systems are among the most common technologies used by schools. Generally, schools that are large, at the secondary level, with many safety rules and procedures, with high rates of school crime/disorder, with high levels of police and community presence, located in high crime neighborhoods, Southern, and urban schools use more security products. Interestingly, school wealth is not a significant predictor of technology use. Further, school and contextual characteristics are better than school crime/disorder as predictors of security technology adoption in

AN EXAMPLE OF AN ABSTRACT

ABSTRACT

The use of the detainer in correctional settings is the result of a technologically and legally sophisticated criminal justice system. The detainer has become the primary method of regulating additional charges on incarcerated offenders. For the most part, detainers represent criminal warrants from other counties, states, or the federal government, but they may also be civil orders such as those filed by the Immigration and Naturalization Service. This study examines the use of the detainer within a conflict framework. Past treatments of the prison by conflict theorists have been general and ideological, and little attempt has be made to explore and critique policies based on administrative data. An analysis was conducted of all detainers currently in the Department of Corrections. Characteristics of the inmates' prison experience focused on their criminal history and current prison status. Comparisons of inmates with and without detainers and between inmates with various types of detainers were made to determine whether there was support for conflict propositions regarding detainers. Though there is no direct finding that detainers were used more often against blacks, the inclusion of alien inmates under the punitive effects of criminal detainers may be unwarranted. When analyzing the types of crimes for which detainers were placed, there appears to be a greater number of public order crimes than normally found in convictions being served. This indicates that misdemeanor charges follow the inmate into prison and cause additional, secondary punishment. Finally, while most detainers appear to be placed and removed in a timely fashion, those that remain unprosecuted for years may do so because of neglect and the absence of an effective administrative policy regulating detainers.

AN EXAMPLE OF A TABLE OF CONTENTS

TABLE OF CONTENTS

Chapter 1 Introduction...1

  Overview of DWI Today 2

  Significance of the Study..7

  Statement of the Research Problem 9

Chapter 2 Literature Review...11

  Theoretical Framework 12

    The Concept of Deterrence 14

    Social Learning Theory...19

    Cognitive Behavioral 24

  Program Initiatives...27

    Interlock Devices 27

    Alcoholics Anonymous 30

    Victim Impact Panels...34

    DWI Education Classes 37

    A Notebook Program...39

  Summary of Results from the Literature Review.......................41

Chapter 3 Methodology 42

  The Setting..42

  Data...43

  Sample...46

  Variables...47

    Content of DWI Articles 47

    Type of Article..48

    Source of Article 48

    Relation to Alcohol..48

pages that come between the table of contents and the first page of the text usually have small Roman numerals (i, ii, iii) and not Arabic numerals (1, 2, 3). Your table of contents may start with a list of tables and a list of figures that will be numbered sequentially with small roman numerals.

In this case, the beginning of your table of contents would look like this:

List of Tables i
List of Figures ii
Chapter One Introduction 1

Acknowledgments

Most students are inclined to compose a short statement of acknowledgments. Traditionally, they thank their committee members, any additional faculty members or professional contacts who may have supplied data, access to interviewees, edited draft material, or contributed to the project in any meaningful way. It may also be appropriate to briefly thank family or friends who supported you during the thesis or graduate school period. However, it is important to keep the content short and professional. Again, it should be stressed that the thesis will be a permanent part of your library's collection and comments that are too personal or esoteric should be avoided.

> **Do:** I would like to thank my committee members Dr. Jeff Ferrell and Dr. Chip Burns for their assistance in this project and especially my chair, Dr. Robert Bing. Mr. Lu Wang at The Office of Legal Assistance at the State Penitentiary was directly responsible for assisting me in the gathering of the data for this study, and I appreciate his kind efforts. I would also like to thank my husband Rob for all his patience and encouragement during my graduate program.

> **Don't do:** What can I say, Geeezzz Dr. Ferrell and Dr. Burns you were the greatest and Dr. Bing, I could not have done it without you, literally man. To my dog Bonzo, I am sorry that I didn't get to pay more attention to you during those three years I was glued to my keyboard but I will make it up to you, I swear. To my old Frata Capa fraternity brothers, thanks for all the beer and shots during the all-nighter sessions, you guys rock.

Remember you will want to have your final proofread and edited version to your committee members in enough time for them to read and make comments before the defense. It is in your best interest to have them submit any concerns and go over your work carefully prior to the presentation, as the best defense has no surprises and no unexpected committee feedback.

THE PRESENTATION

Your success in the prospectus defense should have done much to alleviate some of the presentation fears you had early in the thesis process. Attending as many final thesis defenses as possible will be very important at this stage as the best way to learn is to observe. As Susan explained, she was quite relieved to find out that the defense was not what she had originally feared.

> The misconception that I had before starting the process was that of being tortured and scrutinized with very specific and detailed questions at both the prospectus and thesis defense. I think attending other prospectus and thesis defenses helped me in preparing myself for my defenses. This gave me an idea of what I was going to walk into and what positions and questioning I was to be prepared for.

Your committee will again advise you of the expectations they have for your final presentation. Generally, however, some assumptions about the nature of a defense may be possible at this point. Unlike the prospectus defense, there may be less emphasis now on the exact procedures you followed and the details of your methodology, and more on the findings, particularly what they mean. A conceptual model for the thesis defense may be diagrammed as almost the opposite of the prospectus defense:

The diagram indicates that more discussion may be placed on your reflections on what the thesis accomplished, what you might have done differently, and what you learned from the study beyond the specific findings. Another difference between the final thesis defense and the prospectus is that you may have more discussion with the members about the significance of your work, more questions and answers, and broader comments about the meaning of the concepts under study. Because you now know quite a bit about the topic, you should be more comfortable with this direction. If you expect a great deal of professorial input and sometimes even argument among your committee during the defense, then you shouldn't have a problem with the usual defense process. This give-and-take discussion is part of the teaching process that faculty enjoy most, and it is not unusual for them to get very vocal and expressive, even carried away discussing the research.

To best prepare for your defense, discuss your presentation plan with your chair and committee. For example, Terry's chair suggested that he do about 5 to 10 minutes on his interest in the topic, some historical background

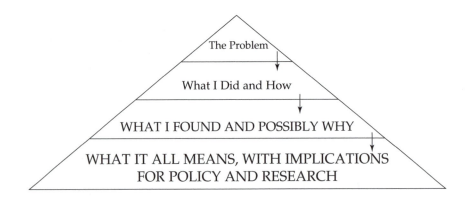

on the issue, a literature review, and a summary of previous research findings. The chair then indicated that he should spend another 5 to 10 minutes on the study design and data gathering process, explaining any difficulties he encountered and how he resolved them. The findings were expected to add 10 more minutes. After that, they collectively anticipated that Terry would spend about 15 minutes discussing the implications of the study and his insights as he reflected on the study and its meaning. The chair noted that committee members would likely react to Terry's commentary and ask questions or begin to discuss relevant issues during this final part of the presentation.

Each thesis defense will be different and, even if you attend several prior to your own, you must tailor yours to your individual style and needs. One way is to get a clear picture of how much time or how much detail your committee chair would like you to include in each of the sections or segments of your defense. That determination may be tied to the method of presentation you choose.

Choosing a Presentation Style and Format

Lecture

The standard format for the defense has traditionally been the lecture with notes. This might include charts, diagrams, or handouts. Handouts might include the tables from your analysis, or other significant charts, graphs, or diagrams. When Judith presented her ethnographic study of the homeless, she positioned several large photographs she had taken of some of her subjects in black and white on easels at the front of the room. Blown up into 3 x 5 posters, at a reasonable rate at a local copy shop, they made a dramatic accent to her narrative. Lois had several large color geographic profiles of the jury pool areas blown up for display which she was able to reference during her presentation. While this may not be suitable for many different types of thesis topics, it may provide an alternative to duplicating expensive color handouts of your graphs and charts for members of the audience.

Electronic Presentation

For a PowerPoint presentation, you may want to duplicate some or all of the slides as handouts or create a combined slides/notes handout so the audience has something to take away from the session as a summary of your findings. Handouts are also valuable as a way to help the audience follow the presentation of your findings. Even if you don't duplicate the slides, you should develop handouts for some of the most significant tables, figures, or conclusions.

The Defense as Presentation

Regardless of your style of presentation, there are only a few presentation tips to keep in mind during your defense. Remember to go slowly and make eye contact with those in attendance. Be aware of the amount of time you have already used and the time left for your scheduled delivery. There should be plenty of time at the end for members of the committee and the audience to ask questions. In fact, committee questions usually take up as much time, if not more, than the presentation itself. Try not to let any questions unnerve you or disrupt your concentration; such questions are to be expected, and you are unlikely to have prepared an answer to every type of question. Do not be afraid to say that you do not know, or to give several possible or different answers to a question depending on different considerations and scenarios. Remember, those in attendance are there out of interest for you and your topic, so relax as much as possible and enjoy your opportunity to convey the results of your hard work.

The Results of the Defense

According to one student, Laura, completing the thesis not only meant that she felt good about herself, but also it was a defining moment in her professional career as well. "The organizational skills, working with different offenders in a research setting, research on a particular agency problem has interest for both you and your department." She believes that earning a master's degree is necessary for all who are interested in gaining promotion to a management position in the field.

Remember that there are essentially three results for a defense: pass, pass with minor revisions, and fail. The latter result almost never occurs, primarily because few chairs will let a student go to the defense if there are still major problems. On the other hand, requiring some minor corrections is commonplace. These might be typos, a statement that a committee member wants qualified, or even a new journal article on your topic that someone feels needs to be included. For this reason, you might ask your chair if you can wait until after the defense to put the final copy on the type of paper required by the university (usually an expensive rag bond paper). It is probably a good idea to *expect* minor revisions so you don't feel like you didn't "pass." Anticipating the necessity ahead of time also means you have programmed the time necessary to do these corrections. There are usually very short extension periods during which you must make all final revisions in order to meet graduation deadlines. Don't let this bother you. After all, your thesis will be in the university library, and you want it to reflect the good job you have just done.

Successfully defending your thesis is an exciting experience. Relief and personal satisfaction are just some of the overwhelming emotions students feel at this time. However, do not let the celebration distract you from the reality of the bottom line—you aren't done until all of the paperwork is finished!

Depending on the process used by your institution, the responsibilities you may have at this time are to ensure that right number of final copies are on the correct bond paper, all signatures have been obtained on the correct forms, and you have delivered the thesis copies to the proper source for binding. Don't forget that there are also fees to be paid and the usual bureaucratic forms to be submitted. Ask your graduate coordinator for a checklist of final requirements—most departments (or the graduate school) have one.

Seeing your thesis on the shelf at the library is a very special milestone and evidence of your status in the academic world. Congratulations.

REFERENCES

COON, J. (2007). Crime prevention technology and public schools. N.Y.: LFB Scholarly.

13

REVISING YOUR THESIS INTO ARTICLES AND PRESENTATIONS

Because a thesis represents such a concentrated academic effort, it is logical to consider to convert the work into additional products, such as a paper presentation and possibly even a published article or book chapter. Though your advisor and committee members may be in the best position to give you advice and to help you with these activities, there are some general considerations that hold true across related disciplines. The best way to begin is to present a paper at a scholarly conference. First, pick a proper size conference. A state or regional meeting is the probably best option for a paper presentation. These types of meetings offer advantages of associated costs and time consumed by the presentation, as well as the presence of other students who can act as a support source for first-time presenters. The other alternative, journal publication, is a bit more difficult because it requires knowledge of how journals process and accept manuscripts. Journals have a range of demands and expectations, and it would be best to submit to one where articles are routinely similar to the one you have prepared.

PAPER PRESENTATION

Students may wish to consider making a paper presentation either prior to defending the thesis or after. You can frequently get feedback during a presentation that might help you prepare for your defense or help you shape your conclusions and implications. In criminal justice there are a number of conference possibilities for presenting your work, and you may do this on your own or with a professor who will assist you.

Most conferences require that paper topics and abstracts be submitted four months or more in advance of the conference presentation. Watch for calls for papers by visiting the Web sites of academic organizations, or consult with your committee for further ideas about where to submit. Some meetings, particularly those at the national level, set aside special panels and forums for student papers. The intent is to make students feel more comfortable presenting their work in a venue that is clearly identified as student work, though you are not restricted to applying in that context. You may want to talk to your chair about whether a student panel section is right for you.

POSSIBLE SCHOLARLY VENUES

There are generally four types of professional and scholarly conferences in which papers might be presented. From more localized to more distant, they are local and state professional meetings, state scholarly conferences, regional scholarly and professional conferences, and national and international scholarly and professional conferences. In general, the more geographic area covered by the association meeting, the larger the conference will be and the more papers presented. Expense of attending also tends to vary in the same way. Here are some ideas for finding presentation venues:

- **Local and State Professional Meetings**
  - State or area probation professionals' meeting
  - State or area meeting of law enforcement officials
  - State or local judges, attorneys, or courts professionals
  - State or area meeting of women, minorities, or specialized professionals in Criminal Justice
- **State Scholarly Conferences**
  - State criminal justice educators' associations
  - State social science educators' associations
  - State criminal justice justice researchers' associations
- **Regional Criminal Justice Conferences**
  - Western and Pacific Association of Criminal Justice Educators (annually in October)
  - Western Society of Criminology (annually in February)
  - Regional Social Science Associations' Criminal Justice & Criminology Section (Southern, Northeastern, Midwestern, Southwestern, Western—annual meeting dates differ)
  - Southern Criminal Justice Association (annually in September)
  - Northeast Association of Criminal Justice Sciences (annually in June)
  - Midwestern Criminal Justice Association (annually in October)
  - Southwestern Association of Criminal Justice (annually in October)

- **National and International Criminal Justice Conferences**
  - Academy of Criminal Justice Sciences (annually around March)
  - American Society of Criminology (annually in November)
  - American Academy of Forensic Sciences (annually in February)
  - American Society of Victimology (annually in March)
  - American Jail Association (annually in May)
  - American Correctional Association (annually in August)
  - American Probation and Parole Association (annually in July)
  - National Association of Blacks in Criminal Justice (annually in July)
  - International Association of Chiefs of Police (annually in October)
  - International Society for Criminology (every five years)
  - World Society of Victimology (annually in August)

Many regional criminal justice associations edit and publish journals. The conference would be a good place for you to meet the journal editors and get some feedback on the feasibility of submitting your paper. Here are four associations with journals:

Regional Association	Journal
Southwestern Association of Criminal Justice	Southwest Journal of Criminal Justice
Midwestern Association of Criminal Justice	Journal of Criminal Justice
Southern Criminal Justice Association	American Journal of Criminal Justice
Western Society of Criminology	Western Criminology Review

PAPER COMPETITIONS AND AWARDS

Most of the associations listed also sponsor paper competitions and student research awards as a way to encourage graduate student development and participation at the meetings. Prizes include funding to attend annual meetings, or simply prize money, and the expectation that the student's paper will be presented at the meeting. Having a paper selected for one of these awards is particularly prestigious for those who plan on continuing their graduate education. It is also a distinction for the résumé, especially for those desiring work in management, research, or agency planning.

Organizations Typically Sponsoring Student Paper Competitions

Not all scholarly or professional organization sponsor student paper competitions, but there are several that do, with both monetary prizes and/or award certificates. Some societies have multiple sections or divisions, each with their own award competition. A few of these are listed below.

- Academy of Criminal Justice Sciences
  - Minorities and Women Section
- American Society of Criminology
  - Division on Corrections and Sentencing
  - Division of International Criminology
  - Division on Women and Crime
- Northeast Association of Criminal Justice Sciences
- Southern Association of Criminal Justice
- Southwest Association of Criminal Justice

PUBLICATIONS

One of the first decisions you must make about publishing an article from your thesis is the question of authorship. If you are simply going to cut your manuscript down to an interest article for a professional publication such as a newsletter or monthly magazine or news bulletin, you will probably be able to do this yourself in a single-author piece. Still, you should have faculty members review your work before submitting it for formal review.

Coauthoring with your chair or other members of your committee is a practical avenue if you are targeting a fairly competitive journal with a reputation for rigorous peer review. This is not uncommon, and the faculty involved dedicate substantial effort and experience to bring your work to a level that will withstand such review. The prestige of publishing in these venues is often considered worth the additional coordination necessary for such a collaborative effort. In most cases, if the faculty members assisting you serve mostly as editing and support, they will designate the student as primary author. There are circumstances, however, where the graduating student may be publishing research from their thesis but may not serve as the primary author.

Secondary author situations generally occur when the faculty members or outside researchers designed the initial study and collected the data. In these cases, the student is usually allowed access to the data for the purposes of their thesis, or perhaps the student conducted a secondary analysis incidental to a major research project already underway by the primary investigators. For various reasons, these latter situations are not uncommon but the primary reason revolves around the benefits of using large data sets—as we have already discussed. One of the benefits of using data analyses from such projects for publication is that the data and methodologies are probably already rigorous enough that few will be challenged under the scrutiny of publication review. Another possibility of a secondary author publication occurs when a faculty member has to make changes that create a final product substantially different from the material in the original thesis. Acceptance in some prestigous journals literally requires manuscripts with writing and analytical skills beyond that of most master's graduates.

Publishing a Journal Article: What to Expect

Publishing an article can be a stressful process and one that any student should investigate thoroughly before undertaking. You should use the web to begin researching information about journals. The information you need will be general as well as specific and technical. General information includes the goal of the publication, its mission, its audience, how often it publishes the types of manuscripts it is seeking, whether it is currently seeking submissions, and its submission process. You should spend some time reviewing articles in that journal and determining whether they match the type of paper you are preparing for your thesis.

A second type of information is technical, including the specific style of writing and formatting used, the way citations are done, and presentation of the bibliography. It is best to prepare your manuscript in a way that is consistent with the structure a journal uses for its abstracts, subheadings, references, and so forth, so that the editors can see that you paid attention to such details. While it may appear mundane, these details get close scrutiny. Sometimes using the correct structure and formatting means the difference between getting a borderline manuscript accepted with revisions, or rejected.

Another factor you should be aware of before submitting to a journal is the publication's normal acceptance rate. Journals with low acceptance rates (high rejection rates) are usually not a good prospect for a thesis product. You should also check to see what the publication schedule of the journal or magazine has been, in particular determining if recent issues have been delayed. If so, you need to ask if current issues are backlogged and lengthy delays anticipated.

Finally, the normal processing time—when you submit to when you receive notice of the status of your manuscript—is a valuable piece of information. You cannot send the manuscript to two journals at once; therefore, a submission is usually deemed to be a promise that the manuscript is not under consideration elsewhere. The editorial process of some journals seems to take forever, and, in others, there is a turnaround time of only a month or so. You cannot afford to have a manuscript sitting too long in the editorial and printing process. Your review of the literature will get old, and, perhaps, there will even be another article published doing exactly the same research you did.

All of these are important aspects in making a choice about where to submit, especially when two journals appear to be equally appropriate. Ask your chair and committee members about these, and other, facets of the publishing process. Another good source of information about journals in the field is an article by Michael Vaughn, Rolando del Carmen, Martin Perfecto, and Ka Xiong Charand (2004).

Outlets and Time Frames

Peer Reviewed versus Nonpeer-Reviewed Journals

Generally there are two types of article outlets, which are distinguished by the type of review process they employ. Peer-review journals are academic periodicals that generally submit manuscripts anonymously to two or three outside reviewers who are known to have researched and published on the topic of the manuscript or one closely related to the field it reflects. This process is more time-consuming as the reviewers may take anywhere from six to eight weeks to return manuscripts with their comments and recommendations. Coupled with the editor's processing time, a peer review can take anywhere from three to six months.

Acceptance and Revisions

The full range of decisions that may be rendered on a manuscript usually include wording as described below:

- *Accepted for publication as is* (with perhaps minor, typographical edits). This decision is relatively rare.
- *Accepted for publication, contingent upon the author making minor changes.* The editor will be responsible for assuring that the changes are made and that the reviewers do not need to see the manuscript again.
- *Revise and resubmit.* Reviewers see promise in the manuscript, but suggest changes, some of which are potentially major ones. The manuscript will be returned to the same reviewers to ensure that the author has complied with the spirit, if not the letter, of the requested changes. An explanation of changes made in response to reviews is usually required. This decision is the most common one. Variations on this decision are
  - The paper needs major revisions in specific areas, perhaps including more explanation of the methodology and elaboration of the analysis.
  - The paper needs to be significantly expanded or reduced in size, requiring substantial rewriting and restructuring.
- *Reject.* The paper is rejected as the subject matter is really not within the focus of the journal, or the paper is rejected as not meeting the standards of the journal.

Even when reviews are favorable, reviewers will often suggest a number of changes, edits, or revisions for the manuscript. You need to have a tolerance for criticism, even when that criticism is designed to improve your manuscript. Sometimes the revisions will be minor, and the editor will simply ask you to make those changes and extend an acceptance pending those changes. Alternatively the reviewers and the editor will classify their evaluation as "Revise and Resubmit" and ask you to make revisions with the implication that acceptance will likely follow after a review of those changes determines that concerns have been met.

As Miller & Harris (2004, p. 76) explain, when substantial editing is required, the author must make a decision about whether the changes required are worth the effort.

> A decision to withdraw may result if the authors deem that the scope of the required revisions is too large or impossible. Once withdrawn, the manuscript can be submitted for peer review to another journal. If the authors decide to revise the manuscript, they are typically given a time frame in which to complete the revisions.

Once your revisions have been incorporated into the manuscript, and you also provide the editor with your own comments about the changes that you have made, or an explanation of why certain revisions were not made, the manuscript will most likely be sent back to the reviewers to assure that their concerns have been addressed. With revisions, it is not unusual for the peer review process from original submission to seeing the manuscript in print to take anywhere from a year to eighteen months.

Nonpeer reviewed sources are also appropriate outlets for many topics, particularly those with practical policy implications for practitioners and administrators in criminal justice agencies. Often these bulletins, newsletters, magazines, and professional journals are published much more frequently than academic journals so that they accept a greater number of submissions. Moreover, editors may have sole authority to accept or reject manuscripts. This means that turnaround time is usually shorter, as is the time to publication. Examples of these include *American Jail, Corrections Today, Police Chief,* the *FBI Law Enforcement Bulletin,* and *Federal Probation.* Some of these publications are well respected in the field.

PREPARING A MANUSCRIPT FOR SUBMISSION

The most common revisions applied to a publication from a thesis are reducing the size and revising the traditional thesis terminology. In addition, you should prepare the manuscript according to the format guidelines of the journal, including electronic and hard copy specifications. You should also prepare a letter to accompany the manuscript.

Reducing the Size of the Thesis

Most theses will have to be reduced in size to be appropriate for a journal article as the standard article length is about twenty-five manuscript pages. One of the best ways to do this is to eliminate any lengthy definitions. If needed, definitions can be put into footnotes. Likewise, much of the methodology can be condensed to just the basic facts one would have to know to understand the conditions, most likely those affecting the validity or reliability of the research. Again, sometimes footnotes are appropriate for additional methodological information. A thesis frequently can be reduced even further to create a shorter "research note" that some journals offer, or perhaps a magazine article.

Revising Thesis Terminology

Theses, and even doctoral dissertations, tend to contain phrases and terms that are rarely found in published materials, and the author will need to remove some of the most conspicuous "thesis jargon." That may mean substituting standard academic headings such as discussion, literature review, and so forth, for more descriptive phrases that are more useful to practitioners, students, and a more general consumer audience.

For example, the standard language of various thesis chapters might be transformed as demonstrated below:

Traditional Chapters	Changed to
Introduction	Skateboarding: Teen Fun or Delinquent Menace?
The Literature Review	Measuring Social Distance: Research Findings
Methodology	Data Collection and Methods of Analysis
Analysis	Analysis of Social Control Variables in Drug Use
Summary and Conclusions	Legislative Reform and the Future of Insider Trading

COVER LETTER

Gump (2004) reminds authors to make sure their cover letter is professional and designed to make a good impression. A cover letter should contain the manuscript title, word or page count, and some indication of familiarity with the journal and its submission requirements. The author should also include current contact information to make it easy for editors to contact you whether it is in the next week or the next three months. Gump argues that the letter should establish a good rapport and suggests reflecting a willingness to adjust the manuscript as reviewers might see necessary and to be able to provide revisions in a timely and effective manner in whatever format is required.

DETERMINING A SUITABLE JOURNAL OUTLET

There are many ways to review the wide variety of journals available for criminal justice audiences today. Both the ACJS and the ASC Web sites link you to a descriptive listing of journals in the field and their calls for the submission of papers. Most of these announcements also include direct links to the Web sites of these journals, their instructions and specifications for submission, or the e-mail addresses of the editors where questions can be directed and additional information obtained.

There are several approaches to selecting a periodical to which you will submit your work. Most journals can be researched online, and most have a

Web site of their own which provides suggestions for authors and details on the types of manuscripts sought. Your library's online databases will indicate which journals are on schedule in their production. After careful research you may be able to directly match your topic with a more narrowly defined journal. For example, a paper from a thesis evaluating a training program for bank employees on detecting money laundering might be sent to the *Journal of Money Laundering Control*. It is obviously a good topic fit. However, the author may want to broaden the scope of the potential audience by submitting to a more general publication, *Journal of Financial Crime*. On the other hand, there may be more submissions to compete with from a journal encompassing the nature of the crime, criminals, and detection, as well as prevention of a wider range of financial crimes. Upon further investigation, the author may decide that since both of these journals are international and the editor is located out of the country, it may be more practical to work closer to home.

An author may want to publish in a journal of a regional organization of which he or she is a member, knowing that the paper will be reviewed by those you might know. Thus, you would be more familiar with the reviewers' expectations and perhaps even their general philosophy about supporting the work of their members. In that same way, some beginning writers might find it more difficult to submit to international journals or interdisciplinary journals where the competition is likely to be stronger.

Some Journal Suggestions

The list below of some possible journal sources, by major components of the criminal justice field, is just suggestive in nature and does not imply that these publications will accept your material. You should discuss your intentions to publish with faculty members in your department who have experience in publishing in a variety of outlets, particularly your committee members. Also, it is best to review several of these journals' back issues to get a feel for the type of articles they publish and the likelihood of finding an article along the same line as yours. You can even contact the editor in advance if you are still unsure about the fit of your work to that publication.

- **Police**
  - *Police Chief*
  - *Police Studies*
  - *Police Quarterly*
  - *Police Forum* (Journal of the Police Section of the Academy of Criminal Justice Sciences)
- **Courts**
  - *Judicature*
  - *Justice System Journal*
  - *Criminal Law Bulletin*
  - *Criminal Law*

- **Corrections**
  - *Corrections Today* (Magazine of the American Correctional Association)
  - *Federal Probation* (Publication of the Office of the U.S. Courts)
  - *Prison Journal*
  - *American Jail*
  - *Corrections Compendium*
  - *Journal for Juvenile Justice & Detention Services*
- **Policy & Management**
  - *Justice Policy Journal*
  - *Security Management*
  - *Criminology and Public Policy*
- **Other Specialized Topics**
  - *Critical Criminology*
  - *Journal of Ethnicity in Criminal Justice*
  - *Journal of Drug Issues*
  - *Journal of School Violence*
  - *The Security Journal*
  - *Women and Criminal Justice*
  - *Youth Violence & Juvenile Justice: An Interdisciplinary Journal*

A FEW LAST RULES

Everyone in the academic world has had their share of publication experiences that are both rewarding and disappointing. You should not be discouraged by any initial negative feedback you might receive. The best approach is to adjust to the circumstances, reevaluate your course of action, and listen to the advice of your academic mentors. Editors often suggest that potential contributors research their selection of a publication source well, and make sure that the relevance, significance, and contribution of the manuscript are stated clearly and early in the work.

If you receive feedback on an manuscript indicating that it would need substantial revisions and you decide to submit the article to another publication, make sure that you notify the original editor in writing that your are withdrawing the article from consideration. Never submit to more than one source at a time. Though your committee members will be able to guide you in the proper methods of submission, the bottom line is to present your work honestly and be open to suggestions and revisions. As Hauptman (2005, p. 116) warns,

> Avoid at all costs, plagiarism, fabrication, falsification, and fudging, cooking, or trimming of data. Research misconduct, though more widespread than commonly acknowledged, is unacceptable behavior; it harms editors and readers, and it sullies the perpetrator's integrity and reputation.

Many academics know a colleague who was charged with plagiarism or research misconduct. Such charges are normally enough to ruin careers—don't ruin yours before it begins. It is important to remember that publishing is a time-honored academic tradition. Hard work and good faith efforts in the pursuit will last longer and go further than any short-term benefit from bringing a less worthy article to print.

EXAMPLES OF STUDENT PUBLICATIONS FROM THESIS

Below are just a few examples of the student theses that have been crafted into articles for publication in the field of criminal justice. In many of these cases, the student retained first authorship as evidence of their primary contribution to the work. We have purposefully added first names to these examples, so they are not in APA style nor are they listed alphabetically (do not use these for formatting purposes in your thesis!).

ANTOINETTE R. LOZANO, G. LARRY MAYS, and L. THOMAS WINFREE, Jr. Diagnosing Delinquents: The purpose of a youth diagnostic center. *Juvenile and Family Court Journal, 41*(2), 25–39, 1990.

BARBARA J. PEAT AND L. THOMAS Winfree, Jr. Reducing the intra-institutional effects of prisonization: A study of a therapeutic community for drug-using inmates. *Criminal Justice and Behavior, 19*(2), 206–225, 1992.

E. LYNN WHITE AND FRANK P. WILLIAMS III. Legislative actions against drunken driving: An assessment with additional evidence on the open container. *Criminal Justice Policy Review, 1*(3), 286–304, 1986.

CHRISTOPHER HOWARD, L. THOMAS WINFREE, JR., G. LARRY MAYS, MARY K. STOHR, AND DENNIS L. CLASON. Processing inmate disciplinary infractions in a federal correctional institution: Legal and extralegal correlates of prison-based legal decisions. *Prison Journal, 74*, 5–31, 1994.

NOREEN PURCELL, L. THOMAS WINFREE, JR., and G. LARRY MAYS. DNA evidence and criminal trials: An exploratory survey of factors associated with the use of genetic fingerprinting in felony prosecutions. *Journal of Criminal Justice, 22*(2), 145–157, 1994.

YANG FANG, MARILYN MCSHANE, AND FRANK P. WILLIAMS III. Concepts and theories in the use of mediation: Shaming models in American and Chinese cultures. In Charles B. Fields and Richter Moore (Eds.), *Comparative Criminal Justice: Traditional and Nontraditional Systems of Law and Control*, pp. 379–389. Prospect Heights, IL: Waveland Press, 1996.

ANDREW F. SELPH, L. THOMAS WINFREE, JR., AND G. LARRY MAYS. Serving juvenile time in New Mexico: A comparison of institutionalized and reintegrated male offenders. *Juvenile and Family Court Journal 47*(2), 1–14, 1996.

JAMES BRECKENRIDGE, L. THOMAS WINFREE, JR., JAMES W. MAUPIN, AND DENNIS L. CLASON. Drunk drivers, DWI-drug court: treatment, and recidivism: Who fails? *Justice Research and Policy, 2*(1), 87–105, 2000.

DAVID MARSHALL AND MARILYN MCSHANE. First to fight: An analysis of the marine subculture and domestic violence. In Peter Mercier and Judith Mercier (Eds.)., *Domestic Violence in the Military*, pp. 15–29. Springfield, IL: Charles C. Thomas, 2000.

DANA PETERSON LYNSKEY, L. THOMAS WINFREE, JR., FINN-AAGE ESBENSEN, AND DENNIS L. CLASON. Linking gender, minority group status, and family matters to self-control theory: A multivariate analysis of key self-control concepts in a youth-gang context. *Juvenile and Family Court Journal, 51*(3), 1–19, 2000.

ELIZABETH K. BUTLER, L. THOMAS WINFREE, JR., AND GREG NEWBOLD. Policing and gender: Male and female perspectives among members of the New Zealand Police. *Police Quarterly, 6*(3), 298–329, 2003.

DEYANDRA ZAMORA (2005). Levels of academic achievement and further delinquency among detained youth. *Southwest Journal of Criminal Justice, 2*(1), 42–53. Online at *www.cj.txstate.edu/SWACJ/Z%20SWACJZamora.pdf.*

FINAL REMARKS

The thesis can be a very demanding and challenging experience. However, it is also the capstone of a master's program and the hallmark of scholarly achievement at this level. As Dey looks back on the process, as many students have, she appreciates the rewards of the endeavor. She writes

> For me the thesis gave me not only the opportunity to write about a topic of interest to me, but allowed me to share the results of my study with others in the academic field through publication of my study as well as presentation of my results at a professional conference. I'll tell you, when I first thought "thesis project," I never would have imagined all the avenues through which I would be sharing my information or of how others were actually interested in learning about what I had found. It truly was an amazing experience and one that I never expected but will always treasure.

We suggest you do all you can to make your thesis experience just as rewarding.

REFERENCES

GUMP, S. E. (2004). Writing successful covering letters for unsolicited submissions to academic journals. *Journal of Scholarly Publication, 35*(2), 92–102.

HARMAN, E., MONTAGNES, I, MCMENEMY, S., AND BUCCI, C. (Eds.) (2003). *The thesis and the book: A guide for first-time academic authors.* 2d Ed. Toronto: University of Toronto Press.

HAUPTMAN, R. (2005). How to be a successful scholar: Publish efficiently. *Journal of Scholarly Publishing, 36,* 115–119.

MILLER, C. and HARRIS, J. (2004). Scholarly journal publication: Conflicting agendas for scholars, publishers, and institutions. *Journal of Scholarly Publication, 35*(2), 73–91.

VAUGHN, M. S., DEL CARMEN, R. V., PERFECTO, M., and CHARAND, K. X. (2004). Journals in criminal justice and criminology: An updated and expanded guide for authors. *Journal of Criminal Justice Education, 15,*(1), 61–128.

LITERATURE REFERENCES AND RESOURCES

There are several types of resources that will be important for researching your thesis topic, including journals and books, case law and penal codes, government publications, other theses and dissertations, reference books, Web sites, trade journals or magazines, and newspapers. Some will only be available in or through your library while others will be accessible online. Many of these and their uses are described in further detail below.

ACADEMIC JOURNALS

Academic journals are the best source of information on research studies conducted to test various theories, theoretical discussions of the structure and function of crime and delinquency in society, and scholarly discussions and research on the components of the criminal justice system. Literature related to crime and criminology may be found in journals in a wide range of disciplines, especially sociological and social science ones. Criminal justice–related articles will be found in a wide array of journals and publications focusing on police, courts, juvenile delinquency, drugs, violence, victims, and corrections.

Databases such as *Sage, Academic Search Premier, Criminal Justice Periodical Index,* and *Criminal Justice Abstracts* are a good place to start. Once you locate an article, you might want to use the *Social Science Citation Index* to quickly find other articles that cited the first article. Some of the most commonly used journals available in these databases are listed below.

American Bar Association Journal
American Behavioral Scientist
American Criminal Law Review
American Journal of Orthopsychiatry
American Journal of Sociology

American Political Science Review
American Sociological Review
Annals of the American Academy of Political & Social Sciences
Australian & New Zealand Journal of Criminology
British Journal of Criminology
Canadian Journal of Criminology and Criminal Justice
Contemporary Crises
Contemporary Issues in Criminal Justice
Contemporary Justice Review
Crime and Delinquency
Crime and Social Justice
Criminal Justice and Behavior
Criminal Justice Ethics
Criminal Justice Policy Review
Criminal Justice Review
Criminal Law Bulletin
Criminal Law Quarterly
Criminal Law Reporter
Criminal Law Review
Criminology and Public Policy
Criminology: An Interdisciplinary Journal
Critical Criminology
Critical Perspectives in Criminology
Federal Probation
Feminist Criminology
International Criminal Justice Review
International Journal of Comparative and Applied Criminal Justice
International Journal of Offender Therapy & Comparative Criminology
Journal of Contemporary Criminal Justice
Journal of Contemporary Ethnography
Journal of Crime and Justice
Journal of Criminal Justice
Journal of Criminal Justice Education
Journal of Criminal Law & Criminology
Journal of Ethnicity and Criminal Justice
Journal of Family Law
Journal of Homicide Studies
Journal of Offender Counseling Services & Rehabilitation
Journal of Offender Monitoring
Journal of Police Crisis Negotiations
Journal of Psychiatry & Law
Journal of Research in Crime & Delinquency
Journal of School Violence
Judicature
Justice Quarterly

Justice System Journal
Juvenile and Family Court Journal
Juvenile Court Digests
Juvenile Justice
Juvenile Justice Digest
Law & Society Review
Police Forum
Police Practice and Research
Police Studies
Prison Journal
Psychiatry and Law
Public Opinion Quarterly
Qualitative Sociology
Security Journal
Social Casework
Social Forces
Social Justice
Social Problems
Social Science Quarterly
Sociological Perspectives
Sociological Quarterly
Sociology & Social Research
Trends in Organized Crime
Victimology
Women and Criminal Justice
Women's Policy Journal of Harvard John F. Kennedy School of Government

MAGAZINES AND TRADE JOURNALS

Because most magazines and trade journals do not go through an extensive referee process, they usually have a rapid publication process. Often the most recent population statistics and up-to-date information on programs can be found in these resources. Many of the policies and programs popular in addressing crime-related issues are found in these reports. Some of the most useful trade journals are

American Jails
American Probation and Parole Association Perspectives
Corrections Today
FBI Law Enforcement Bulletin
Police Chief

INTERDISCIPLINARY DATABASES

Because criminal justice is an interdisciplinary field, law journals, as well as journals in sociology, psychology, philosophy, political science, management, administration, and economics will be useful. Databases that will help you in these areas are

JSTOR — older issues of journals in social sciences and business, some from as far back as 1831.

EMERALD — over 130 journals focusing on management, leadership, criminal justice, and human resources. Most from 1994 on.

American Periodical Series — a valuable historical resource with professional and general interest news stories from magazines and journals published between 1740 and 1900.

NY TIMES (historical) database with high-quality PDF image articles from 1851 to 2002.

THESES AND DISSERTATIONS

Most college libraries have holdings with theses produced at that campus. You may also search for dissertations that may be related to your topic through the Web site for Dissertation Abstracts, as well as the site for University Microfilms. Your reference librarian may be able to assist you, or you may be able to access it online. Another valuable resource for examining research studies that may be related to yours in either methodology or topic is the LFB Scholarly Publications series called Criminal Justice: Recent Scholarship. This company publishes quality dissertations that are marketed to libraries as regular book acquisitions. Visit the Web site of the series at *www.lfbscholarly.com* to see if any of the resources are relevant to your work, and then discuss obtaining one with your library.

LEGAL RESOURCES

The most commonly used legal resources for course work in criminology are law reporters, law journals, and penal codes. Your school library should have either the Lawyers Edition, Supreme Court Reporter, or U.S. Reports version of U.S. Supreme Court cases. Libraries vary on which online database they use for legal referencing — LEXIS or WESTLAW — but either should allow you to find information about the specific content of the various laws both historically and currently. Check with your reference librarian for more information on any of these legal resources.

GOVERNMENT PUBLICATIONS

There are many useful government publications for reference use. Your state department of corrections annual report should give current statistics about offenders both demographically and by the various offense types. The Bureau of Justice Statistics, the National Institute of Corrections, and the National Institute of Justice all publish timely pamphlets and regular reports in the areas of drugs, violence prevention, the use of weapons, incarceration, juvenile delinquency, and new innovations in fighting crime.

One of the key statistical documents used by persons in this field is the *Sourcebook of Criminal Justice Statistics*. This annual is published by the U.S. Department of Justice, Bureau of Justice Statistics (BJS), Washington, D.C., U.S. Government Printing Office. The volume includes many useful charts and data sets, including investigative reports, characteristics offenders and employees in the criminal justice system, public attitudes and opinions on crime issues, and information on sentencing and criminal careers. Another useful BJS publication is the *Report to the Nation on Crime and Justice*. This volume has a variety of information tables on police, court, and corrections data and a section on the costs of operating the criminal justice system.

THE WORLD WIDE WEB

Many of the sources noted earlier are now available on Web sites, as is a wealth of other information. Often you will have the choice of downloading materials in standard text format, known as ASCII format — which can be read across computer platforms — or of downloading the materials in PDF (portable data file format). The PDF format developed by Adobe allows the document to be downloaded with all its graphic characteristics. The advantage of PDF is that the printed document can be almost indistinguishable from the original document, whereas ASCII text strips bold, underlining, graphics, and other font styles from the document. To read or print documents downloaded in PDF format, you must obtain the Adobe Acrobat File Reader, which is free and can be downloaded from the Adobe Web site, *http://www.adobe.com/acrobat/*.

THE TYPICAL WEB SITE ADDRESS (URL) FORMAT

URL	The Web site address, universal resource locator, usually expressed in the format: *http://www.domainname.suffix/nameofspecificpage*
http:	hypertext terminal protocol — indicates the site is in standard web page format
https:	secure hypertext terminal protocol
// or /	File path specifier used in UNIX — do not confuse with the DOS backslash (\)
www	indicates a Web site
wwws	indicates a secure Web site
com	suffix after the Web site name indicating it is a business site
edu	suffix after the Web site name indicating an educational institution
org	suffix after the Web site name indicating it is an organization's site
gov	suffix after the Web site name indicating it is a government site
html	indicates a file written in hypertext markup language — the format for web browsers

SEARCH INFORMATION

The three most commonly used search sites and their URLs are:

Google *http://www.google.com* (searches several search engines at once)
Ixquick *http://www.ixquick.com* (searches several search engines at once)
Yahoo *http://www.yahoo.com*

In particular see *http://www.yahoo.com/Society_and_Culture/Crime/*.

Caution: Web sites change addresses often. Some of these site addresses may already be outdated.

JUSTICE-RELATED WEB RESOURCES

Note: This is far from a complete guide to justice resources on the World Wide Web. New sites are constantly being developed.

DRUGS

CEDAR: Center for Education and Drug Abuse Research
  http://www.pitt.edu/~mmv/cedar.html
Drug Text USA
  http://www.calyx.com/~mariolap/drugtext.html
Drugs and Crime
  http://amcom.aspensys.com/ncjrs/drguse.htm
Drug Use Forecasting
  http://ncjrs.org/drguse.htm
National Clearinghouse for Alcohol and Drug Information
  http://www.health.org
National Household Survey on Drug Abuse
  http://www.health.org/hhs/93hhsrvy.htm
National Institute on Drug Abuse
  http://www.nida.nih.gov/
Substance Abuse and Mental Health Services Administration (SAMHSA)
  http://samhsa.gov//
United Nations International Drug Control Program
  http://www.undcp.org/index.htm
Web of Addictions
  http://www.well.com:80/user/woa/

ONLINE JOURNALS

Cornell Law Review
  http://www.law.cornell.edu
FBI Law Enforcement Bulletin
  http://www.fbi.gov/leb.htm

International Journal of Drug Testing
http://www.stpt.usf.edu/journal/index.html
Journal of Criminal Justice and Popular Culture
http://www.albany.edu/~gh7878/cjhome.html
Journal of On-line Law
http://www.law.cornell.edu/jol/jol.table.html
Justice Policy Journal
http://www.cjcj.org/jpj
National Institute of Justice Journal
http://ncjrs.aspensys.com:81/news2/nijour.txt
Online Quarterly Review of Crime, Ethics, and Social Policy
http://www.erces.com/journal/journal.htm
Southwest Journal of Criminal Justice
http://swjcj.cjcenter.org/archives/
Terrorist Profile Weekly
http://www.site.gmu.edu:80/~cdibona/
U.S. Law Week: The Supreme Court
http://www.bna.com/supreme.html
Western Criminology Review
http://wcr.sonoma.edu

LEGISLATION RESOURCES FOR IDENTIFYING AND TRACKING

California Legislative Information
http://www.leginfo.ca.gov/
Federal Legislative Information—Thomas, Library of Congress Legislative Resource
http://thomas.loc.gov/

OTHER JUSTICE RESOURCES

1994 Crime Bill:
http://gopher.usdoj.gov/crime/crime.html
Central Intelligence Agency: Offers access to publications, country, and intelligence information.
http://www.odci.gov/cia
Code of Federal Regulations, a House of Representatives Site
http://law.house.gov/cfr.htm
Home Office Research and Statistics Department, United Kingdom
http://www.open.gov.uk/home_off/rsdhome.htm
International Centre for Criminal Justice Policy: Located at the Institute of the United Nations in Vancouver, BC
http://view.ubc.ca:80/1/acad-units/crim-justice

OIJC: Office of International Criminal Justice
http://www.acsp.uic.edu/
Partners Against Violence (PAVNET)
http://www.pavnet.org
RAND Corporation
http://www.rand.org
State Court Locator—Villanova University's State Court Listings
http://www.law.vill.edu/State-Ct/
United Nations Crime Prevention and Criminal Justice
http://www.ifs.univie.ac.at/~pr2gql/uno
United Nations Online Justice Information System (UNOJUST)
http://unojust.mitre.org/
http://www,ifs,univie.ac.at/-uncjin/uncjin.html
Vera Institute of Justice
http://broadway.vera.org
World Factbook:
http://www.odci.gov/94fact/fb94toc/fb94toc.html

LAW RESOURCES

California Codes
http://www.leginfo.ca.gov/calaw.html
Emory University School of Law, U.S. Federal Courts: Finder includes Federal Circuit, DC Circuit, U.S. Court of Appeals, First through Eleventh Circuit cases, U.S. Constitution and Declaration of Independence
http://www.law.emory.edu/
Inter-Law's 'Lectric Law Library
http://www.inter-law.com/
Law Marks: Legal Resource Database
http://www.iwc.com/entropy/marks/bkmrk.html
Legal Information Institute (LIL): Cornell Law School (U.S. Supreme Court decisions, search by subject)
http://www.law.cornell.edu
gopher.law.cornell.edu:70/
RefLaw: The Virtual Law Library Reference desk, Washburn University School of Law Library.
http://lawlib.wuacc.edu/washlaw/reflaw/reflaw.html
The SEAMLESS WEBsite:
http://starbase.ingress.com/tsw/
U.S. House of Representatives Internet Law Library, U.S. Code:
http://www.pls.com:8001/his/usc.html
U.S. Supreme Court Decisions, A Cornell University Site
http://supct.law.cornell.edu/supct/

Virtual Law Library, University of Indiana
http://www.law.indiana.edu/law/lawindex.html
Wadsworth Publishing
http://www.thomson.com:9966/rcenters/cj/cj.html
West Publishing
http://www.westpub.com/

MEDIA RESOURCES

CNN
http://www.cnn.com
Court Law Center: Court TV home page
http://www.courttv.com/
Crime and Media: criminology course taught entirely over the World Wide Web
http://www.fsu.edu/~crimdo/gradc&m.html
Los Angeles Times
http://www.latimes.com/
Media Literacy Project
http://interact.uoregon.edu/MediaLit/HomePage
Television News Archives: National newscasts from 1968 to present.
http://tvnews.vanderbilt.edu/
USA Today
http://www.usatoday.com/

ORGANIZATIONS

Activist Groups — includes sections on drug law reform, forfeiture, and the jury system.
http://www.calyx.net/activist.html
American Civil Liberties Union
http://www.aclu.org
ARC's Access to Justice Project (mentally retarded and criminal justice)
http://www.metronet.com/~thearc/ada/crim.html
Community Policing Consortium
http://www.communitypolicing.org/
International Association of Chiefs of Police
http://www.amdahl.com./ext/iacp/
International Association of Court Officers and Services
http://www.sheriffs.org/iacos.html
National Association of Counties
http://www.naco.org/
National Center for State Courts
http://ncsc.dni.us/ncsc.htm
National Center for State Courts — Institute for Court Management
http://www.ncsc.dni.us/icm.htm

National Sheriffs Association
   http://www.sheriffs.org/
State Justice Institute
   http://www.clark.net/pub/sji/home.htm

OTHER USEFUL RESOURCES

California Criminal Justice Statistics Center
   http://www.caag.state.ca.us/cjsc/
California Office of Criminal Justice Planning
   http://www.ocjp.ca.gov/
California Youth Authority
   http://www.cya.ca.gov/
Crime Statistics Guide
   http://www.crime.org
ERIC Database
   http://ericir.syr.edu/ERIC/eric.html
Hourly Depiction of Radar Weather Echos — Southwestern United States
   http://www.intellicast.com/weather/lax/radsum/
Sourcebook of Criminal Justice Statistics
   http://www.albany.edu/sourcebook
U.S. Census Bureau
   http://www.census.gov/
U.S. Census Bureau Tiger Maps (Lets You Create Maps to Street Level Detail)
   http://tiger.census.gov/cgi-bin/mapsurfer?

POLICE

Cop Net/Police Resource List:
   http://police.sas.ab.ca/prl/index.html/
Law Enforcement Agencies on the web: university, city, county, and state police departments.
   http://www.fsu.edu/~crimdo/police.html

PRISONS

Alcatraz
   http://www.nps.gov/alcatraz/
Amnesty International
   gopher://gopher.icg.apc.org
Prison Legal News:
   http://www.ai.mit.edu:8O/people/ellens/PLN/pln.html
The Keeper's Voice: The International Association of Correctional Officers
   http://www.acsp.uic.edu/iaco/kv1603tc.htm

U.S. DEPARTMENT OF JUSTICE

Department of Justice — Home Page
http://justice2.usdoj.gov/
Antitrust Division
http://justice2.usdoj.gov/atr/atr.htm
Bureau of Justice Assistance
http://www.ojp.usdoj.gov/BJA/
Bureau of Justice Statistics
http://www.ojp.usdoj.gov/bjs/
Civil Division
http://justice2.usdoj.gov/civil/civil.html
Civil Rights Division
http://justice2.usdoj.gov/crt/crt-home.html
Community Oriented Policing — Home Page
http://justice2.usdoj.gov/cops/
Community Relations Service
http://justice2.usdoj.gov/offices/crs.html
Criminal Division
http://justice2.usdoj.gov/criminal/criminal-home.html
Criminal Division — International Inter Agency Fugitive Lookout
http://justice2.usdoj.gov/criminal/oiafug/fugitives.htm
Drug Enforcement Agency — Home Page
http://justice2.usdoj.gov/dea/deahome.htm
Drug Enforcement Agency — Fugitives List
http://justice2.usdoj.gov/dea/fugitive/fuglist.htm
Environment and Natural Resources Division
http://justice2.usdoj.gov/enrd/enrd-home.html
Executive Office for Immigration Review
http://justice2.usdoj.gov/eoir
Executive Office for United States Attorneys
http://justice2.usdoj.gov/offices/eousa.html
Executive Office for United States Trustees (Bankruptcy)
http://justice2.usdoj.gov/offices/ust.html
Federal Bureau of Investigation — Home Page
http://www.fbi.gov/
FBI Most Wanted
http://www.fbi.gov/wanted.htm
FBI Wanted — Fugitive Publicity — Other Fugitives
http://www.fbi.gov/fugitive/fpphome.htm
FBI Publications (Includes the UNIFORM CRIME REPORTS)
http://www.fbi.gov/publish.htm
FBI Publications — NCIC 2000 Newsletter
http://www.fbi.gov/2000/2000newl.htm

Federal Judicial Center
http://www.fjc.gov/
Federal Web Locator
http://www.usdoj.gov/other-link.html
Immigration and Naturalization Service — Home Page
http://justice2.usdoj.gov/ins/
Immigration and Naturalization Service — Form 1-9, Employment Verification Form
http://justice2.usdoj.gov/ins/forms/i-9.htm
Immigration and Naturalization Service — Forms Available by Mail or Download
http://justice2.usdoj.gov/ins/forms/index.html
National Criminal Justice Reference Center — Home Page — System Wide Resources
http://www.ncjrs.org
National Criminal Justice Reference Center — Federal Grants
http://www.ncjrs.org/fedgrant.htm
National Criminal Justice Reference Center — Victims' Resources
http://www.ncjrs.org/victhome.htm
National Criminal Justice Reference Center — Victim Statistics Including the NCVS
http://www.ncjrs.org/ovchome.htm
National Institute of Corrections
http://www.bop.gov/nicpg/nicmain.html
National Institute of Justice — Home Page (A Criminal Justice Research Resource)
http://www.ncjrs.org/nijhome.htm
National Law Enforcement and Corrections Technology Center
http://nletc.aspensys.com:83/nletchome.html
Office For Victims of Crime
http://www.ncjrs.org/ovchome.htm
Office of the Attorney General (Limited Resource Reno's Speeches and another picture)
http://justice2.usdoj/gov/offices/oag.html
Office of Information and Privacy (Freedom of Information Act — Guidelines)
http://justice2.usdoj.gov/offices/oip.html
Office of the Inspector General (Links to Audit/Inspection Reports)
http://justice2.usdoj.gov/oig/ighp01.htm
Office of Justice Programs — Home Page (Federal Justice Programs/Grant Information)
http://www.ojp.usdoj.gov/
Office of Juvenile Justice and Delinquency Prevention — Home Page
http://www.ncjrs.org/oijhome.htm
Office of Tribal Justice — Links to other Native American Resources
http://justice2.usdoj.gov/otj/otj.html

U.S. Attorney's Office For the Southern District of California
http://justice2.usdoj.gov/usao/sdc/
U.S. Federal Courts Homepage
http://www.uscourts.gov/
U.S. Marshal's Service
http://justice2.usdoj.gov/marshals/
U.S. Marshal's Service — 15 Most Wanted Fugitives
http://www.usdoj.gov/marshals/wanted/wanted.html
U.S. Parole Commission — To Be Phased Out By 2002
http://justice2.usdoj.gov/bureaus/parole.html
Violence Against Women Office
http://justice2.usdoj.gov/vawo/

U.S. DEPARTMENT OF THE TREASURY

Financial Crimes Enforcement Network
http://www.ustreas.gov/treasury/bureaus/fincen/
Internal Revenue Service — Home Page
http://www.irs.ustreas.gov/prod/
Internal Revenue Service Forms and Publications
http://www.irs.ustreas.gov/prod/forms_pubs/pubs.html
U.S. Secret Service
http://www.ustreas.gov/treasury/bureaus/usss/usss.html

INDEX

A

abbreviations, 72–73
abstraction, triangle of, 138
abstracts, 177, 178–179, 187
academic writing style, 66–67
acknowledgments, 177, 181
acronyms, 72–73
Adobe Acrobat, 202
agency permission, 61
alcohol abuse, data sets on, 49
American Psychological
   Association. *See* APA
   (American Psychological
   Association) style
analysis, 4, 145–161
   bivariate, 145, 146–149
   content, 27–28
   cost-benefit, 28–29
   detail in, 158
   empirical, 22–23
   limitations of, 125–130, 169–170
   multivariate, 149–152
   regression, 152–157
   statistical models in, 123–125
   tables and figures in, 157–160
analysis chapter, goals of, 145
anecdotes, 129–130
Antisocial Behavior Scale, 33
APA (American Psychological
   Association) style, 16–17,
   176–177
Arrestee Drug Use Monitoring
   data, 128

ASCII format, 202
assessment instruments, 33–34
association, measures of, 146–149,
   148
attitude surveys, 31
authorship, 189–190
awards, 188–189

B

backup copies, 16
The Belmont Report, 52–53
Best, Joel, 74
bias
   participant observation and, 35
   unobtrusive measures
      and, 24
   value neutrality of research
      questions and, 38–39
bibliographic references
   importance of, 102
   original vs. secondary sources
      for, 73
   plagiarism and, 67
   style guides on, 16–18
bibliographies, 176
   compiling, 5
   style guides on, 16–18
bivariate analysis, 145,
   146–149
   dual, 148–149
brainstorming, 6
Burns, Chip, 44

C

calendars, 10. *See also* deadlines; time lines
Callanan, Valerie, 95–96
"can't find time" writers, 19
Carlan, P.E., 56
Carroll, Leo, 21
case examples, 81–82
case studies, 30–31
    in legal theses, 21
causal propositions, 34
chairperson
    in committee member selection, 13
    as proofreader, 74
    role of, 14
    selecting, 5
charts, 100, 176
Chicago School, 30, 35
Chicago style, 18
child abuse, data sets on, 48–49
chronological order, 91, 92
citations, 176. *See also* bibliographies; documentation; sources
    importance of, 102
    keeping track of, 102
    original vs. secondary sources for, 73
    plagiarism and, 67
    style guides on, 16–18
clarity, in writing, 72–73, 94, 166
codebooks, 112
Code of Federal Regulations, 54
coding
    in content analysis, 27–28
    describing in methodology section, 116
    examples of, 118–119
    missing information, 114
    in NACJD data sets, 45
    secondary data, 40, 42
    suggestions for, 111–114
coercion, 59. *See also* informed consent
committee

agreed upon approach with, 131–132
    changes to, 13–14
    defense date and, 132–133
    in editing process, 19
    expectations of about sources, 73–74
    expectations of for defense, 182
    format decisions with, 15
    functions of members in, 14–15
    outside members in, 14–15
    prospectus expectations of, 77
    selecting, 5, 13–15
    in time line development, 8–9
    in topic selection, 12–13
concept operationalization, 90–91
conciseness, in writing, 71
conclusions, 162–171
    importance of, 170
    limitations and, 127, 169–170
    organizing, 166
    policy implications and, 166–168
    research implications and, 168–169
    section containing, 165–166
    summary section, 163–164
    writing, 4
    writing style for, 162–163
conference presentations, 187–188
confidentiality, 159–160
conflict theory, 22–23
consent, informed, 58–60
consistency, in committee oversight, 14
contact information, 193
content analysis theses, 27–28
    examples of, 28
    resources for, 28
control groups, 34–36
corrections, journals on, 195
correlation coefficients, 154–155
    Beta, 154–155
cost-benefit analysis, 28–29
    resources for, 29

survey research for, 31
"countdown" approach
 to writing, 19
courts, journals on, 194
cover letters
 for informed consent, 59, 60
 in IRB applications, 61, 62
 for IRB exemptions, 56, 57
 for submission for
  publication, 193
credibility, 73–74
Crimes of Style (Ferrell), 31
critiques, in theoretical theses,
 22–23
current issues, in introductory
 chapter, 80–81

D

data
 analyzing and presenting,
  145–161
 availability of, 137
 coding, 27–28, 111–114, 117–118
 collection levels for, 113
 describing sources of, 110–111
 existing, 54
 file management and, 18
 finding and assembling, 39–51
 finding good, 44–51
 general criminal justice and
  criminology, 46–48
 government data sets, 37, 41,
  44–51
 IRB exempt, 54–56
 limitations in, 127–128
 methodology for collecting,
  116–121
 methodology selection and, 30
 original vs. secondary, 37, 39
 from participant observation,
  35–36
 with quantitative methodologies, 107–108
 secondary, 37, 40–44

databases, 198–200
 interdisciplinary, 200–201
deadlines, 4
 official university, 9
 for prospectus defense, 132–133
 self-paced, 18–19
 time lines for managing, 6, 8–9
defense process, 5
 costs of, 185
 electronic presentations as, 183
 as end result, 3–4
 final, 175–185
 first person language in, 67
 lectures as, 183
 nervousness about, 132–133,
  181–182
 paperwork in, 185
 practical preparation for, 142
 preparation for, 77, 139–140,
  181–182, 182–183
 presentation of, 137–139, 181–185
 prospectus, 132–140
 results of, 184–185
 setting a date for, 132–133
 style and format for, 183–184
 technology problems in,
  140–141, 142
definitions, 192
departmental research, ongoing,
 64–65
detail
 in analysis, 158
 in methodology section, 111, 116
Dewey, L., 82–84, 166
discussion section, 165
dissertations, 201
documentation. *See also* citations
 of data sets, 43
 plagiarism and, 67
Dolny, H. M., 111
downloadable files, 41
drafts, 4
 feedback on, 19
 time line for, 9

drug abuse
  data sets on, 49
  journals on, 203
Drug Use Forecasting, 128
Dugdale, Richard, 30

E

edge-work, 108
editing process, 4, 5
  committee input in, 15
  for conciseness, 71
  perfection seekers and, 19
  proofreading and, 74
  for publication in journals,
    191–192
  technical vs. substantive, 19
  time line for, 9
Edmunds Act of 1882, 80
Eith, C. A., 93–94
emotions
  defense process and, 139
  neutral perspective vs., 11
empirical analysis, 22–23, 107
Environmental Protection Agency
    (EPA), 44
Erickson, K., 31
error, potential sources of, 169–170
"Ethical Principles and Guidelines
    for the Protection of Human
    Subjects of Research," 53
ethics, 52–53, 195–196. *See also*
    institutional review boards
    (IRBs)
ethnography, 108
Everything in Its Path (Erickson), 31
expectations
  about sources, 73–74
  of committee member in defense
    process, 182
  limiting scope and, 84–85
  narrowing the parameters of, 85
  for prospectus, 77
  of readers, 110
  research settings and, 110
experimental design, 34–36

  in methodology chapter, 106
  expertise, demonstrating, 90

F

faddish words, 72–73
feedback, 6
  maximizing, 4
  negative, 195
  perfection seekers and, 19
  systematic, 132
  in time line development, 8–9
  waiting for, 8–9
Ferrell, Jeff, 31
figures, 181
file folders, 15
file management, 16, 18
filing systems, 15–16, 100
first person language, 66–67
footnotes, 192
format, 176–177
  for literature reviews, 92–93
  for meetings, 15
  page, 16
  for prospectus defense, 139
  for publication, 190
  style guides and, 16–18
front material, 175, 177–181
full board reviews, 53–54
  submitting proposals for,
    56–64

G

Garson, G. David, 155
Gentry, H. M., 169–170
Gibson, Camille, 159
GIS-based mapping information, 50
Goddard, Henry, 30
Google, 203
government data sets, 41, 110
  on child abuse, 48–49
  cost of, 42
  on criminal justice and criminol-
    ogy, 46–48
  finding good, 44–51
  list of, 45

government publications, 201–202
grant writing, 3
Gump, S. E., 193

H

Hamm, Mark, 31, 33
Hardy, R., 82
Harris, J., 192
hate crimes, 50
Hauptman, R., 195
headings, 16, 176–177
  APA style, 17
  in literature reviews, 91
highlighters, 15
Hirschi, Travis, 148–149
historical background, 80
  in literature reviews, 91
historical theses, 26–27, 80, 108
  resources for, 27
Holmes, Oliver Wendell, 68
Holt v. *Sarver*, 21
html format, 73
human subjects, 53–56. *See also*
  institutional review boards
  (IRBs)
  controversy over use of, 65
human subjects review committees. *See* institutional review
  boards (IRBs)
hypotheses
  analysis and, 147
  bivariate sub-, 145
  how to phrase, 116
  null, 115
  one-tailed, 116
  operational, 84, 115–116
  statement of, 114–116
  stating, 84
  theoretical, 84, 115
  two-tailed, 116

I

ICPSR. *See* Inter-university
  Consortium for Political
  and Social Research (ICPSR)

identity theft, 81
Iglesias, S., 81
impact studies, 23
implementation evaluations, 24
implications
  limitations of, 169–170
  for policy, 166–168
  for research, 168–169
inferential statistics, 151
information gathering, 24, 39–51
informed consent, 58–60
  documenting, 61
  elements of, 59
institutional review boards (IRBs),
  52–65
  application materials for, 59, 60,
    61–64
  applications to, 56, 58
  cover letters for, 56, 57
  examples of research designs
    and, 62–64
  exempt categories and, 54–56
  full review by, 53–54
  informed consent and, 58–60
  methodology oversight by, 65
  ongoing departmental research
    and, 64–65
  prospectus defense approval by,
    135
  role of, 52–53
  secondary data and, 50–51
  submissions to for full review,
    56–64
  Web sites on, 65
instruments
  describing in methodology
    section, 116
  for interviews, 32–33
  in IRB applications, 61
  in methodology section, 116
  pretesting, 33
  reliability of, 107
  scales and assessment, 33–34
  topic size and, 11–12
  validity of, 107
interdisciplinary studies, 14

interpretations, 158
  limitations of, 169–170
Inter-university Consortium for
  Political and Social Research
  (ICPSR), 42
interviews, 31, 32–33
  example of methodology section
    describing, 120
  informed consent for, 59
  using quotes from, 159–160
introductory chapter, 79–89
  case examples in, 81–82
  current issues in, 80–81
  elements in, 79
  facts and figures in, 81
  historical background in, 80
  importance of, 170
  limitations stated in, 84–85
  narrowing topics in, 82–84
  outlines for, 82–84
  purpose statements in, 84
  transitioning from, 85–88
IRBs. *See* institutional review
  boards (IRBs)
italics, 176
Ixquick, 203

J

The Jackroller (Shaw), 30
jargon, 72–73
Jordan, J. Michael, 68–69
journals, academic
  acceptance rates of, 190
  data sets published in, 44
  listed by field, 194–195
  list of, 198–200
  manuscript preparation for,
    192–193
  nonpeer-reviewed, 191
  peer-reviewed, 44, 191
  revising theses for, 189–197
  selecting for publication,
    193–194
journals, online, 203–204

journals, trade, 188, 200
Jukes (Dugdale), 30
jury duty, 82–84
juvenile delinquency, data sets on,
  49–50
juvenile justice, data sets on, 49–50

K

Kallikaks (Goddard), 30
Kent v. United States, 68
knowledge base, contributions
  to, 11, 132
  topic selection and, 13
Krizan, V., 82, 167

L

layering tables, 150–151
learning styles/preferences, 6
legal resources, 201
legal theses, 20–22, 108
  examples of, 21–22
  legal research data and, 50
  limitations in, 126
  resources for, 21–22
legislation resources, 204
life history method, 21, 30–31
lifestyle theory, 22
limitations, 5
  in discussion section, 165
  general, 126–128
  of implications, 169–170
  of interpretations, 169–170
  methodological, 105, 125–130
  in methodology chapter, 106
  in prospectus, 137
  of secondary data, 127–128
  stating in introductory chapters,
    84–85
  subject, 84–85
  ways to address, 126
line spacing, 176
literature reviews, 90–104, 136–137
  analysis plans and, 124

avoiding unnecessary information in, 71
benefits of, 91
checking citations in, 102
concluding, 102–103
drafting, 5
formatting, 92–93
frequently discussed items in, 97
generalized findings in, 95–96
grouping studies in, 92, 100
methodology and, 105
narrowing focus in, 94
organization of, 91–95
purpose of, 90–91
quotes in, 69
research summary charts for, 97–98, 99–100, 101
selecting studies for, 97
specific results in, 96–100
studies included in, 93–94
summarizing results in, 100, 102
systematic, 98
transitioning from, 103
transitioning to, 85–88
logistic regression, 155–157
Lynch, Mike, 44

M

machine-readable files, 45
coding and, 111–114
macrolevel implications, 166–168
magazines, 200
margins, 176
McShane, M. D., 111
measures
of association, 146–149, 148
in data sets, 43–44
describing/defining, 121–123
limitations of, 125–130
of strength, 154–155
unobtrusive, 24
Mebane, D., 86–87, 168–169
media resources, 206
meetings, format of, 15

mentors, 14
methodologies
appropriateness of, 30
case studies, 30–31
information availability and, 30
IRB oversight of, 65
limitations of, 85, 169
literature reviews and, 90–91, 102
matching with research questions, 37–38
in prospectus, 137
qualitative, 108
quantitative, 107–108, 117, 120
selecting, 5, 12, 30
surveys, 31–33
types of, 29–36
methodology section, 105–130
coding suggestions for, 111–114
contents of, 106–107
data collection methodology in, 116–121
data sources in, 110–111
defending the methodology in, 129–130
detail in, 111, 116
examples of, 117–121
explanation of methodology in, 105–107
first person language in, 66
general statistical models for, 123–125
goals of, 105
hypothesis statement in, 114–116
introductory paragraphs in, 109
limitations explained in, 105, 125–130
operational hypotheses in, 84
overview of research design in, 108–109
population in, 109–110
research question statement in, 114–116
research setting in, 109–110
sampling procedures in, 110–111
systematic review in, 117

variables in, 121–123
microlevel implications, 166–168
Miller, C., 192
MLA (Modern Language
Association) style, 18
Modern Language Association. *See*
MLA (Modern Language
Association) style
Mole People (Toth), 31
Monitoring the Future, 49
Morrill (Anti-bigamy)
Act of 1862, 80
multiple regression, 154–155
multivariate analysis, 149–152
Murphy, David, 169

N

NACJD. *See* National Archive
of Criminal Justice Data
(NACJD)
National Archive of Criminal
Justice Data (NACJD), 41, 42,
44, 45–46
directions for downloading data
sets from, 47–48
juvenile justice data in, 49–50
National Consortium of Violence
Research, 46
National Crime Victimization
Survey (NCVS), 46, 127–128
National Criminal Justice Data
Archive (NCJDA), 41
National Incident Based Reporting
System (NIBRS), 45, 46
National Institute of Health, 44
National Institute of Justice, 44
National Longitudinal Survey of
Youth, 49
National Youth Risk Behavior
Survey, 49
National Youth Survey, 49, 127–128
needs assessments, 31
Neglekerke's R-square, 155
neutral perspective, 10, 11
non-PRE measures, 146
note taking, 139, 159–160

O

observation, 108
Oklahoma City bombing, 31
ongoing research, 64–65
Open Records Act, 54
operationalization of concepts,
90–91
opinion polls, 3, 31
oral presentations. *See* defense
process
organization. *See* structure
organizations, regional, local, and
national, 194, 206–207
orphans (typographic), 176
outcome evaluations, 23
outlines
chapter organization and, 86–88
for conclusions chapters, 170
for introductions, 82–84
overview of research design, 107,
108–109

P

page numbers, 176
Palmigiano v. *Garrahy*, 21
paper competitions, 188–189
paraphrasing, 67
Parker, Mary, 21
partial regression, 152–154
participant observation, 35–36
pdf format, 73, 202
Pearson's *r*, 152, 153
percentages, calculating for tables,
157
personal support, 1–2, 6
perspective, neutral, 10, 11
pilot studies, 11–12
plagiarism, 67, 195–196
police resources, 50–51, 207
journals on, 194
policy, journals on, 195
policy analysis theses, 25–26
resources for, 26
survey research for, 31

policy evaluation, 3
policy implications, 166–168
populations, 12, 109–110
positivist tradition, 30
Post-it notes, 15
PowerPoint, 77, 183
  preparation for using, 139
  resources on, 141
preliminary assessments, 11–12
PRE measures, 146
preparation phase, 1–75
presentations
  defense process as, 137–139,
    181–185
  electronic, 183
  PowerPoint, 77, 139, 141, 183
  preparing from theses, 186–188
  resources on oral, 141
principle investigators (PIs), 58
prisons, resources on, 207
probability, one-tailed, 153
problem statements, 136
process evaluations, 24
professional conferences, 187–188
Professional Thief (Sutherland), 30
program evaluations, 3
program evaluation theses, 23–25
  experimental design for, 34–36
  participant observation
    for, 35–36
  resources for, 25
  survey research for, 31
proofreading, 74, 175
  checklist for, 175–177
proposals. *See* prospectus
prospectus, 77–142
  content of independent
    document, 136
  content of thesislike, 135–136
  copies of, 139–140
  data availability in, 137
  defending, 132–142
  as document, 133–136
  elements found in all, 136–137
  expectations for, 77

first person language in, 66, 67
goals of, 131–132
information in, 77
introduction and problem statement in, 79–89
limitations in, 137
literature review and, 90–104,
  136–137
methodology and, 105–130, 137
problem statement in, 136
steps leading to, 4, 5
title page for, 133, 134
publication, 189–197
  cover letters for, 193
  examples of student, 196–197
  manuscript preparation for,
    192–193
  multiple submissions for, 195
  revising for, 191–192
  selecting a journal for, 193–195
publications, revising theses for,
  189–197
purpose statements, 84, 145

Q

qualitative methodologies, 108
quantitative methodologies,
  107–108, 117, 120
quasi-experimental design, 34–36
questionnaires, 31–32. *See also*
  surveys
  cover letters with, 56
  informed consent for, 59
  in IRB applications, 61
  IRB exempt, 55, 56
questions
  rhetorical, 73
  in thesis defense, 184
quotes
  effective use of, 68–69
  from interviews, 159–160
  in literature reviews, 96
  overuse of, 67–69
  plagiarism and, 67

R

R. J. Reynolds Tobacco Company,
68–69
random assignment, 34–35
reading aloud, for proofreading,
74
recidivism, 94–95, 124–125
regression, 152–157
  logistic, 155–157
  multiple, 154–155
  partial, 152–154
reliability, 12, 107
  describing in methodology
    section, 116
reluctant writers, 18
repetition, avoiding, 69–71
research
  brainstorming ideas for, 6
  explaining setting for, 109–110
  human subjects in, 52–61
  implications for future, 168–169
  informed consent in, 58–60
  IRB exempt vs. full review of,
    62–64
  misconduct in, 195–196
  ongoing departmental, 64–65
  original vs. secondary sources
    for, 73
  question development for, 37–51
research questions, 37–51
  examples of good, 38
  methodology selection and,
    37–38
  narrowing the topic for, 37
  statement of, 114–116, 136
  value neutrality of, 38–39
  wording of, 38–39
research skills, uses of, 3
research summary charts, 97–98,
  99–100, 101
resources, 198–210
  academic journals, 198–200
  for case studies, 31
  for content analysis theses, 28

for cost-benefit analysis, 29
for experimental design, 35
government publications,
  201–202
for historical theses, 27
legal, 201, 205–206
for legal theses, 21–22
on legislation, 204
on logistic regression, 155–156
magazines and trade journals, 200
online, 202–210
on oral presentations, 141
on participant observation, 36
for policy analysis theses, 26
on PowerPoint, 141
for program evaluation theses, 25
on scales and assessment
  instruments, 34
for secondary data, 40–41
on statistical programs, 154
on statistical tests, 125
theses and dissertations, 201
U.S. Department of Justice,
  208–210
U.S. Department of the Treasury,
  210
Web-based, 73
on writing for publication, 190
results
  limitations of, 85
  promising, 39
  summarizing, 163–164
rhetorical questions, 73
Richardson, T., 102
risk assessments, 3
running heads, 176–177

S

samples
  describing procedures in, 110–111
  as limitations, 128
  population for, 109–110
  size of, 11
  for surveys, 31

Samuels, L., 94–95, 168
SAS program, 45–46, 47
scales, 33–34
scholarly conferences, 187–188
Schubert, C., 129–130
Scott, Yolanda, 70
search engines, 45, 203
secondary data, 37, 40–44
  accessing, 41
  advantages and disadvantages
    of, 40
  assessing, 41
  authorship issues and, 189–190
  cost of, 42
  data collection methods
    of, 41–42
  describing sources of, 110–111
  on drugs and alcohol abuse, 49
  finding, 41, 44–51
  IRB exemptions and, 54–56
  on juvenile delinquency and
    juvenile justice, 49–50
  limitations of, 127–128
  police data, 50–51
  qualities of good, 43–44
  quality of, 44
  with quantitative methodologies,
    107–108
  quantitative methodologies
    with, 107
  questions to use when consider-
    ing, 42–43
  research setting expectations
    and, 110
  systematic literature reviews
    and, 98
self-report studies, 32
sentence length, 72
Shaw, Clifford, 30
signature pages, 177
significance tests, 151
slang, 72–73
Social Competence Scale, 33
social control theory, 148–149,
  150–151

Social Science Citation Index, 198
software, statistical programs,
  45–46, 154
Sourcebook of Criminal Justice
  Statistics, 202
sources
  academic journals, 198–200
  credibility of, 73–74
  magazines and trade journals, 200
  in methodology chapter, 106
  primary vs. secondary, 73
  reliability of, 73–74
  secondary, 73–74
  Web-based, 73
spreadsheets, 100
SPSS program, 45–46, 47
STATA program, 47
statistics. See also analysis
  bivariate analysis, 146–149
  controlling variables and, 151–152
  data set case numbers and, 43
  distortion of, 74
  general models to apply,
    123–125
  in introductory chapters, 81
  in methodology chapter, 106
  multivariate analysis and,
    149–151
  quantitative methodologies
    and, 107
  resources on, 125
  software for, 45–46, 47
stepwise multiple regression, 155
storytelling, 129–130
strength, measures of, 154–155
structure, 4
  chapter-based, 86–88
  for coding, 113–114
  of literature reviews, 91–95,
    94–95
style guides/manuals, 16–18
subheadings, 16, 91
subject limitations, 84–85
summaries
  of analysis plans, 145

in conclusion section, 163–164
in literature reviews, 95–96, 97, 102
supplies, 15–16, 18
support, personal, 1–2, 6
surveys, 31–33
 cover letters with, 56
 example of methodology section describing, 119, 121
 interviews, 32–33
 in IRB applications, 61
 IRB exemptions for, 56
 questionnaires, 31–32
Sutherland, Edwin, 30
systematic literature reviews, 98, 117

T

tables, 146, 157–160
 controlling for variables in, 149–151
 cross-tabulation, 148–149, 157
 describing, 158
 layering, 150–151
 lists of, 181
 multivariate analysis and, 149–152
 numbering, 176
 proofreading, 176
 significance testing and, 151
tables of contents, 87–88, 177, 180
tape recordings, 159–160
technology, practicing with, 140–141
"Telling the truth about damn lies and statistics" (Best), 74
terminology, revising, 193
theoretical theses, 22–23
 examples of, 22–23
 participant observation for, 35–36
 structure of, 86–88
 survey research for, 31
theory construction theses, 22–23, 108
theory testing theses, 22–23

theses
 choice to participate in, 1–2
 content analysis, 27–28
 cost-benefit analysis, 28–29
 distributing, 181
 final defense of, 175–185
 first step in, 9–10
 getting started on, 20–36
 historical, 26–27
 legal, 20–22
 limiting scope and expectations of, 84–85
 ongoing departmental research and, 64
 order of steps in, 4
 organization of, 85–88
 policy analysis, 25–26
 as process, 3–10
 program evaluation, 23–25
 as resources, 201
 revising for publication, 188–197
 revising into presentations, 186–188
 social aspects of, 6
 theoretical, 22–23
 time line for, 6, 8–9
 types of, 20–29
 value of, 3
third-order partials, 153–154
third person language, 66–67
time lines, 6, 8–9
 committee member feedback on, 12–13
timer technique for writing, 18
title pages, 133, 134, 177
titles, for tables, 157
topics
 appropriate, 10
 arguing the importance of, 81
 contribution to knowledge and, 13
 finding, 13
 fit with committee members and, 12–13

narrowing, 5, 12, 37–38, 82–84, 138
qualities of good, 10–11
selecting, 5, 10–13
size of, 11–12, 13
triangle of abstraction and, 138
Toth, Jennifer, 31
transcriptions, 159–160
treatment groups, 34–36
triangle of abstraction, 138
Turabian style, 18

U

Uniform Crime Report (UCR), 45, 46, 127–128
unobtrusive measures, 24
URLs, 73, 202
U.S. Census Data, 127–128
U.S. Department of Justice, 208–210
U.S. Department of the Treasury, 210

V

validity, 12, 107
participant observation and, 35
of secondary data, 40
value neutrality, 38–39
variables
in analysis chapters, 145
bivariate analysis of, 146–149
controlling for in tables, 149–151
controlling statistically, 151–152
describing, 121–123
limitations of, 128
in literature reviews, 93–94
logistic regression and, 155–157
methodology and, 12
in methodology chapter, 106, 121–123
multivariate analysis of, 149–152
names of in tables and text, 158
selecting, 94

victims, ethics of research on, 54
voluntariness, 59. *See also* informed consent

W

Walker, Jeff, 91, 92–93
Warren, D., 87–88
Web sites, 202–210
changeable nature of, 73, 203
on child abuse, 48–49
credibility of, 73–74
on drug and alcohol abuse, 49, 203
for general criminal justice and criminology data, 46–48
government-sponsored, 41, 42
on IRB reviews, 65
journals listings in, 193
on juvenile delinquency and juvenile justice, 49–50
legal research, 50, 205–206
legislation resources on, 204
on logistic regression, 155
media resources on, 206
NACJD, 45–46, 47–48
of online journals, 203–204
organizations on, 206–207
page numbers in, 73
on plagiarism, 67
police data, 50–51, 207
on prisons, 207
for publication information, 190
on secondary data, 40–41
secondary data sets on, 41, 45–51
on statistical programs, 154
U.S. Department of Justice, 208–210
U.S. Department of the Treasury, 210
validating, 176
Weiss, M. S., 103
widows (typographic), 176
Williams, F. P., III, 111

writing
  clarity in, 72–73, 94, 166
  first person language in, 66–67
  plagiarism and, 67
  self-paced, 18–19
  transitions between chapters,
    85–88, 103
writing style
  academic, 66–67
  clarity in, 72–73
  conciseness in, 71
  in conclusions, 162–163
  first person in, 66–67
  in implications sections, 167–168
  methodology section and,
    129–130
  overuse of quotes and, 67–69
  for policy analysis, 25
  for publication, 193
  repetition and, 69–71
  third person in, 66–67
  varying phrasing in, 69–71

Y

Yahoo, 203
Yearbook of Mental Measurements, 33

Z

Zamora, D., 169